D1498687

EXISTENCE AND BEING

Martin Heidegger

EXISTENCE AND BEING

Introduction and analysis by
Werner Brock

REGNERY/GATEWAY, INC.
SOUTH BEND, INDIANA

SANFORD, FLORIDA
32771

First American edition published 1949
by the Henry Regnery Company, Book Publishers

This edition published 1979 by Regnery/Gateway, Inc.
120 West LaSalle Avenue, South Bend, Indiana 46601
by arrangement with Vision Press, Limited
Manufactured in the United States of America, 9-79

International Standard Book Number: 0-89526-935-X

CONTENTS

Foreword   ix

Introduction   2

  Prefatory Note   2

  A Brief Outline of the Career of M.
    Heidegger   6

  An Account of "Being and Time"   11

        1. The three main problems: Dasein,
           Time and Being. The project and
           the published version

        2. Some aspects of the analysis of
           Dasein

        3. Dasein and Temporality

        4. Some reflections on the signifi-
           cance of the work

  An Account of "The Four Essays"   117

        1. A brief general characterization of
           the four essays

        2. On the Essence of Truth

v

3. The Essays on Friedrich Hölderlin

4. What is Metaphysics?

Note   232

Remembrance of the Poet   233

    Translated by Douglas Scott

Hölderlin and the Essence of Poetry   270

    Translated by Douglas Scott

On the Essence of Truth   292

    *Translated by R. F. C. Hull and
    Alan Crick*

What is Metaphysics?   325

    *Translated by R. F. C. Hull and
    Alan Crick*

Notes   363

Warum ist überhaupt Seiendes und nicht vielmehr Nichts?
— Das Nichts als das Andere zum Seienden ist der Schleier des Seins.

MARTIN HEIDEGGER

FOREWORD

In appearance, Professor Heidegger is short and slight; his hair is thick and jet black with occasional white streaks. When he emerged from the small skiing hut, high up in the mountains, to greet me, he was dressed in the costume of a Swabian peasant, a dress he often also used to wear when he was Rector of Freiburg University. His heavy, squarish skiing boots (it was summer) emphasized still more strongly his relationship to the soil. He was born in 1889, in Messkirch and his brother still farms in the region. Martin Heidegger, too, has never left it. When Hitler called him to Berlin in 1935, he rejected the offer. The world had to come to him, to Freiburg. There he lives, with Hellingrath's edition of Hölderlin's works. This closeness to Hölderlin is no accident but an essential key to an understanding of Heidegger's own philosophy. For Hölderlin came from the same physical region, he faced the same spiritual problems, and he experienced more lucidly and bitterly the ultimate meaning of nothingness than any other person who could give expression to it in song. The parallel with Heidegger is close, indeed, if "thought" is substituted for "song."

On both occasions when I met Professor Heidegger, in June, 1946, and in October, 1947, I had to drive for an hour to the small town of Todtnau in the Black Forest Mountains, then to climb still further until the road became a path and all human habitation scattered and invisible. There on top of a mountain, with the valley deep down below, with nothing but space and wilderness all around, in that small skiing hut, I spoke to the philosopher. He had not been to Freiburg for six months when I saw him for the second time. His living conditions were primitive; his books were few, and his only relationship to the world was a stack of writing paper. His whole life revolved within those white sheets and it seemed to me that he wanted nothing else but to be left in peace to cover those white sheets with his writing.

The atmosphere of silence all around provided a faithful setting for Heidegger's philosophy. I could not help comparing it with the atmosphere I had encountered in the house of Professor Berdyaev near Paris and that of Professor Jaspers in Heidelberg. In every case, the external world faithfully reflected the world of the mind. In Berdyaev's case it was the spirit of communion; in Jaspers's that of spiritual engagement. But in Heidegger's case it was the spirit of overwhelming solitude.

With the four essays in this book, which Professor Heidegger gave me, this much-discussed philosopher now appears for the first time before the English-speaking world. As Professor Heidegger pointed out to me, the four essays are complementary and have an organic unity. Two deal with the essence of metaphysics, the other two with the essence of poetry. The two Hölderlin studies, in Heidegger's words, were "born out of a necessity of thought" conditioned by the questions raised in the metaphysical papers.

STEFAN SCHIMANSKI

ACKNOWLEDGEMENT

I wish to thank Professor Dr. Heidegger who, through Mr. Schimanski and the publishing firm, expressed the desire some time ago that I should write an Introduction to his essays. Furthermore, I wish to thank most warmly my friend Mr. E. K. Bennett, the President of Gonville and Caius College and Senior Lecturer in German at the University of Cambridge, for his constant encouragement in carrying out this task as well as for making some most valuable suggestions in the final phrasing of mainly the second part of this Introduction. Moreover, I should like to thank the Society for the Protection of Science and Learning for their encouragement and support. My sincere thanks also go to Mr. R. P. Friedmann who assisted me in the final phrasing, especially of the first part of this Introduction and shared with me the task of proof-reading.

WERNER BROCK, DR. PHIL.

Sometime Lecturer in Philosophy at the University of Freiburg i.B.

Cambridge,
January 31, 1949

PREFATORY NOTE

I have been asked to write an Introduction to this edition of four essays of the German philosopher Martin Heidegger, the first publication of a selected portion of his work in English. And I have agreed to do so, believing as I do that his theoretical work, above all his early systematic treatise "Sein und Zeit" (Being and Time), Part I (1927), represents a valuable and most stimulating contribution to philosophical studies. It provoked great interest in Germany and abroad, and is likely eventually to arouse such an interest also among the philosophically-minded English-speaking public. I am of the opinion that this contribution made to philosophic thought can be and should be considered and appreciated independently of any question of politics in which Professor Heidegger was involved during the early period of the Nazi régime. The publication of the essays, two on the work of the eminent German poet Friedrich Hölderlin and two on relevant philosophic problems, seems to me timely in view of the great recognition which the thought of the author has received elsewhere. And I look forward to the day when his main philosophic work published hitherto, "Being and Time," will be similarly accessible to the English-speaking reader. Although the essays presented here can make the reader acquainted with only a few aspects of the work of this contemporary thinker, it is hoped that they will prepare the ground for a more profound study of his thought, once "Being and Time" itself has been translated into English.

The following Introduction deviates from the established form by being considerably more extensive. It has been felt that it may be of help to many of his readers if Heidegger's thought, which, particularly in the two essays on philosophic topics, offers marked difficulties of comprehension through its new terminology as well as through the original ideas behind it, were reproduced in a simpler way. With regard to the essays themselves I envisage my task as that of emphasising and explaining some fundamental ideas and concepts advanced in them with a view to facilitating the reader's study and assimilation of the text. Criticism is not required from an Introduction. Such criticism, good, incisive and helpful or arising from misunderstanding and irrelevant, is bound to come, once Heidegger's ideas are submitted to intelligent discussion. My main aim is interpretative, on the assumption that I myself understand the text of the essays, as least in most points; and I shall raise a doubt only very rarely. The first essential is a proper understanding of Heidegger's thought. Judgement on his work and valid criticism can only come afterwards.

But this Introduction will not restrict itself to a discussion of the essays themselves. The thought in all of them, as well as some specific ideas and terms, is inevitably, related to "Being and Time," even though the substantial content can be understood independently. Moreover, the name of

Heidegger has become associated, mistakenly or not, with the movement now commonly termed "Existentialism." And though he himself emphatically insists, and I think he is fundamentally right, that he has nothing whatever to do with it, the fact remains that it was his work "Being and Time," together with Professor Karl Jaspers' philosophic thought, both being stimulated by Kierkegaard in this respect, that gave rise to the movement in our age. Thus it would seen arbitrary and inappropriate to concentrate here exclusively on the four selected essays with the ideas which they single out and present. The reader, unacquainted with both the Philosophy of Existence, as developed in Germany, and the outlook and main aim of Heidegger's thought, has a right to expect from an Introduction to the first writings published in English-speaking countries that these more general problems should be discussed as well, and that especially some kind of preliminary account of "Being and Time" should be given in order to clarify the approach of the thinker. For without some notion of this work the reader of these essays is apt to grasp only aspects of thought, however relevant and stimulating, but not the profound and comprehensive homogeneity of outlook, which inevitably belongs to an original thinker of rank.

This Introduction, therefore, falls into two parts. First I shall try to characterise "Being and Time" in its main problems and to give a somewhat detailed account of the fragment as published, basing my account strictly on the text, even to the point of a literal rendering as far as is possible. Afterwards I shall give a preliminary outline of the ideas contained in the four published essays.

A brief outline of the career of the thinker may preface the more general considerations.

Martin Heidegger, born at Messkirch in the Black Forest in 1889 and, as a Roman Catholic, well acquainted with Thomistic thought from his early youth onwards, received his first philosophic training in the Neo-Kantian school of Windelband and Rickert. The thinkers of this school distinguished themselves in two main respects. They analysed the epistemological difference between the objects studied and the concepts applied in history and in kindred branches of knowledge and those of the natural sciences; and it was found that all historical studies, by their nature, were concerned with phenomena of an "individuality" of some kind or other, which were essentially related to "values." At the same time, they approached the history of philosophy in a manner, novel at the time, by emphasising the great and fundamental problems advanced in the various periods of Occidental philosophy, from the days of the early Greeks to those of their own age. Heidegger's first published work, his Thesis for the Lectureship, dealt with "Duns Scotus' doctrine of categories and of concepts," with the outlook of that medieval thinker whom Windelband appraised as the most acute and most profound of all. Thus Heidegger rooted himself at the start in the study of one great figure in the tradition of European philosophy, a tradition in relation to which all his later work was to be conceived. In his first lecture, given at Freiburg i.B. in the summer semester 1915, he discussed "the concept of Time in historical studies," which likewise points from afar in the direction of his later great work "Being and Time."

It was, however, in close contact with Edmund Husserl, the founder of phenomenology, Professor of Philosophy at Freiburg i.B. from 1916 to 1929, that he developed his own method of the interpretation of the texts and ideas of great philosophers of the past, and of the exposition of systematic problems to which the tradition, from the Greeks to Husserl, and other eminent thinkers of the present age, gave rise. For to Heidegger, the study of the philosophic tradition and of systematic problems has been but one. He was and is convinced that only he who is steeped in the philosophic tradition, understanding the thought of a great thinker of the past as if it were his own, philosophising with him, as it were, in dialogue and only then criticising him constructively, would eventually develop philosophic problems in an original manner worthy of being contemplated by his own contemporaries and by posterity.

Solely on the strength of his stimulating and instructive teaching in lectures, the first form of publicity in which he embodied many of his own profoundly new investigations, he was appointed Professor of Philosophy in the University of Marburg a L. in 1923. During this period he produced and, in 1927, published his greatest work hitherto "Being and Time," Part I. Despite its fragmentary character—only the first two out of six planned sections of the book were published—and despite the novelty of its approach to fundamental problems, which involved the use of a new philosophic language, difficult to understand,* the work made at once a profound impression upon the philosophically-minded public, even outside the sphere of the trained philosophers, and was soon considered to be a landmark in philosophic studies.

Elected as Husserl's successor to the Chair of Philosophy in Freiburg in 1929, and undoubtedly also spurred by the exceptionally widespread recognition of his work, its rank and originality, he published in quick succession three works of varying length. In the historical study "Kant and the Problem of Metaphysics" he gave a new interpretation of the "Critique of Pure Reason," particularly its first half, placing in its centre the transcendental power of imagination as the "root" of the two stems of knowledge, intuition and understanding, and

---

* His employment of a new philosophic language arose probably first in connection with his intense study of Greek and medieval philosophy, and with his endeavour to find an adequate terminology for the new problems which he was analysing; this tendency seems to have been strengthened by his belief in the wisdom embodied in language. It seems to me essentially to resemble the treatment of words by the modern German poets Stefan George and Rainer Maria Rilke who, likewise, felt incapable of expressing their visions and thought with the help of the traditional and generally accepted language.

8

he related his own endeavours in "Being and Time" to Kant's work as a renewed attempt at laying a foundation to metaphysics. In the systematic study "On the Essence of Cause (or Ground)," an essay dedicated to Husserl in honour of his 70th birthday, he discussed the fundamental problem of transcendence as the realm within which an enquiry into the nature of cause could be made, analysed the concept of the "world," as well as transcendence, as the "Being-in-the-world" of Dasein, and distinguished three different kinds of "ground," each of which is rooted in transcendence: (a) the "founding" (Stiften), (b) the "gaining of ground" (Boden-nehmen) of Dasein amidst all that is and (c) the more especial function of "reasoning" (Begründen), understood as Dasein being enabled to ask the question "why." The third of these works was his Inaugural Lecture "What is Metaphysics?", one of the essays published in the present English collection. All of these publications were closely connected with the problems of his main work, particularly the first two, elucidating its theme and purpose in a relevant way.

In 1933, under the National Socialist régime, Professor Heidegger was elected Rector of Freiburg University, in which capacity he also delivered and published an Address on the position of German universities. He resigned this post early in 1934.

A new departure in his philosophic thought was indicated by his essay on "Hölderlin and the

Essence of Poetry" (1936); for the realm of poetry had so far not appeared to belong to his philosophic problems, still less to be outstanding among them. Interpretations of three individual poems of Hölderlin, two hymns "Wie wenn am Feiertage" (As when on a Festal Day), 1941, and "Andenken" (Remembrance), 1942, as well as one elegy "Homecoming," 1944, have since been published; in addition an analysis of "Plato's Doctrine of Truth" (1942), a systematic essay of considerable import, "On the Essence of Truth" (1943), and a likewise important "Letter on 'Humanism'" (1947). Of these more recent publications by Heidegger two essays on Hölderlin and the one on the Essence of Truth have been selected for this edition.

1

THE THREE MAIN PROBLEMS: DASEIN, TIME AND
BEING. THE PROJECT AND THE PUBLISHED VERSION

One important criterion for assessing the rank of
a thinker is the relevance of the problem or
problems originally envisaged by him, the intensity and consistency of thought with which he
contemplates it or them and the lucidity of the
exposition. Another criterion is that, under
the impact of a philosophic work, the reader is
induced to consider life and the world in a new
way and that relevant aspects, unthought of or
left in the background before, are brought into
the full light of conscious reflection. A true
philosopher differs from the scientist and scholar,
with whom he is bound up by their common
search for truth, not only through the fact that
his problems are on a greater scale and more
fundamental. But if his exposition is of weight,
it implies a new outlook with the force of
affecting, changing or stimulating that of the
reader.

Judged by these criteria, M. Heidegger's
"Being and Time" is a work of high rank. And
it must be my first task to make its main purpose
clearer.

The aim of this great work, and indeed of all
of Heidegger's publications, is the re-awakening
of the question: what is meant by "Being"?

This problem belongs to the tradition of European philosophy from the Greek philosophers Anaximander and Parmenides onwards; more than that, it was its central problem. In Heidegger's view, it guided the exertions of the greatest among the Pre-Socratic thinkers as well as those of Plato and of Aristotle—but after Aristotle it ceased to be the thematic problem of a genuine philosophic enquiry.

The achievement of elucidation attained until Aristotle affected vitally the medieval discussion of the problem and the whole of the Christian theological outlook; and through many changes the tradition of the problem kept alive down to Hegel's "Logic."

To-day, and in fact throughout the last century, the problem of "Being" has fallen into oblivion.*

According to Heidegger, the concept of "Being" is the most universal one, as was also realised by Aristotle, Thomas and Hegel; and its universality goes beyond that of any "genus." At the same time it is obscure and indefinable; "Being" cannot be comprehended as anything that is (Seiendes); it cannot be deduced from any higher concepts and it cannot be represented by any lower ones; "Being" is not something like a being, a stone, a plant, a table, a man. Yet "Being" seems somehow an evident concept. We make use of it in all knowledge, in all our statements, in all our behaviour towards anything

* Cf. "On the Essence of Truth," Section 6 and the corresponding commentary remarks in the Introduction.

that "is," in our attitude towards ourselves. We are used to living in an "understanding of Being" (Seinsverständnis), but hand in hand with it goes the incomprehensibility of what is meant by "Being." *

Heidegger's aim in "Being and Time" is to revive the question about the meaning of "Being," in the sense in which it was the guiding problem of Greek thought until Aristotle and its express theme of enquiry. In this respect he takes the Greek thinkers as his model.

But he deviates from them fundamentally in his starting-point. They reflected upon the things encountered in the world, that could be seen and thus known. And the thing that was perceived and about which statements could be made in various relevant respects, i.e. by way of "categories," was their paradigma.

Heidegger's starting-point is not the perceptible things, but what he terms: human "Dasein," a phenomenon fundamentally, i.e. in its ontological structure, not contemplated and not analysed by the Greeks or ever since in later philosophic tradition. His endeavour in this respect is to give an analysis of the "existentialia" and of the "existentialistic" structure of human Dasein in a way in which the Greek thinkers developed the "categories" of a thing that "is." But this analysis, profound and original as it is, is to him nothing but the starting-point. It is from this new angle that he intends to unfold the problem of "Being"

* The statements made in this paragraph are strictly based on "Being and Time," pp.2/4.

afresh. And the final guiding aim should not be overlooked when the attention is drawn to the new starting-point. The analysis of "Dasein" is of an exclusively preparatory nature.

Heidegger realised that "Dasein"—what is usually called "human life," though both are not entirely the same—differed ontologically from all the things which are not "Dasein" in essential respects. These things, when they are there by nature, are termed "vorhanden" ("existent" in the usual sense of the word, literally: before one's hand, at hand, present); and when they are made by men, such as utensils, they are termed "zuhanden" close at hand, in readiness, at one's disposal); but occasionally, the term "Vorhandenes" and "Vorhandenheit" applies to all that is not "Dasein."

(1) "Dasein" is always my own "Dasein." It cannot be ontologically grasped as the case or the example of a genus of beings, as can be done with things that are "vorhanden." This by itself causes considerable difficulties for the adequate ontological exposition. Besides, the being of the kind of "Dasein" is in its Being concerned about its Being and behaves towards its Being as towards its own possibility. It chooses and decides and it may gain or may lose itself, inasfar as its Being is concerned. All this cannot be said of the things that are "vorhanden." Two fundamental modes of Being, authenticity and unauthenticity, are distinguished, both of them depending on the fact that "Dasein" is essentially always my own.

(2) Of all the things that are "vorhanden" it

14

can be stated that they are of a special "genus," e.g. a house or a tree, and that they have special "qualities." In other words, their "essence" is always ascertainable. In contrast to them, the characteristics of "Dasein" are not "qualities," but possible ways of "Being." Therefore the term "Da-sein" is to express not its "essence," but its "Being"; it means "Being there." To distinguish further the kind of Being, peculiar to "Dasein," from all "Vorhandenheit," the term "Existence" is applied exclusively to it. And the fundamental characteristics of "Dasein," corresponding to the categories of "Vorhandenheit," are therefore termed "existentialia." *

Heidegger's own philosophic thought is grounded and deeply at home in the whole of the Occidental philosophic tradition from the earliest Greek thinkers to Kant and Hegel and beyond that to Kierkegaard, Husserl, Dilthey, Scheler and Jaspers. It would go beyond the framework of this brief introductory characterisation to consider the relatedness of "Being and Time" to any endeavour in thought of one of his great predecessors or contemporaries.†

But it would seem appropriate to refer in passing to its relatedness to two more recent or contemporaneous tendencies: to the Philosophy of Existence, as inaugurated by Kierkegaard and

* For the last two paragraphs cf. "Being and Time," pp.41/45.
† For the relatedness of "Being and Time" to Kant's "Critique of Pure Reason" cf. Heidegger's own book "Kant and the Problem of Metaphysics," especially Section 4, pp.195/236.

15

prominently represented today by Jaspers; and to the method of phenomenology, as introduced by Husserl.

Heidegger characterised his own attitude towards Kierkegaard, as follows: "In the nineteenth century S. Kierkegaard expressly seized upon and penetratingly thought out the problem of Existence as an existential one. But the existentialistic kind of problems (Problematik) is so alien to him that he is entirely under the sway of Hegel, and of the ancient philosophy seen through him, in ontological respect. Therefore more can be learnt philosophically from his 'edifying' writings than from the theoretical ones —with the exception of the treatise on the concept of dread." *

This distinction between "existential" (existenziell) and "existentialistic" (existenzial) is a fundamental one. When Kierkegaard criticised Hegel that he had omitted the problem of the actual Existence of the individual in his apparently all-embracing speculative philosophy and when he wrote his own works of philosophical elucidation, his aim was primarily not a "theoretical" one, but he wished by his "existential" elucidations to serve and to guide other people in their conduct of life. The "elucidation of Existence" in Jaspers' philosophy† takes fun-

* "Being and Time" (German edition), p.235.
† Cf. "Philosophy," Volume II, 1932. The impulse to "existential" reflections and the emphasis of the import on Kierkegaard's work can be noticed in his earlier publication "Psychologie der Weltanschauungen," 1919, to which reference is made on occasion in "Being and Time."

damentally the same line. In the meditation upon Existence the knowledge of the objects of the "world" is transcended; but such meditation aims at appealing in communication to others and to clarify, stimulate and strengthen them in their striving for Existence in their actual conduct; "Dasein," which is here taken to mean the same as life, and "Existence," which is of an absolute significance to the individual, are radically distinguished. Existential philosophy is, by its nature, inseparably related to both insight and conduct.

Heidegger's interest in "Existence" is essentially different from that of either Kierkegaard or Jaspers. He regarded it as his task to analyse "Dasein" ontologically, as had not been done by the Greeks and was never attempted afterwards. In this respect "Existence" seemed to him the fundamental characteristic of "Dasein." But one important difference between science and learning on the one hand and philosophy on the other seemed to him to consist in the fact that every kind of scientific and scholarly knowledge was concerned with a limited set of objects, of what he termed "ontic," whereas philosophy strove to envisage and analyse the far more hidden structure, and the guiding concepts, of the phenomenon basic to the "set of objects," a visualisation and an analysis which is "ontological." In this sense he states that "philosophical psychology, anthropology, ethics, 'politics,' literature, biography and history" have been the studies of some aspects of Dasein and

17

may have been "existentially genuine" (exist-enziell ursprünglich). But it remained an open question whether these investigations had been carried out in an equally genuine "existentialis-tic" (existenzial) manner, i.e. with a philo-sophic insight into and grasp of the "ontologi-cal" structure of Dasein. It is therefore with the "existentialistic" structure of Dasein, with what is basic to "Existence," that Heidegger is con-cerned. Otherwise he could not compare the "existentialia" to the "categories," analysed by Aristotle and since, of what is "vorhanden." *

Similarly he adapts the method of phenome-nology, as introduced by Husserl, for his own philosophic purpose. The method was applied to prevent any arbitrary and ready-made epistemological constructions and to study and describe the whole range of the phenomena given to consciousness from the standpoint of "transcendental subjectivity." In the last chap-ter of the "Ideas to a Pure Phenomenology and Phenomenological Philosophy" Husserl express-ly discussed the problem of a formal "ontol-ogy," of the transcendental constitution of a thing and of other "regional ontologies."

Heidegger adopted this method of philo-sophical analysis for "Being and Time," and he adopted the aim of a "regional ontology,"

* About the concept of "ex-sistence," first introduced in the essay "On the Essence of Truth," which is likely to have played an important part in the third Section of "Being and Time," about "Time and Being," cf. that essay, Section 4 and the corresponding remarks in the Introduction.

namely of "human Dasein," which, however, he considered to be the fundamental one preparing for an exposition of the meaning of "Being." But his attitude is not that of a "transcendental subjectivity" and of a study of the phenomena given to consciousness in the reduced state of a "phenomenological ἐποχη." But his intention is to overcome the attitude of "subjectivity," assumed by Husserl and by most thinkers since Descartes and Kant. His aim is to analyse the structure of Dasein, as it actually is, in its relations to the things in the "world," non-human and human; and though it is a transcendental analysis and though its problem is fundamentally different from that of Greek philosophy, it may be said that it is in its spirit and standpoint much nearer to Greek thought than perhaps any other work of philosophy in our age. The terms "objective" and "realistic" in their usual sense would not seem appropriate. But Dasein is envisaged in the light of "Being" and not primarily as a theme and "transcendental object" of human consciousness and "subjectivity." The phenomenological method, as applied by Heidegger, is thus as subtle in its descriptive analyses as is that of Husserl, but the attitude in which the phenomena are studied and the final aim towards which the enquiry is directed radically differ from that of his predecessor.

If the aim of "Being and Time" is the reawakening of the question: what is meant by

Being? and if its starting-point is an ontological analysis of Dasein, the one main problem not yet considered is that of <u>Time</u>. <u>The problem of Time is the link between the analysis of Dasein and the revival of the question of the meaning of Being.</u> Here again Heidegger's approach seems to be in vital contrast to that of the Greeks and the ontological tradition which they initiated.

In Heidegger's view, the meaning of "Being" is intimately bound up with the phenomenon of Time and has been bound up in this way since the beginning of philosophic thought. For the Greeks the definition of the Being of the things that are was, he points out, παρουσία or ουσία, not only in its ontological, but also in its temporal meaning. The things that are were envisaged in their Being as "present." This basis of the interpretation of the things in their Being has never been fundamentally questioned.

The temporality of Dasein, with its relations to future, past and present—to what Heidegger terms the three "ecstasies" * of temporality— opens up the "horizon" for the question about "Being" in an entirely new way so that this question can be re-asked only after this analysis of temporality. The relevance of Existence becomes clearer here through its prevalent relationship to the future; and it may be said that

---

* About "ecstasy" in the philosophical sense *cf.* the brief remark in my Introduction to "On the Essence of Truth" in connection with the concept of "Existence" as an "ex-position."

all
their
its tem
entirely a
rality of D
lichkeit); and
as well as the u
grounded in "hist
tated upon in more
by Dilthey and Niet
this aspect by itself open

The aim of the expositi   ...ity
of Dasein is to gain an insi   ...ature
of Time itself, an insight whic   ...degger's
view, has hitherto not advance   ...bstantially
beyond Aristotle's interpretation of Time in the
"Physics." An analysis of Hegel's concept of
Time and an expounding note on Bergson's
conception of Time tend to substantiate his
view. The explication of Time as the "transcendental horizon" for the problem of "Being" was
to lead to the aim: the analysis of what is meant
by Being.

But now it seems appropriate to state what
was the original plan of the work, as set out
in the beginning, and what has been published
of it hitherto.

The work was to consist of two main parts.
Each of them was divided into three divisions.
The first part was to contain the preparatory
fundamental analysis of Dasein, the analysis
of the temporality of Dasein and the analysis

...zon of the
...part was to offer
...omenological destruc-
...of ontology, guided by the
...mporality. It was to analyse criti-
...ral doctrines of Kant, of Descartes and
...Aristotle and to show where their essential
limitations lay, thereby clarifying Heidegger's
own exposition of Time and of Being. In this
way there were to be investigated Kant's doctrine of the schematism and of Time as a
preparatory stage for the analysis of the problem of temporality; the ontological basis of
Descartes' "cogito sum" and his transformation
of the medieval ontology into the problem of
the "res cogitans"; and Aristotle's treatise on
Time as the discrimen of the phenomenal basis
and of the limitations of Greek ontology.

The project comprising the two parts forms
a whole. Only when Aristotle's doctrine of Time
was scrutinised and the limitations of Greek
ontology and of their influence on the ontology
of the middle ages and of later times was made
plain, only when the import of the conception of
subjective consciousness in Descartes' work and
its bearing upon subsequent philosophy right
down to Husserl was exposed, and only when
the analysis of the temporality of Dasein was
brought into clear comparison and contrast
with Kant's doctrine of Time could Heidegger's
systematic enquiry stand out in full relief.

Of this project only the first two Sections,
a formidable work of concentrated systematic

22

analysis of more than 400 pages, were published. The publication breaks off at the end of the analysis of the temporality of Dasein and before the most important exposition of the work to which everything else had been preparatory: the problem of Time and Being.* Nor have any of the historical analyses of Kant, Descartes and Aristotle, directly concerned with the problem of "Being and Time," been published since, though the book on "Kant and the Problem of Metaphysics" arose in connection with the greater work and has a close bearing on it.

This fragmentary character of the work had, inevitably, a great influence on the understanding of its readers. What was aimed at and what was guiding the whole trend of thought, the problem of Being, was mostly overlooked; and it may well be said in defence of the interested and enlightened public that at the time it could hardly be grasped in its full and absorbing significance. In contrast to this, the novel exposition of the "existentialia" of Dasein, among them an analysis of phenomena such as dread, care, the Being-towards-one's death, the call of conscience and resolve, held the attention of many and it was rarely realised, though plainly stated by the author, that this ontological analysis of the structure of Dasein formed nothing but the preparatory starting-point. The philosophic study of human Dasein,

---

* About the reason given for the fragmentary character of the work by the author himself cf. the end of the Introduction to "On the Essence of Truth."

though here undertaken from the unusual angle of a descriptive analysis of "existentialia," seemed the more to fulfil a requirement of the age, as Nietzsche and particularly Dilthey and his school had for long demanded a "philosophy of human life," as Simmel's philosophy had tended in the same direction and as Scheler had proclaimed the task of a "Philosophical Anthropology" during the very years when "Being and Time" was prepared and published. Heidegger may well meet with a similar fate as did Hume, in that his greatest contribution to philosophic thought, held back at the time, will be recognised only very slowly and gradually, while other more congenial results of his thought found a ready acceptance and, however much distorted, helped to stimulate what is now commonly termed the movement of "Existentialism."

The fact that the actual second part of the work, the investigations of the history of European ontology, i.e. of the philosophic interpretation of Being and beings, at some of its most decisive turning-points, was not published, impairs the work further. The reader is thereby deprived of an insight into the great historic tradition and perspective in which the work stands, as conceived and understood by the author himself. The "phenomenological destruction" of this history, as Heidegger points out in the Introduction to "Being and Time," was to lay bare, under the distorting and obscuring cover of more recent problems and interpretations which stand between us and the great thinkers of the past like a barrier, the actual problems with which Kant, Descartes and Aristotle were concerned. It had thus a positive aim. But it desired at the same time to bring into the open the essential limitations implied in Kant's, Descartes' and Aristotle's approach to ontology. The historic analysis would have made the hardened and fixed tradition come to life again and would, at the same time, have enabled the philosophically-minded people of our age to realise in what essential respects the problem of "Being" and the interpretation of the things that are had not come into full grasp or had even been obscured once more in Aristotle's philosophy.

Thus "Being and Time," in the way in which it was published in 1927, is a fragment in two important respects: it does not contain that part of the systematic enquiry to which all the preceding and preparatory analyses lead up and by which, actually, they are guided; and it does not contain the historical exposition of those great figures of the ontological tradition against the background of which the systematic work itself with its high aspirations was to be measured.

Only with this reservation, and with the repeated emphasis on the great import of the Sections that are unknown for the time being, may now a few remarks be added about the general content of the first two Sections: the ontological structure of "Dasein" and the problem of temporality. These remarks are not intended to give a proper and detailed account of the phenomena that are analysed—a task which, as has been said in the beginning, cannot be undertaken here—but only to indicate the general framework of the exposition so as to allow the reader to see in what context some phenomena, which are of import also in one or the other of the four essays, were viewed and analysed in this work.

2

SOME ASPECTS OF THE ANALYSIS OF DASEIN

Human Dasein is characterised as "Being-in-the-world." This is its fundamental constitution, its innermost essence. The characterisation is not meant in the factual, i.e. "ontic," sense. For it is not essentially necessary that a kind of being, such as human Dasein, exist factually. It may not exist. Thus taken merely ontically, the proposition would even be wrong. It is an "ontological" definition, which means that Dasein can *be* in existence, i.e. as *"Dasein,"* because its essential constitution is "Being-in-the-world."

"World" is the rendering of the Greek conception of κόσμος in the sense used by Parmenides, Melissus, Heraclitus, Anaxagoras and others and indicates the "state," the "how" in which the beings are "in the whole"—a term often employed in the subsequent essays—before any special kind of beings is considered separately. "World" is that whereto Dasein transcends" so as to be what it is.*

Furthermore, the term "World" designates primarily, in Heidegger's view, neither the sum total of the things of nature nor a fundamental characteristic of the community of men, a new tradition introduced by St. Paul and St. John and continued by St. Augustine and by Thomas Aquinas, and also carried on in more recent and different connotations; but it means originally the "how" in which the things are "in the whole" as implicitly related to human Dasein, though for historical reasons this relationship was not given prominence in the strictly philosophic exposition.†

When it is stated in the essays that man is placed amidst a multitude of other beings "in the whole" or that man "lets" the things "be" such as they are, the fundamental characterisation that human Dasein is "Being-in-the-world" is in the background; and it should be borne in mind that this proposition is essentially different from any statement that something that is "vorhanden," e.g. a tree or a star, is in the world.

"Being-in-the-world" is analysed as a unitary phenomenon. The "in" in this connection is of a nature entirely different from the "in" applied to any phenomenon that is "vorhanden." If a thing is said to be "in" something else, this relationship is "spatial." If a being of the kind of

---

* Cf. "The Essence of Ground," pp.12/15.
† "The Essence of Ground," p.25.

Dasein is said to be "in" something, the relationship is not meant to be primarily "spatial," but means to "dwell," to "sojourn," to "stay," in the sense of the Latin word "habitare." E.g. a match is in a box in the plain spatial sense; but if a man is in his home or in his office or in a seaside-resort, obviously this relationship is not primarily spatial.

I have expressly referred to the "in-Being" (In-Sein), as Heidegger terms this structural characteristic of human Dasein, because it plays a great part in the analysis of the first Section, with its three fundamental modes, the *"Befindlichkeit"* of Dasein and its "Gestimmtheit," the *"Verstehen"* (understanding) of Existence and of the world and *"Rede,"* i.e. speech and language; and with the "Verfallen" (the potentiality of Dasein of falling a prey to the things in the world and of becoming alienated to its own authentic possibilities, intentions and endeavours), another outstanding trait of the "in-Being" of Dasein in its everyday state. But this "in-Being" is of considerable import also for the understanding of the essays, since the "Befindlichkeit," the "Gestimmtheit" and the phenomenon of language are expressly referred to or even discussed in some detail in one or the other of them. To these traits we shall return later.

Heidegger's first concern is to analyse the *"worldliness"* of the "world" and it is noteworthy that he observes and emphasises the point that Descartes, whose conception of "res extensa" he examines critically, had omitted to analyse the phenomenon of the "world" itself, restricting his analysis to the study of the physical and of the mental "things"; and that a similar omission belongs to the whole of European philosophic tradition as such, explicitly so in and since Parmenides.

In order to open up the philosophic study of the phenomenon of the "world" itself, his approach is a new one, different from that of the tradition, in that he analyses the constitution not of the things as given by Nature (das "Vorhandene"), but of the "utensils" ("Zeug," das "Zuhandene"), as they are encountered in daily life. This analysis offers two advantages: (1) Dasein is primarily not concerned with the things of nature in an exclusively theoretical attitude, but in its foreground of attention and interest are the *"utensils,"* this term taken in the widest sense of a product made by man in the state of civilisation. The things of Nature were originally encountered and discovered only in connection with such practical pursuit and they commonly form its background. Thus an analysis of "utensils," as that of one kind of beings, would seem to be as good for the opening up of the problem of the phenomenon of the world as an analysis of the things of Nature and would seem more appropriate in an exposition of the constitution of human Dasein. (2) Two different kinds of beings, "Zuhandenes" and "Vorhandenes," both belonging to the phenomenon of the "world," thereby come into sight and discussion.

In the course of this enquiry, Heidegger comes to define the worldliness of the world as "the Being of the ontic condition of the possibility of the discoverability of any beings encountered in the world." *

On the basis of the preceding analyses of the "utensil" and of "worldliness" the "spatiality" of Dasein as "Being-in-the-world" and the concept of space are discussed. It is shown that neither the space is in the subject nor the world is in space, but that space is "in" the world and a characteristic of it, inasfar as Dasein as "Being-in-the-world" is of its own spatiality and has disclosed space.

The second main concern is the question about the *"who"* of Dasein. Though this "who" was formally characterised in advance as "I," this must not be taken as an isolated "subject" or "self," independent of the "world," of what is "zuhanden" and "vorhanden," and of the other fellow-beings together with whom the "I" is there. In a similar way in which Heidegger gave an exposition of the "worldliness" of the "world" by way of an analysis of the "utensil," he starts here from the "everydayness" in which the "self" exists together with its fellow-beings and indeed in many respects not as an "Ich" (I), but as a *"Man,"* i.e. as "one like many." Since it will be one of the problems of the subsequent analysis:

* It is in the analysis of the actual care for a "utensil," a "Zuhandenes" that Heidegger introduces the concept "letting-be" which becomes one of the key-terms in the essay "On the Essence of Truth," *cf.* "Being and Time," pp.84/85.

in what way does a Dasein become "authentic"?, the averageness of the way in which the "self" is together with others in daily life, the sway which these others hold over it and the resulting levelling tendency in community life are emphasised. Primarily there is not "I" as my own "self," but the others, and "I" as one among many others, in the way of "one" (in German: "man"). I behave as "one does," I avoid doing something, because "it is not done." The "one" (or in the more common English usage of the passive tense, the "it") is the "neuter" or even the "no one," as Heidegger in his characterisation of the "man" once calls it. Yet this "one like many" is a genuine existentialistic trait of the constitution of Dasein; and the authentic self-Being (Selbstsein) is not something entirely separate from the "one like many," but is an "existential modification" of it.

"Umwelt" (the relationship to the "environment" of Dasein in its widest sense, including all that is "zuhanden" and "vorhanden") and "Mitwelt" (one's being together with a vast multitude of beings of the kind of "Dasein") as well as the rudimentary "self-being" in the form of the "one like many" are the first structural characteristics studied in this analysis of the ontological constitution of Dasein as "Being-in-the-world." They are followed up by the analyses of "in-Being," mentioned above, and of "Care" as the Being of Dasein, to which a briefer characterisation of "dread" is a preliminary.

In view of their relevance for one or the other

of the essays these two structural characteristics of Dasein as "Being-in-the-world" are to be discussed in slightly greater detail.

The "in-Being" (In-Sein) of Dasein,* as analysed in this work, is one of the most profound and stimulating enquiries of this Section, complemented at a later stage by the equally profound investigation into the "ecstasies" of temporality in which the modes of "in-Being" are thought grounded.

The analysis of "in-Being" is to clarify what is meant by the "Da," the "There," of human Dasein, what, in Heidegger's terms, is its existentialistic constitution.

One fundamental trait of Dasein, which is expressly discussed at various points of the published work, but which is in the centre especially in the analysis of "in-Being," is its "Erschlossenheit," i.e. the "disclosed," "discovered," "unveiled" state of Dasein. Referring to the well-known metaphor of the "lumen naturale" in man, Heidegger points out that this metaphor illustrates the way in which the "Da" of Dasein actually is. Dasein is "enlightened" or "illuminated" not by another kind of being, but it itself

* The account of the "in-Being," of "dread" and "Care" and of the whole of the structure of Temporality keeps to the text of "Being and Time" as closely as possible so that this account may assist the reader with a sufficient knowledge of German to find his way better through the text of the original and also in order to make a philosophic discussion of Heidegger's problems possible, while "Being and Time" is not available in an English translation.

is what sheds light. And only to an "enlightened" being (for which the shedding of light is existentialistically constitutive) is what is "vorhanden" accessible in light and concealed in darkness. It is the essential "Erschlossenheit" of Dasein, in one with that of the existence of the world, that would seem to be aimed at in the metaphor.*

This phenomenon of the "Erschlossenheit" of Dasein should be borne in mind, when various modes of "in-Being" are considered.

(1) The first of these "existentialia" is termed *"Befindlichkeit,"* which indicates the way in which a Dasein is "placed" in life and in the world.†

But this "ontological" characterisation of Dasein being "placed" in life and in the world in a specific way manifests itself in another more concrete phenomenon, or, as Heidegger would say, is the same as the well-known "ontic" phenomenon, of "Stimmung" (mood) or *"Gestimmtsein"* (being "tuned," being in a humour, spirit, mood). Thus the way in which a human being is placed in life and generally in the world would reveal itself to himself (or to others) in and

* This "Erschlossenheit" of Dasein is expressly in the centre of the analysis at the end of the whole of the first Section, in the discussion of the problem of truth; and it may be said to be the theme also in the essay "On the Essence of Truth."

† *Cf.* the contrast, in Section 2 of the essay "What is Metaphysics?", between our being "placed" (Sichbefinden) amidst the multitude of things in the whole, which situation repeats itself constantly in our Dasein moment for moment, and the comprehension of the whole of the things in themselves, which is impossible for man on principle.

through his "moods" in a very general and vague, but somehow telling manner. (The power in man of shedding a "light" on Dasein and on the beings that are met in the world will be remembered, here as in the discussion of "understanding.")

The "Befindlichkeit" and its self-revelation through "moods" is analysed in three main respects: (a) Though the "wherefrom" and the "whereto" of Dasein remain veiled, the fact "that it is," i.e. the "thrownness" (Geworfenheit) of Dasein into its "There," and that it is left to its own devices and responsibility (Ueberantwortung) is disclosed to it undisguisedly. The "mood," in its deeper meaning, brings the Dasein face to face with the "That," the fact, of the "There." (b) The "mood" has already always disclosed the "Being-in-the-world" as a whole and makes it possible that the Dasein directs itself towards, and concerns itself with, some things, persons, itself in the world. (c) The Dasein which is circumspect can be affected, impressed, and also threatened, in its "There" by the things and the persons. In the "Befindlichkeit" there is implied a disclosing persistent reference (Angewiesenheit) to the world of a somewhat compelling force; and man may encounter anything that approaches him and concerns him out of the world. He is in some way constantly exposed to the world; and this, too, is vaguely and implicitly revealed to him through his "moods." The concepts "Befindlichkeit" and "Gestimmtheit" are explicitly referred to in some of the essays; and the problem underlying them, the "in-Being" of human Dasein in the world, is common to all of them.

In "Being and Time" itself, one special mode of "Befindlichkeit," that of fear, is analysed, to prepare for the characterisation of another mood, that of dread, which in its turn is relevant for the analysis of Care.

(2) The second of these "existentialia" of "in-Being," co-original with the first, is that of "Verstehen" (understanding). It sheds light on the "There" of Dasein in a way fundamentally different from that of the "gestimmte Befindlichkeit." Taken in its deepest and, in Heidegger's view, most original meaning, the "understanding" discloses to the Dasein "for the sake of what" (the "Worumwillen," the τοῦ ἕνεκα) it "exists," "Existence" here understood in the strict and modern sense. Things and persons and the whole of one's "Being-in-the-world" gain their "significance" (Bedeutsamkeit) from the dominant purpose or aim, for the sake of which man understands himself to "exist."

Dasein means primarily to have the "potentiality of Being" (Seinkönnen). And "potentiality" (or "possibility") is of an essentially different meaning for Dasein and for anything that is "vorhanden." For anything that is "vorhanden" it means what is not yet real and what is never necessary. It is what is "only possible" and is ontologically less than reality and necessity. As for Dasein, on the other hand, it is the most genuine and final positive characterisation. And "understanding," as one of the "existentialia," unveils man's "potentialities" of Being to him.

Both the "Befindlichkeit" and the "Verstehen" belong together and are inseparable from one another. Dasein, as essentially "placed" in life and the world, is always face to face with some definite "potentialities," has let some of them pass and continues to do so, while it seizes upon other ones and materialises them, for good or for bad. Dasein is "thrown potentiality" through and through; and it is the potentiality of becoming free for its own and innermost potentiality of Being. Dasein as "Verstehen" always knows in some way and to some extent what is the matter with itself, i.e. with its own "potentiality of Being." But such knowledge does not arise from, and is not dependent on, introspection: it belongs to the Being of the "There," which, in one respect, essentially consists in "understanding."

However, this "understanding" of one's own potentialities does not restrict itself to the "Existence" of the individual human being. In the "light" of these potentialities what is "zuhanden" is seen and discovered in its serving function, its applicability or its harmfulness; the potentiality of the interconnectedness of all that is "zuhanden" is seen and discovered as is the "unity" of the manifold things that are "vorhanden," i.e. Nature, namely on the basis of its disclosed "potentiality."

The counter-phenomenon to the "throwness" (Geworfenheit) of Dasein as "Befindlichkeit" is termed "project" (Entwurf). The "project" of "understanding" is always essentially concerned with "potentialities," in all possible respects. The "understanding" conceives "for the sake of what" the Being of Dasein is to be as well as the "significance" to be attached to any utensils or things or persons and to the worldliness of the world. Such "projecting" has nothing to do with a well thought-out "plan" which would only be a remote derivative of it. Dasein has always "projected" itself already and continues to "project," as long as it is. In the same way as Dasein is always essentially "thrown" into its "There," it always "projects" essentially potentialities.

The "project" concerns the full revealedness of "Being-in-the-world." But the "understanding" has two primary tendencies of dealing with this "Being-in-the-world," in accordance with the realm that is discoverable to it. It may primarily concern itself with the disclosed state of the world, i.e. Dasein can primarily understand itself from its world. Or it may primarily project itself into the "for the sake of . . ." (the "Worumwillen"), in which case the Dasein "exists" as itself. In this sense the "understanding" is either an "authentic" one, arising from one's own self as such, or an "unauthentic" one, though this does not presuppose that the self is ignored and only the world understood and though the world belongs essentially to one's self-Being.

Starting from his exposition of "understanding" as a fundamental mode of "in-Being," Heidegger analyses in some greater detail two "derivatives" of "understanding": "interpretation" (Auslegung) as the elaboration of the understanding of something as something and of "meaning" (Sinn); and the nature of "propositions" (Aussage) as a derivative mode of interpretation.

In contrast to the phenomena of "Befindlichkeit" and "Gestimmtheit," those of "understanding" and of "project" are not explicitly referred to in the subsequent essays. But this does not mean that they are not fundamental to the problems which are analysed there. In the concluding note to the essay "On the Essence of Truth," it is expressly emphasised that the decisive question about the "meaning," i.e. the "realm of project" (Entwurfbereich), remained intentionally undiscussed. Obviously, the aim, approach and treatment of the essay would have gained much in the way of elucidation, had this dominant and, as Heidegger calls it, "decisive" question been brought into the discussion, too; and it seems fortunate that both its relevance and its omission are clearly stated. Similarly, the conception of "project" would seem to be of great relevance for the essays on Hölderlin, especially that on the poem "Homecoming" and the outlook developed there by the poet, but also that on "Hölderlin and the Essence of Poetry," particularly in view of the great, and even extraordinary, significance which Heidegger ascribes to the work of poets for the life of the human race and its history as a whole.

(3) The third of the "existentialia" of "in-Being," co-original with "gestimmte Befindlichkeit" and "Verstehen," is "speech" (Rede). "Speaking" is the "signifying" articulation (Artikulation, Gliederung) of the "Being-in-the-world" in the way in which it is "understood." The "understanding," arising for human Dasein in the "There" in which it is "placed," expresses itself as "speech"; and the totality of the "significances" articulated by "understanding" and "interpretation" comes to "word."

"Listening" (Hören) and "silence" (Schweigen) belong as potentialities essentially together with "speech." Constitutive characteristics of "speech" are: "what is spoken of" (das Worüber der Rede, das Beredete), "what is said as such" (das Geredete als solches), "communication" (Mitteilung) and "the information given" (Bekundnng). As Heidegger points out, these are not "qualities" empirically to be gathered, but existentialistic traits rooted in the constitution of Dasein, which make something such as language ontologically possible. The attempts at grasping the "essence of language" have usually taken their orientation from one or the other of these traits. The task would be to elaborate the whole of the structure of "speech" on the basis of the analytics of Dasein.

The interpretation by the Greeks of the essence of man as ζῷον λόγον ἔχον, the living being which speaks, gives point to the import of the phenomenon. For "speech," in this sense, refers not to voice and sounds, but to the way in which the world and Dasein itself are discovered.

In this connection it seems noteworthy that Heidegger points out some shortcomings of the philosophic reflections on the nature of language, which are due to the Greek tradition. The λόγος was principally grasped as "proposition" (ἀπόφανσις) and the fundamental structure of only its forms and elements was elaborated. Furthermore, the foundation of Grammar was sought in Logic and the traditional Logic, on its part, arose from the ontology of what is "vorhanden." These limitations are thought to have essentially affected the subsequent study and theory of language; in the view of the author, this kind of learning requires a genuine philosophic refoundation.

The problem of the nature of language is discussed in the essay on "Hölderlin and the Essence of Poetry." There it may be remembered that "speech" is regarded and analysed as a fundamental mode of the "in-Being" of human Dasein, equally essential as the "Befindlichkeit" with its "moods" and the "understanding" of potentialities, of the "for the sake of what" and of "significances."

The analysis of the three "existentialia" of "Befindlichkeit," "understanding" and "speech" forms only the first part of the characterisation of "in-Being." Its second part resumes the investigation of the "everydayness" of Dasein, i.e.

the "in-Being" of the "one like many" (in German: "man"), the primary "who" of Dasein. This aspect of the analysis is of considerable import in "Being and Time," where "authentic Existence" is to be developed from its common background of the average and levelled kind of life of the "one like many." But it has relatively little bearing on the problems of the four essays and thus it may be treated more briefly here.

Three characteristics of the "in-Being" of everyday Dasein are analysed at first: (a) "Talk" (Gerede), a modification of "speech" in which what is and what is spoken of is not so much understood, but where one listens only to what is said; it implies an indifferent and superficial, but no "genuine" understanding and moves in the wide realm of common and accepted interpretations; like the other two it is a positive and constitutive mode in which everyday Dasein understands and interprets events, things, persons, the world and Dasein itself. (b) "Curiosity" (Neugier), a modification of the "vision" (Sicht) based on the power in man of shedding forth light, a tendency of a peculiar perceptive encounter with the world, not in order to understand what is seen, but merely in order to see what things look like; the new attracts for the sake of its novelty; it is usually bound up with restlessness and distraction. (c) "Ambiguity" (Zweideutigkeit), implying the difficulty in everyday Dasein of discerning what is disclosed (erschlossen) in genuine understanding and what not; all may look as if it were genuinely understood, taken up and spoken and fundamentally this is not so, and reversely, all may look different and yet attitude and behaviour are genuine.

The fourth characteristic, the "Verfallen" of Dasein, is of a more fundamental nature and is also basic to the three fore-mentioned ones. It means primarily that the Dasein is entirely concerned and occupied with the "world" of its care. But an undercurrent of its meaning is that the Dasein lost itself in the publicity of the "one like many" and in the "world" which belongs to its Being. Here, as everywhere, Heidegger is interested in the phenomenon not as an "ontic" peculiarity, but as an "existentialistic," i.e. "ontological," mode of "in-Being"; and he describes in a most elucidating and impressive way this mode of "unauthentic" Existence and the structure of its inner "movement."

Dasein with the publicity of the "man" in its various forms offers to itself constantly the "temptation" (Versuchung) of "Verfallen." Yet when the Dasein is actually falling a prey to the publicity of the "man," this publicity itself, and the Dasein's trust in it, exercises a profoundly appeasing influence (Beruhigung) as if everything was in the best order. But this appeasement by itself intensifies the "Verfallen," driving to a restless activity and bringing Dasein into a state of "self-estrangement" (Entfremdung) in which its own innermost "potentiality of Being" becomes concealed to it. However, this self-estrangement which denies to Dasein its authenticity and best potentialities, as it were, locking it up from what it genuinely can be, does not hand it over to something which it is not itself, but presses it into its unauthenticity, a potential mode of Being of itself; in it Dasein catches itself up and entangles itself (Sichverfangen). This way of inner movement of Dasein in its own Being is termed the "fall" (Absturz): the Dasein falls from itself to itself, namely to the groundlessness and irrelevance of unauthentic everydayness. Its kind of motion is characterised as the "whirl" (Wirbel) which swings it down into the "man." But this whirl itself reveals the "thrownness" (Geworfenheit) itself in its moving and throwing force. For thrownness is not a finished fact, but Dasein, as long as it is, remains in the state of throw and may thus be whirled into the unauthenticity of the "man."

This constitution of "Verfallen" as a mode of "in-Being" is not anything that speaks against the existentiality of Dasein, but on the contrary is a weighty proof for it. For throughout the whole of the process of "Verfallen" Dasein is concerned about nothing else than its own potentiality of "Being-in-the-world."

"Being-in-the-world" is a unitary structural whole. Up to this point the phenomenon was analysed in its various constitutive aspects: the worldliness of the world; the Being-together-with-others, the self-Being and the "one like many"; the in-Being, the "There" of Dasein. The new problem is the unity of the structural whole. The question in this "ontological" enquiry, i.e.

the philosophical investigation into the Being of . . . , is: what is the Being of Dasein? It is defined as "Care"; and in preparation for its exposition the fundamental "Befindlichkeit" of dread is analysed. But the analytics of Dasein is, as we know, not the main aim, but only the starting-point. Thus we shall have to bear in mind the one guiding question: what is the meaning of Being as such? especially while the Being of one kind of beings, of Dasein, is under consideration.

The concept of "dread" (Angst), introduced into the modern philosophic discussion by Kierkegaard, prepares not only the analysis of "Care" in "Being and Time," but forms also one important link in the sequence of arguments in the essay "What is Metaphysics?"

Both Kierkegaard and Heidegger distinguish "dread" from "fear" (Furcht). "Fear" is always the "fear of something definite." * "Dread" is, as Kierkegaard puts it, "the reality of freedom as a potentiality, before this potentiality has materialised"; it is "a sympathetic antipathy and an antipathetic sympathy" and its object is "the something which is nothing." †

Heidegger analyses fear as a special mode of

* S. Kierkegaard, "The Concept of Dread"; German edition, p.36.
† *Op. cit.*, p.37. It may be of interest to some readers that Freud, in his "Introductory Lectures on Psychoanalysis," distinguished "dread" from "fear" in a similar way: "Dread is related to the mental state as such and disregards the object, whereas fear directs its attention especially to the object"; *cf.* Chapter 25· About Dread, German edition, p.410.

the "Befindlichkeit" of "in-Being" and dread as a fundamental "Befindlichkeit" disclosing Dasein to itself in an eminent way. Both phenomena are considered neither psychologically and psychopathologically nor "existentially" with a view to their relevance for the actual life of the individual, but ontologically with regard to their bearing on Dasein as "Being-in-the-world."

Three structural aspects in the phenomenon of "fear" are especially analysed: what is feared (das Wovor der Furcht), the fearing itself (das Fürchten) and on behalf of what the fear fears (das Worum der Furcht). (a) What is feared is always something which is encountered in the world, either of the kind of the "Zuhandene" or of that of the "Vorhandene" or of that of the Dasein of others. The "What" is threatening. This implies: that it is harmful; that it concerns a definite sphere of what it can endanger; that it comes from a definite "region" which is known, but somewhat uncanny; that it approaches and is imminent; that it may hit or pass by. (b) The fearing leaves room for what is threatening in this way. It allows itself to be concerned about it. It discovers it in its threatening nature, while and even before it approaches. The fear may then clarify the specific kind of the threat by envisaging it expressly, since the circumspection is in the "Befindlichkeit" of fear. (c) The fear fears "on behalf of" the Dasein concerned. The Dasein discloses through its fear its own endangered state and its dependence

45

upon itself. Thus the fear always reveals the Dasein in the Being of its "There," though in different ways, e.g. concerning one's own possessions or the well-being of a friend.

The phenomenon of "dread," though somewhat akin to that of "fear," is essentially different. What is "dreaded" is something that threatens, as is what is feared. But the "something" is different. The "What" of dread is not of the kind that can be encountered in the world, "Zuhandenes," "Vorhandenes" or the Dasein of others. To clarify the nature of the "something" that is dreaded the phenomenon of "Verfallen" is found of help.

When Dasein occupies itself entirely with its world of care and gives itself up to the publicity of the "one like many," something like a flight of the Dasein from itself as from authentic potentiality of self-Being reveals itself. What it flees in this turning away from itself is not grasped and not even attentively experienced. But the "something" from which the flight or rather the withdrawal takes place must be of a threatening nature, though it is not concrete and definite, as is any "What" of fear. The turning away from oneself and the withdrawal from one's authentic potentialities in the "Verfallen" would seem to be grounded in "dread."

What is dreaded in the state of dread is entirely indefinite. As has already been mentioned, nothing of what is "zuhanden" and "vorhanden" within the world functions as what the dread dreads. More than this: all that is discovered in either of these ways is of no interest and the world itself has assumed the character of complete irrelevance. What is dreaded is that what is threatening is nowhere. It is somehow there—and yet nowhere, very close and oppressing—and yet nowhere. What is dreaded reveals itself as "it is nothing and nowhere"; but the atmosphere of profound averseness and oppression implied in the "nothing and nowhere" indicates that what is dreaded is yet "something," namely "the world as such." What the dread dreads is the "Being-in-the-world." The dread discloses the world as world, which does not mean that the worldliness of the world is comprehended in the state of dread.

This is the first aspect of Heidegger's analysis of dread. The second one concerns the question: "for the sake of what" the Dasein is in a state of dread.

Here again it is not for the sake of one definite mode of Being and one definite potentiality of Dasein that the Dasein is in dread. It is for the sake of the "Being-in-the-world" itself or rather for the sake of its authentic potentiality of "Being-in-the-world"; for the world and the Dasein together with others as such cannot offer anything to the Dasein in dread any more. The dread isolates the Dasein for its own innermost Being-in-the-world, it opens up to Dasein, Dasein as "potentiality," namely as what it can be uniquely out of itself as an isolated one in isolation. It can now project itself into potentialities by way of its understanding.

47

In the phenomenon of dread, therefore, both what is dreaded and for the sake of what the Dasein is in dread are substantially the same. The one is the Being-in-the-world in the state of "thrownness"; the other is the potentiality of Being-in-the-world authentically. In this way a "Befindlichkeit" of an eminent kind has become the theme of the exposition which, by its fundamental character, prepares for the subsequent exposition of the Being of Dasein.

The problem with which the reader of the essay "What is Metaphysics?" is concerned is not the analytics of Dasein, but the problem of the nature of metaphysics. In "Being and Time" dread is analysed, as it were, as the stepping-stone to Care, representing the transition from the "nothing and nowhere" to the Being of any Dasein. Here the emphasis lies on the phenomena of dread and Care themselves. In the essay the phenomenon of "nothingness" is in the centre throughout, though it is shown to be grounded in dread. Moreover, the transposition into "nothingness" is thought to be the preliminary and indispensable state, one of "transcendence," to open up the realm of the multitude of beings in the whole and of Being itself of which nothingness is "the veil." Here again a transition, though of a very different character, from nothingness to the beings in the whole and to Being is noticeable, not wholly dissimilar to that from dread to Care. Thus the exposition in "Being and Time" and that in the essay may mutually illustrate and elucidate each other, to some extent at least. Yet the problem of the essay is infinitely vaster. Thus, while in one respect the analysis of dread, including its relation to nothingness and the "Being-in-the-world," and also that of Care would seem of especial relevance for the understanding of the essay, the whole of the analyses of the first two Sections of "Being and Time" appear to be the background for its comprehension, as is definitely so in the case of the essay "On the Essence of Truth."

In the subsequent analyses three ontological characteristics of Dasein show themselves to be the most fundamental ones: "existentiality" with its special reference to the "potentiality of Being" (Seinkönnen), "understanding" and "project"; "Befindlichkeit" or, as it is sometimes termed with a slightly different emphasis, "Faktizität" with its special reference to the fact "*that* Dasein is," that it is "thrown" into the "There" and is in the movement of the "throw"; and the "Verfallensein," which, though it is a movement into "unauthenticity," is manifest in some respects in every Dasein. These three characteristics should not be thought three self-dependent "elements" belonging to a compound; they are in one genuine structural connection one with the others and are of one whole. But it may be well to fasten one's attention upon them when the Being of Dasein is defined as Care, this term again taken in the ontological sense. Three important aspects emerge.

(1) Dasein is a kind of being which, in its

Being, is concerned about its own Being, or, as it may be phrased, is "for the sake of" its own Being. It is free for its own innermost potentiality of Being and thus for the potentialities of authenticity and unauthenticity. This relatedness to its own potentiality of Being means ontologically: Dasein is, in its Being, always already in advance of itself.

(2) But this "Being-in-advance-of-itself" is not to be taken as an isolated tendency of a "subject" without world, for it characterises one aspect of the "Being-in-the-world." It is "thrown" into a world and left there to its own devices and responsibility. It is always already in a world, being in advance of itself.

(3) However, the actual Existence of Dasein does not only consist in a "thrown" potentiality of Being-in-the-world in general and without further qualification. Dasein always engages and spends itself in the world of its care. It is actively concerned with beings that are "zuhanden," i.e. belong to the realm of civilisation, in the world. In this the "Verfallen" manifests itself. Dasein is thus, structurally: Already-Being-in-the-world, in-advance-of-itself, as the Being-concerned-with-beings-encountered-in-the-world.

This is the formula for the ontological whole of the structure of Dasein, i.e. for its Being, to which the title of care (Sorge) is given. The formula may seem formidable at first, but I hope that, once it is seen how it arises, it can relatively easily be understood in its articulated meaning.

Care, taken in this sense, may be a care of . . .

if it concerns anything that is "zuhanden," or a care for . . . if it concerns the Dasein of others.

The term "Care" is not only to characterise the "existentiality" of Dasein isolated from "Fakti-zitat" and "Verfallen," but is to comprise all of them and to indicate their unity.

In view of the import of an exposition concerning the Being of Dasein itself, two investigations of a more general significance are carried out, to make the meaning of "Care" and its philosophic relevance clearer: one into the problem of "Dasein, worldliness and reality," where the problem of the reality of the outer world, Kant's refutation of Idealism, Heidegger's attitude towards "Realism" and "Idealism" as well as to the interpretations of the nature of "reality," more recently undertaken by Dilthey and Scheler, and the problem of the relationship between "reality" and "Care" are discussed; and another one into "Dasein, its disclosed state (Erschlossenheit) and truth." An account of these two investigations cannot be attempted here; a brief reference to the second one will be made in the Introduction to the essay "On the Essence of Truth."

It is needless to say that the concept of "Care," of which only its formal and most general characterisation could be given above, is of special import and interest whenever it occurs in one of the essays: it is used rarely and most thoughtfully.

It is referred to in the Prefatory remarks to the interpretation of Hölderlin's poem "Home-coming" as well as in the interpretation itself, briefly in the beginning and more expressly towards the end. The vocation of the poet, according to Heidegger, is "to name what is holy." His Care, therefore, is concerned with "the way in which he must tell what he contemplates he ought to communicate in his poem." The "Holy" and the "Care" in his choice of the way of its communication and wording are thus the central concern of the poet as poet.

Similarly, the thought of the thinker is considered to be "obedient to the voice of Being" and he must therefore employ all his Care for conveying it in the language which he finds to be most appropriate.

Whenever the term "Care" is used, it refers to, and may even be meant to invoke for the reader the thought of, the Being of either the poet or the thinker or the reader himself. The brief account given above of its significance in Heidegger's main work may help to understand it more precisely in its concrete applications in the essays.

3

DASEIN AND TEMPORALITY

The first Section, the preparatory fundamental analysis of Dasein, leads up to the exposition of Care as its Being. The second Section is devoted to the problem of "Dasein and Temporality." *

* Of the first Section some outstanding characteristics, such as the "worldliness" of the world with its "utensils" and the "who" of Dasein as the "one like many," were

The enquiry aims at a more fundamental (ursprünglich) ontological interpretation of Dasein than has been reached so far, in order to lay bare the "horizon" in which something such as "Being" can become understandable at all and to answer the question about the "meaning" of Being as such. In the preparatory analysis the "unauthentic" Being of Dasein, and in fact without its consideration as a "whole," was in the foreground. Two questions are therefore guiding: (a) in what way can Dasein be approached and analysed as a "whole"? and (b) in what way can it be "authentic"? Both questions are interlinked, though the one or the other of them dominates the investigation at the various stages of its progress.

The problem of "Temporality" begins to be explicitly discussed only from the middle of the

-----

only hinted at and mainly those traits which had a more direct bearing on the problems of the essays were discussed in somewhat greater detail. Thereby the reader may have gained an inkling of the originality and intensity of the exposition, but not a clear insight into the structural complexity and unity in its variety of aspects nor into the forcefulness of the systematic procedure and into its profound consistency.

As for the second Section the subsequent representation aims at bringing this systematic procedure, and with it the treatment of the problem of "Time," before the mind of the reader. For since the exposition of the meaning of Being itself has not been published, this treatment of the problem of "Time" should at least come into clear relief, as otherwise the reader cannot gain even an "impression" of the main purpose of the work nor fully realise what the occasional reference to "Time" at some point or other in the essays signifies. At the same time, the intention of comparative brevity is maintained.

third chapter onwards, i.e. in the course of the third stage of our account. But it is implicitly the one outstanding problem right from the start; and the two "guiding" questions themselves are not only related, but even subservient to it. The analysis of the phenomenon of "death" as well as of those of "conscience," "guilt" and "resolve" is carried out not so much for its own sake as rather to prepare for the exposition of "Temporality" and more especially of the "future" which, in and for Dasein, is its dominant mode. Therefore the reader may do well to bear the problem of "Temporality" in mind even during the initial stages of the enquiry, though the problem is only implicitly posed there.

(1) The first step taken to envisage, grasp and define ontologically, i.e. existentialistically, Dasein as a "whole" is the analysis not of "death" as such, but of the "Being-towards-one's-own-death" (Sein zum Tode). The meaning of the term and the reason why this is the theme of the analysis will explain itself from what follows.

"Death" is the "end" of Dasein whereby it becomes a "whole." But to arrive at this boundary of Dasein is at the same time the loss of Dasein. The transition to Dasein-no-more makes it impossible for Dasein to experience the transition and, having experienced it, to "understand" it. There is the experience of the "death" of others and this phenomenon is first characterised. But for the problem under review, i.e. death as the "end" of Dasein which always means my own

Dasein, the phenomenon of the death of others is not of relevance. However much one Dasein may be able to replace another one in the activities of the community, no one can relieve another one of his own dying. Death is irreplaceable. Dasein, as long as it lasts, is always and essentially a "not yet" of what it will be; and the others who are dead are "no more" in the "There," which is an essential trait of Dasein, too, when its "end" is reached.

The first question is: in what sense must death be comprehended as the "ending" of Dasein. Such "ending" does not necessarily mean "fulfilment," but it does also not merely mean "ceasing," as of rain, or "completion," as of a work, or "vanishing." The kind of "ending" meant by death would appropriately be characterised not simply by being *at* the end" of Dasein, as if it were the actual outer close of it, symbolised, e.g. by the cutting of the thread by one of the three Parcae, but by "Being-*towards*-the-end." For death belongs to the "Being" of Dasein; and it is a mode of its Being to which Dasein is exposed and which it must take upon itself, as soon as it is.

After this initial clarification the existentialistic analysis is distinguished from other possible interpretations of death, such as the biological one of the death of plants and animals (Verenden), the physiological and medical one of the death of Dasein (Ableben), the psychological one of the states and the ways of the experience accompanying the "Ableben," the ethnological one concerning the conceptions of death by the primitives and their attitude towards it in magic and cult, furthermore especially the "existential" attitude towards death in its great variety, the theological interpretation and the one within the larger framework of "theodicy." To all these "ontic" interpretations with the rich multitude of their material the ontological exposition is methodically prior, even though its results are of a formality peculiar to all ontological characterisations.

The actual exposition starts by demonstrating that, and in what sense, the "Being-towards-one's-death" belongs genuinely and essentially to the "Being" of Dasein, i.e. to "Care." "Care" was analysed with regard to its three main constituent aspects: "Existentiality," "Faktizität" and "Verfallen." The "Being-towards-death" is, first of all, characterised in these three respects as well.

(Existentiality.) Death is of the character of something towards which Dasein behaves: it is an "imminence" (Bevorstand) in an eminent sense. It is a potentiality of Being which Dasein, each in its way, has to take upon itself. With death Dasein in its own and *innermost* potentiality of Being is imminent to itself. In death the "Being-in-the-world" is at stake. It is the potentiality of no more being able to be there. In this imminence Dasein is compelled to take entirely its recourse to its own potentiality of Being. For in it *all relations* to the Dasein of others are *dissolved*. This innermost potentiality, without any relationship to others or to things, is at the same time the *extreme* one. As the potentiality of Being which it is, Dasein cannot overcome the potentiality of death. For death is the potentiality of Dasein being entirely and absolutely impossible. Thus death reveals itself as the innermost (eigenst) and irrelative, i.e. absolute (unbezüglich) potentiality, not to be overcome (unüberholbar).

(Faktizität.) Dasein does not adopt this potentiality afterwards and on some occasion or other in the course of its Being nor does it arise by way of a personal attitude that is taken up by some and at some times. But whenever Dasein exists, it is also already "thrown" into this potentiality. At first and mostly, Dasein has no express, and even less a theoretical, knowledge of the fact that it is handed over to its death. The thrownness into death unveils itself more genuinely and more penetratingly in the "Befindlichkeit" of dread. The dread of death is dread of one's own innermost and irrelative potentiality of Being, not to be overcome. What is dreaded in this state of dread is the "Being-in-the-world" itself. For the sake of what Dasein is in a state of dread is the "potentiality of Being" of Dasein as such. The dread of death is no arbitrary and chance mood of the individual, but, as a fundamental Befindlichkeit of Dasein, the disclosure that Dasein exists as the thrown "Being-towards-its-end."

(Verfallen.) At first and mostly, Dasein obscures and conceals its own "Being-towards-death," fleeing from it. Dasein dies factually, as long as it exists, but at first and mostly in the mode of

"Verfallen." For the actual Existence engages and spends itself always already also in the world of its care. In this state of preoccupation with what is cared for the flight from the "uncanny" announces itself, i.e. in this context, the flight from its own "Being-towards-death."

Before Heidegger endeavours to develop the full existentialistic concept of death, he considers it first in its best known concrete mode, that of everydayness.

In the publicity of the "one like many" death is "known" as an event which constantly occurs, as something which happens "in" the world, i.e. as something which is "vorhanden," but not yet "vorhanden" for the person concerned and thus of no threatening character. "People die" (man stirbt). This "man" is "not just I"; it is "no one." The publicity of the "one like many" intensifies the "temptation" of concealing to oneself one's own "Being-towards-death" as well as the constant "appeasement" about it, even in the conventional consolation with which the "dying" is often persuaded he would escape death. The publicity of the "one like many" does not allow the courage required for the dread of death to arise. An indifferent tranquillity is expected in view of the "fact" that "one" dies. The development of such "superior" indifference "estranges" the Dasein from its innermost, irrelative potentiality of Being.

The mode of "Verfallen" is obvious in such "temptation," "appeasement" and "estrangement." The everyday Being-towards-death is a constant flight from it and has the mode of avoiding it by way of its misinterpretation, unauthentic understanding and disguise. But with all this, Dasein in its everydayness, shows itself to be essentially concerned about this innermost and irrelative potentiality of Being, if only in the mode of its care for an undisturbed indifference to the extreme potentiality of its Existence.

In the continued examination of the Being-towards-death in its everydayness two further essential traits emerge and are discussed: the kind of "certainty" (Gewissheit) implied in death and its "indefinable" character ("Unbestimmtheit") as to its "when."

"Certainty" is grounded in truth and one mode of certainty is conviction. But the way in which Dasein in its everydayness is mostly convinced of the "certainty" of death is that it is an "event" somehow encountered in the world. Even in serious theoretical reflection death is regarded as merely a "fact of experience" which can be observed daily and which therefore is undeniable. It is usually overlooked that Dasein, i.e. my own Dasein, must be certain of its own innermost and irrelative potentiality of Being in order to be able to be certain of death.

One way of obscuring the "certainty" of death in everyday Dasein results from its "indefinable" character as to its "when." It is interpreted and thought of as the "not yet for the time being."

Dasein in its everydayness tries to cover up that death, as the "end" of one's own Dasein, is imminent every moment.

Death is thus defined as the innermost and irrelative potentiality of Being, certain and indefinite as to its "when" and not to be overcome. And the problem that now arises, and for which the whole of Heidegger's preceding analysis prepares, is: in what way can Dasein "understand" its own death "authentically" and what is the "authentic" attitude and behaviour towards one's own death, i.e. the authentic "Being-towards-death."

The authentic "Being-towards-death" will not evade its own innermost and irrelative potentiality nor obscure or conceal it in such an escape nor misinterpret it in the way of the intelligibility of the "one like many."

It will "understand" the Being-towards-death as a Being concerned with a "potentiality" and in fact an eminent potentiality of Dasein. This potentiality, however, does not belong to the realm of what is "zuhanden" or "vorhanden," where something is to be attained or brought into control and "realised" in some way. It is a potentiality of the Being of Dasein. If it is to be "authentically understood," it must be understood, developed and endured in one's practical attitude and behaviour as a "potentiality" and no obscuring of it should be allowed.

"Expectation" is the behaviour of Dasein towards something possible in its potentiality. But this phenomenon is ambiguous in that it is mostly related to "realisation" and "reality" and to what is possible or potential there. But the attitude towards one's death is to be such that it unveils itself in and for its Being as "potentiality." Such Being towards a potentiality is termed a *"running forward in thought"* (Vorlaufen) to the potentiality. It does not aim at bringing something "real" into one's control, but approaches it in its potentiality most closely. In fact, the closest proximity of Being-towards-death is as remote from anything "real" as possible. The less this potentiality is understood in an obscured way, the more genuinely does the understanding penetrate into the potentiality as the impossibility of Existence as such. Death is the potentiality of the impossibility of every kind of behaviour towards . . . , of every mode of Existence. This "running forward in thought" to the potentiality of death makes it truly possible as such and makes the Dasein "free" for it.

Such "running forward in thought" to the potentiality of Being, as here with regard to one's death, is a very important mode of the constitution of Dasein itself, as will be seen later. As to death, Dasein discloses itself thereby in its extreme potentiality. Owing to such "running forward in thought," one's own and innermost extreme potentiality of Being can be understood, i.e. understood as the potentiality of authentic Existence.

In this perspective the five main characteristics of "Being-towards-death" are examined.

(a. Death as the innermost potentiality of

Dasein.) The Being-towards-death discloses for Dasein its innermost potentiality of Being, in which the Being of Dasein is at stake. Dasein can become aware that, in this eminent potentiality of itself, it will be aloof from the "one like many" and that, in the "running forward in thought" to death, it can separate itself from this unauthentic mode, enabling itself to stand aloof.

(b. Death as the irrelative potentiality of Dasein.) Dasein can learn to understand that it has to take upon itself this potentiality of Being, involved in death, when "running forward in thought" to it. Death does not belong to Dasein in an indifferent way, but claims it in its individuality. The irrelative nature of death singles the Dasein out and refers it to itself. It makes it aware that all concern for the world of one's care and for other people fails, when one's own potentiality of Being is at stake. Dasein can be "authentic" only when it has enabled itself to be so. Dasein is "authentic" only when it is primarily concerned with its own potentiality of Being, and not with that of the "one like many," while taking care of things and of one's fellow-men.

(c. Death as the potentiality of Dasein not to be overcome.) It can learn to understand that the extreme potentiality of Existence is one of ultimate renunciation. The "running forward in thought" does not try to evade it, but makes Dasein free for it. But this liberation for one's own death frees man also from the danger of losing himself to chance possibilities and allows him to understand and choose his actual potentialities, which precede the one which cannot be overcome. Free for his own potentialities, which are determined by the "end," that is to say, are understood as "finite" ones, he will also free himself from the danger of misunderstanding the existential potentialities of others or from forcing them into the framework of his own potentialities by way of misinterpretation: for death as an irrelative potentiality singles man out and, as it were, individualises him to make him understand the potentiality of the Being of others, when he realises the inescapable nature of his own death. Because the "running forward in thought" to the potentiality that cannot be overcome implicitly discloses all the potentialities that precede it, it can envisage existentially the "whole" of Dasein, i.e. "exist" as a "whole" potentiality of Being.

(d. Death as the certain potentiality of Dasein.) The certainty of death cannot be calculated from the observation of deaths nor does it belong to the realm of the truth of what is "vorhanden": it has nothing to do with the order of degrees concerning the "evidence" of things or events that are "vorhanden." The kind of certainty, here involved, discloses itself only when the "running forward in thought" renders the potentiality of death actually potential. Then it will be found to be more "fundamental" than any kind of certainty of the things that are encountered or of formal objects. For it ascertains the Being-in-the-world itself and the innermost Being of Dasein as a "whole."

(e. Death as the potentiality of Dasein indefinite as to its when.) In realising the certainty and at the same time the "indefinite" character of death, Dasein opens up for a constant threat arising from its own "There." The mood in which it meets this threat of an absolute nature is that of dread. In it Dasein is face to face with the "nothing" of the potential impossibility of Existence and thereby discloses the extreme potentiality.

The characterisation of the "authentic" Being-towards-death is summarised as follows. "The running forward in thought reveals to Dasein that it is lost in the 'oneself' and brings it face to face with the potentiality of being itself, primarily unaided by the care of others, but itself in the passionate, actual Freedom-towards-death (Freiheit zum Tode), being certain of it and dreading it, yet being independent of the illusions of the 'one like many.' "

(2) The second step in the new inquiry is guided primarily not by the problem of Dasein as a "whole," but by that of its "authenticity." The problem is as follows. An "authentic" potentiality of the Being of Dasein, i.e. "self-Being," was presupposed in the last and most relevant formulation of the analysis of "Being-towards-death." If so, such a potentiality of "self-Being" must be "testified." With regard to this

problem three phenomena are ontologically analysed: conscience, guilt and resolve.

(a. Conscience.) The essential character of conscience is found in its "call." Whereas Dasein primarily and mostly "listens" to others, gaining its restricted and unauthentic potentiality of Being and its kind of understanding in the world of its care and in the publicity of the "one like many," the "call" of conscience breaks into such "listening" of the Dasein to the anonymous "one like many" and appeals to the "self" in man to fetch it back out of this anonymity.

Heidegger considers the "call of conscience" to be a mode of "speech" in the strict sense, emphasising again that the voicing of a sound is not essential for "speech" or for a "call" like this one. "Speech" in any of its modes articulates what is "understood"; and so does, in its own way, the "call" of conscience. Heidegger refuses to accept the common interpretation which tries to trace conscience back to one of the presumed "faculties of the soul," intellect, will or feeling or to explain it as the complex product of all of them.

The "call of conscience" is characterised as a mode of speech in the following way. (a) What is spoken of is Dasein itself, not in a vague and indifferent way, but in the way in which it understands itself concretely in its everyday and average kinds of care. (b) What is appealed to is one's own "self"; not what the Dasein is reputed to be, able to do, has achieved or stood up for in the publicity of community life, which, in its "worldly" aspects, is passed by, by the "call" of conscience, but the "self" which is thereby aroused, while the "one like many" collapses. This "self" is not the "object" of introspection and of self-criticism, not something which is separate from the "outer world," which likewise is passed by, but the "self" as one mode of "Being-in-the-world." (c) What is said in this "call" of conscience is in one sense nothing: it offers no information about any events nor does it open up a soliloquy or an inner negotiation. But the "call" appeals to the self's own potentiality of Being. (d) There is no sounding of a voice in this "call." Conscience speaks constantly in the mode of silence and in it alone. Yet it does not lose in audibility thereby, but, on the contrary, forces upon the Dasein which is appealed to and aroused, a silence which is to be of great relevance. (e) The "call" discloses something which is unambiguous, despite the apparent vagueness of its content, namely a sure direction of drive in which the Dasein of the "self" is to move.

The first part of the analysis is concerned with the nature of the "call"; the second part, with that of the "caller." According to Heidegger's interpretation, conscience is the "call" of Care. Here again only a few main points may be mentioned.

(a) Conscience calls the self of Dasein out of the state in which it is lost in the "one like many." The "self" is unambiguously and unexchangeably meant, but beyond this there remains an astonishing vagueness regarding the "What" of the call as well as its source, the "caller." The one main thing is that the call is to be "listened" to. According to Heidegger, Dasein calls in conscience for itself. (b) This call is not planned nor prepared nor voluntarily carried out by ourselves. "It" calls against one's own expectation and even one's own wishes. Yet the call comes not from any one else, but from myself and upon myself.—These characteristics of the phenomenon as such have led to two different interpretations, which go beyond the phenomenon itself: of God as the source of conscience or, as its counterpart, of explaining conscience away in a biological manner. Both of them try to interpret what is, namely the phenomenon of the call, as being "vorhanden." (c) To clarify the "it" that is calling, Heidegger refers to the "thrownness" of Dasein and to Dasein being "thrown into its Existence." The "That" is disclosed to Dasein, the "Why" is concealed. It is suggested that Dasein, being placed in the ground of its uncanniness, is the caller of the call of conscience. A number of phenomena are adduced in its favour, e.g. that the "caller" is unfamiliar to the "oneself" in its everydayness, that the call speaks in the "uncanny" mode of silence to call the self back into the silence of the "existent" potentiality of Being, that "uncanniness" is a fundamental mode of "Being-in-the-world," though concealed in everyday Dasein, and that in the call of conscience tuned by dread, which enables Dasein to "project" itself into its own potentiality of Being, the "uncanniness" follows Dasein closely and threatens its state of being lost in self-forgetfulness. (d) The final proposition is: that "conscience reveals itself as the call of Care." The caller is Dasein which dreads in its thrownness (Already-Being-in-the-world) on behalf of its potentiality of Being. What is called upon is this same Dasein appealed to in its own potentiality of Being (Being-in-advance-of-itself). And Dasein is appealed to by the call out of the "Verfallen" in the "one like many" (Already-Being-concerned-with-the-world-of-its-care).

The main aim of the enquiry at this stage is to make the phenomenon of conscience understandable as a "testimony" of Dasein's own potentiality of Being. The enquiry is continued by investigating what this call of conscience makes Dasein understand. This leads to the analysis of guilt.

(b. Guilt.) Heidegger starts from the double aspect in the "call of conscience": that it points to the Whereto and to the Wherefrom, to the potentiality of Being and to the uncanniness of "thrown" individualisation. (Whereas the "running forward in thought" to death prepares for the analysis of the future as the dominant mode of "Temporality," that of conscience, guilt and resolve prepares for that of the future, the past and the present in their unity.) As the call of conscience seems to make Dasein understand its "guilt" (Schuld, which word means also: what one owes to others, e.g. a debt) this phenomenon is first discussed in its various "ontic" meanings.

Its basic ontological meaning is found to be a "deficiency," a lack of something which ought to be and can be, the ground of a "nullity" (Nichtigkeit). That Dasein is guilty (schuldig), it is pointed out, does not result from one special fault or wrong done, but, reversely, such fault is possible only on the basis of an original Being-guilty of Dasein.

It is shown in a very subtle analysis how Dasein and Care, thrownness and project, are permeated through and through by "nullity" and that "guilt" is thus grounded in the Dasein as such. In this connection Heidegger refers to the "ontological meaning of nothingness (Nicht-heit)," the "ontological essence of the not as such" and the problem of the "ontological origin of nothingness" and its intrinsic conditions—a complex of problems which form the background and also the theme of "What is Metaphysics?"

To understand the call of conscience made upon the "self" (Anrufverstehen) means therefore to realise that Dasein itself, i.e. my own Dasein, is "guilty." Being guilty is a fundamental con-stituent of Care. Being the null ground of its null project of taking over into its own respon-sible Existence what it was "thrown" to be, Dasein is to be fetched back out of its lost state as a "one like many," by the call of conscience, which points forward and backward, and makes man aware that he "is guilty." Only when man projects himself also into the potentiality of being and becoming guilty (which is entirely different from making oneself actually guilty by way of a fault or a neglect), can he be open for his own potentiality of Existence and can he "choose himself" in the existential sense.

The will to have conscience is "chosen" by the self when it understands the call of conscience in the right way. Thereby it becomes free for its own "guilt" as well as for its own potentiality of Being. Understanding the call, Dasein lets its own self "act" in the way of "inner action" out of its "chosen" potentiality of Being. Only in this way can Dasein be "responsible."

(c. Resolve.) The aim of the enquiry at this second stage, the analysis of conscience, guilt and resolve, is: to characterise a "testifiable" authentic potentiality of Being, which is essentially connected with the "running forward in thought" to death so far conceived only in its ontological possibility. Such a "testimony" is found in the phenomenon of conscience and the closely allied ones of guilt and resolve. As with the phenomenon of Care before, the existentialistic structure of the authentic potentiality of Being is here in the foreground. Three main traits are emphasised.

(a) The will to have conscience is a self-understanding in one's own potentiality of Being and, in this respect, a mode of Dasein as being "disclosed" (Erschlossenheit). To understand oneself existentially means to project oneself into an actual potentiality of Being-in-the-world, which is essentially one's own. Only when one actually "exists" in the mode of such a potentiality can it be "understood."

70

(b) The mood that corresponds to such an "understanding" is that not of dread as such, but of a readiness for dread, in view of the uncanniness of the individualisation. In the readiness for the dread of conscience, Dasein is brought face to face with this uncanniness.

(c) The mode of speech here implied is that kind of silence in which the call of conscience brings the self to the realisation of permanent guilt and fetches it back from the talk of the intelligibility of the "one like many."

This projecting of oneself, in silence and in readiness for dread, into one's own Being-guilty—an outstanding mode of the disclosed state of Dasein, testified by conscience—is termed "resolve." The "resolve" is characterised as the "authentic self-Being," which means not a Dasein isolated from the world, but "Being-authentic-ally-in-the-world."

The "for the sake of what" of the self-chosen potentiality of Being makes the "resolute" Dasein free for its world. The authentic fellowship of human beings depends on and arises from the authentic "self-Being" of resolve.

The "resolve" is essentially always of one actual Dasein only. The aim or the ends of the "resolve" depend on the individual Dasein and its thrown and factual potentialities. The existential resolution alone determines and defines them. But even the resolution of the individual remains related to, and in some way dependent on, the "one like many" and its world.

The "resolve" gives to Dasein a peculiar and

authentic lucidity. It discovers in reality actual significant potentialities and deals with them purposefully. Two phenomena especially can be truly approached only by an individual in the attitude of "resolve": a concrete given "situation" and genuine "action."

A concrete given "situation" is the "There" disclosed in its nature by "resolve." It is essentially different from a mixture of circumstances and chance events, from general conditions and opportunities. A "situation" in the sense meant here is unknown to the "one like many." It is the call of conscience that, when arousing the self and its potentiality of Being, calls the Dasein forth into a "situation." Not an empty ideal of Existence is aimed at in the attitude of "resolve," but a situation is, and situations are, to be mastered.

In such a "situation" the Dasein of "resolve" "acts" in the genuine sense, which implies of course the potentiality of "resistance." But the term "action" is very ambiguous and may be misleading. Care, as the Being of Dasein, does not allow for a separation between a "theoretical" and a "practical" kind of behaviour. Therefore it would be a complete misunderstanding of the term "action" if resolve, situation and action were thought to be especially related to practical behaviour. Resolve, intimately related to conscience and guilt, is the "authenticity" of Care.

(3) The two preparatory stages of the investigation into the problem "Dasein and Tempor-

ality" were guided (a) by the question of Dasein as a "whole" and (b) by that of Dasein as "authentic." But the problem of Temporality as such has not been made the explicit theme. This is done, on principle at least, in this third stage of the enquiry. But at first the two most outstanding phenomena of the preceding analyses, the authentic "Being-towards-death" as the "running forward in thought" and the authentic potentiality of Being as "resolve," are interpreted in their essential interconnectedness: the "running forward in thought" is shown to be a most fundamental trait of "resolve," while death is envisaged, besides guilt, in its profound relationship to the "nullity" of Dasein. "Resolve running forward (in thought) to . . ." refers to the one phenomenon which had not yet come into full sight before: the "authentic" potentiality of Dasein as a "whole." This phenomenon had to be analysed first before the phenomenon of Temporality could be discussed.

But this unity of "authenticity" and "whole" in the phenomenon of "resolve running forward (in thought) to . . ." is not the only problem to be clarified in advance. The problem of the fundamental unity of the structure of Care, now implying the "Being-towards-the-end," conscience, guilt and resolve as well, must be elucidated, too. The traditional solution in this respect is found in the "Ego" or the "self" as the basic ground. Heidegger considers this solution to be erroneous. Only when this question of principle has been answered can the exposition of Temporality be carried out.

I am omitting here an account of the phenomenon of "resolve running forward (in thought) to . . . ," to which reference will be made in connection with the exposition of "Temporality" itself, and begin my account with Heidegger's discussion of the problem: what is more fundamental, Care as the Being of Dasein or the authentic Existentiality of the self? and what is their relationship?

Heidegger tries to elucidate the problem of "selfhood" by starting from the self-interpretation of Dasein which, in its everydayness, speaks about "itself" by "saying I" (Ichsagen). This "I" is thought to be permanently the same; and as such it has been discussed by philosophers, e.g. by Kant in his doctrine of the "paralogisms." In this connection Heidegger submits Kant's teaching that the "I think" is "the form of apperception which accompanies and precedes any experience" to a critical examination. Two points are agreed to: that Kant recognises the impossibility of reducing the "I" to a substance in the "ontic" sense; and that he retains the "I" in the sense of "I think." But when Kant takes the "I" again as a "subject," Heidegger holds that he misses his point. For, in Heidegger's view, the ontological concept of the "subject" characterises not the "selfhood of the I qua self," but "the sameness and permanency of something which is always already 'vorhanden.'" Heidegger's further criticisms are: that Kant chooses the formula "I think," instead of "I think something," since the "representations" which the "I think" is said to accompany are "empirical" and not transcendental; that Kant did not characterise the nature of this "accompanying" more precisely; above all, that Kant overlooked the phenomenon of the world, though, then, he was consistent enough to keep the "representations" apart from the a priori content of the "I think," which, in its turn, leads to the result that the "I" is reduced to an isolated subject. The fundamental mistake which, according to Heidegger, Kant made was to force upon the problem of "self" the inadequate "horizon" of "categories" appropriate only for what is "vorhanden."—The fundamental criticism which Heidegger advances against the whole of the European philosophic tradition is that its "ontological" exposition was fundamentally concerned exclusively with what is "vorhanden"; and the criticism on Kant's doctrine of the "I think" is a characteristic and noteworthy instance of this fundamental and, it seems to me, most constructive criticism which pervades the whole of the work.

The criticism of Kant's theory is clarifying because the relationship between "selfhood" and "Care" must be made more lucid if the investigation is to move forward in the right direction. As Heidegger points out, the ontological constitution of the "self" cannot be traced back to either an "I-substance" or a "subject": "selfhood" can be discovered only when the "authenticity" of the Being of Dasein as "Care," especially as the "resolve that runs forward in thought to its potentialities," is analysed. But this does not mean that the "self" is the ground, or ultimate cause, of Care, thought to be permanently "vorhanden." The "self" is "permanent," because it has gained its "stand" and the firmness of its "stand," its independence, by way of its "resolve" in Care. It is the authentic counter-potentiality to the dependence of unresolved "Verfallen." Therefore, Heidegger concludes, Care does not require the foundation in a "self." "Existentiality" as one constitutive characteristic of Care implies the ontological constitution of the "self-dependence" of Dasein, to which, in accordance with the structure of Care as analysed, the actual "Verfallensein" to the dependence on others belongs as well. The enquiry, thus, moves in the direction not of "selfhood" as such, as may have been thought in view of the emphasis placed on "authenticity," but of what Heidegger terms "the ontological meaning of Care."

The phenomenon of "meaning" (Sinn) was studied by Heidegger in the context of the analyses of "understanding" and of "interpretation" when the "in-Being" was investigated. The "meaning," in the sense analysed there, is that within which the "understanding" of something is carried out and by which the "understanding" is guided, but which is not expressly and thematically envisaged as such. The "meaning" signifies the "Whereto" (Woraufhin) of the primary "project," from and by which something can be comprehended as what it is "in its inner possibility." Thus the problem of the "ontological meaning of Care" is the problem: what is the inner possibility of the articulated structural whole of Care as a whole and in its unity? The answer is: *Temporality*. And the phenomenon of "resolve running forward (in thought) to . . ." (vorlaufende Entschlossenheit) is taken as the model phenomenon of "authentic" Dasein as a "whole" to clarify in what way Temporality with its three modes enables it to be such as it is.

(a. *The future*.) "Future," in the sense meant here, does not mean a "now" which has not yet become "real" and will once "be." This is the traditional concept of the "future," based on the ontological exposition of what is "vorhanden" as carried out in Greek thought and adhered to ever since. At the last stage of this enquiry Heidegger endeavours to show how this concept of "Time" as the "sequence of nows" legitimately originates from a more genuine and fundamental kind of "Time," that of the Temporality of Dasein.

The "resolve running forward (in thought) to . . ." is the "Being towards its own eminent potentiality of Being." The reader may think of the indications given of the "Being-towards-death" or, perhaps, of the Being towards one's own profession. What makes such "resolve running forward (in thought) to . . ." possible is that "Dasein can move towards itself in its own potentiality and endures the potentiality as po-

tentiality in this itself-moving-towards-itself."
Heidegger points out that the original phenomenon of the "future" consists in this kind of
"coming," namely in that Dasein comes or moves
to or towards itself in its potentiality, enduring
it. The "running forward (in thought)" makes
Dasein authentically one with the future. But
this is possible only because Dasein as such always and essentially "moves" towards itself.

(b. *The past.*) Here again the "past" does
not mean the "now" which was. The "resolve
running forward (in thought) to . . ." understands Dasein in its essential "Being-guilty." To
take upon oneself in actual Existence such
"Being-guilty," the thrown ground of nullity
and thrownness as such, means to *be* authentically in such a way as Dasein always and already *was* (τὸ τί ἦν εἶναι). But the responsible
acceptance of thrownness is possible only because one's future Dasein can be its own "as it
already always was." Dasein can move towards
itself in the mode of the "future" only by moving backwards towards its past at the same time.
The fact that the call of conscience points both
forward and backward, to the potentiality of
Being and to the "Being-guilty" with its thrown
nullity, will be borne in mind. The analysis of
"historicity," too, at a later stage, will help to
clarify this relationship of Dasein to both future
and past.

However, for the Temporality of Dasein the
future is the somehow "guiding" and dominant
mode. Only when the Dasein "runs forward (in

thought)" to its extreme and innermost potentiality can it, thereby, move backward in "understanding" to its own past. Inasfar as Dasein is of the future can it authentically be of the past.

(c. *The present.*) The Greek and the post-Greek ontology bases its interpretation of the nature of Time on the "present" as the "now" and on the "presence" (παρουσία, Anwesenheit) of what is "vorhanden." The "present" was conceived in that interpretation as the guiding mode. The "present" of the Temporality of Dasein must be characterised differently and, besides, it is not, as it were, its first, but its third mode.

The "resolve running forward (in thought)" discloses the concrete given "situation" in such a way that Existence "acts" with circumspection in its care of what is "zuhanden." The resolute Being-concerned-with what is "zuhanden" in such a concrete given situation is possible only when this "Zuhandene" is "rendered present" (Gegenwärtigen). Only as the "rendering present" or "presenting" can resolve be what it is, the undisguised encountering of what it actively takes upon itself.

To formulate the relationship of the three modes more precisely: Being essentially directed towards the "future" (in the sense indicated above), resolve understands from it the "past" so as to "present" the concrete situation for its circumspect action. The "past" originates from the "future" so as to engender the "present."

In the light of the nature of Temporality the three main characteristics of the structural unity of Care can be understood more appropriately.

(a) The "Being-in-advance-of-itself" of Care is grounded in the "future." The "future" enables Dasein to be concerned about its own potentiality of Being and to "project" itself into the "for the sake of itself." The primary "meaning," i.e. the inner possibility, of "Existentiality" as such is the "future."

(b) The "Already-Being-in-the-world" of Care is grounded in the "past"; and the primary "meaning" of "Faktizität" or "Befindlichkeit" with its "thrownness" is the "past" (in the forementioned existentialistic sense).

(c) The "Being-concerned-with-the-world-of-one's-care" is grounded in the "present," but is of a somewhat different nature. For: the "rendering present," to which it essentially refers and in which also the "Verfallen" is primarily grounded, remains itself "embedded" in future and past. The resolute Dasein, too, which has fetched itself out of the "Verfallen" to be the more "authentically" there in a disclosed situation and to live in the fulfilled moment (Augenblick), is thus related to the future, the past and the "present" as embedded in both these modes.

Another matter of considerable import in this characterisation of Temporality on principle is the statement that Temporality is not at all anything that "is," in the sense of a "being." It "produces Time" (zeitigt sich). Moreover, the "towards itself" of the "future," the "back to" of the "past" and the "encountering of" of the "present" unveil Temporality as the "ἐκστατικόν" as such. Temporality is, as Heidegger emphasises, the original and fundamental "Outside-itself" (Ausser-sich) in and for itself. "Future," "past" and "present" are thus termed the "ecstasies" of Temporality. In the common and public "understanding" and concept of "Time," this "ecstatic" character of original Temporality is levelled.

This first exposition of the nature of original Temporality is made more explicit in the subsequent stages of the enquiry. Its fundamental and profoundly challenging character will, despite the brevity of the account given here, not escape the notice of the reader.

(4) The fourth stage of the enquiry is concerned with mainly two different problems. Firstly, the disclosed nature (Erschlossenheit) of the "There" of Dasein, i.e. "understanding," "Befindlichkeit," "Verfallen" and "speech," is analysed in view of its Temporality. Secondly, the Temporality of "Being-in-the-world" and the genesis of the theoretical discovery of what is "vorhanden" from circumspect care as well as the problem of the "transcendence" of the world are examined. The general tendency of the enquiry at this stage is to elucidate the problems discussed before from the basis of Temporality and to explore thereby the fundamental significance of Temporality further.

The principle of the analysis of the Temporality of "Erschlossenheit" is that Temporality "produces Time" wholly in each of its three ecstasies (future, past and present), i.e. that in the ecstasy of "future" past and present, in that of the "past" future and present, and in that of the "present" future and past, are implied. Thus it is shown that in the ecstatic unity of Temporality the structural whole of Care, i.e. Existentiality, "Faktizität" and "Verfallen," is grounded. The exposition contains a wealth of more concrete analyses.

Primarily the "understanding" is grounded in the "future." Its "authentic" mode is the "running forward (in thought) to. . . ." But there is an "unauthentic" mode, too, e.g. when man becomes aware of potentialities implied in the matters of his care. This "becoming aware of" or "anticipating" (Gewärtigen) is the temporal basis of all kinds of "expectation," e.g. of one's own death in the future when it is not taken as one's own innermost and extreme potentiality. But such "understanding," implying resolve, is also concerned with its "authentic" present, which is termed the "moment," in the fulfilled sense (Augenblick). The "unauthentic" present, where no resolve concerns itself actively with a given situation, is termed the "rendering present" (Gegenwärtigen). Whenever the understanding projects its potentiality from the matters of its care, Time is produced by rendering it present, while the "moment" arises from the authentic future. The "authentic" past, which is taken over in resolve and understood for the sake of one's own "authentic" potentiality of Being, is termed "repetition" or "renewal" (Wiederholung). "Wiederholung" means literally "fetching (something) back" (out of the past). Only here can Heidegger's own intention of a "repetition" or "renewal" (Wiederholung) of the question of the meaning of Being be properly "understood." The problem of Being occupied the great Greek thinkers from Thales and Anaximander to Aristotle. This problem is to be "repeated," i.e. unfolded in the spirit of the thinkers of two and a half milleniums ago by Heidegger. The "unauthentic" past is termed "oblivion" and on its ground arise one's "memories" which are "borne in mind." The "unauthentic" was of understanding, grounded in the ecstasy of the future, is thus here analysed side by side with the "authentic" one.

The Temporality of "Befindlichkeit," grounded in the past, is analysed in a similar way. May it suffice to mention that the Temporality of the moods of fear, of dread and of hope are analysed here especially to show how the present and the future are modified, but as modified ones are implied in the ecstasy of the past.

The Temporality of "Verfallen" is the present and the phenomenon of curiosity is chosen to elucidate the "unauthentic" mode of this ecstasy.

After these analyses the problem of the Temporality of "speech" is outlined in brief. It is not primarily grounded in any one of the three ecstasies, but in language the "rendering present" is thought to have a constitutive function of preference. Special reference is made to the "tenses," and the "is" and a detailed exposition of the "origin" of "significances" is forecast as the theme of a whole chapter in the unpublished third Section.

The second problem studied at this stage of the enquiry is that of the Temporality of the Being-in-the-world.

The investigation starts with an analysis of the Temporality of "circumspect care," where the "anticipating" (Gewärtigen), "bearing in mind" (Behalten) and the "rendering present" (Gegenwärtigen) are thought fundamental for the way in which the "Time" of the "Zuhandene" is produced, though a specific "oblivion" is essential for it, too.

To show more concretely the Temporality of the "Being-in-the-world," the genesis of the theoretical behaviour towards the "world" is traced back to the "circumspect care" of what is "zuhanden." In such a theoretical attitude, the "understanding of Being," which guides the careful handling of the "utensils," has profoundly changed. E.g. in the statement of the physicist: "the hammer is heavy," not only its character of a utensil is ignored, but also its "place" in the specific sense. Its place becomes a space-time-position, a "world-point" undistinguished from any other. What is within the environment (Umwelt) becomes "unbounded" (entschränkt) in some relevant sense. All that is "vorhanden," a phenomenon which only now fully emerges, becomes the theme.

But guided by the understanding of Being in the sense of "Vorhandenheit," what is primarily "unbounded," freed of its character as a utensil in an environment of "a-theoretical" Care, is at the same time confined once more, namely as belonging to the "region" or "realm" of what is "vorhanden." The more appropriately the Being of what is to be investigated is understood and thereby a whole kind of beings is singled out and articulated as a potential realm of matters related to one science or one branch of studies, the more precise will the perspective of methodical questions be. The classical example of such a historical development of a science is the genesis of mathematical physics, which is decisively guided by the mathematical "project" of Nature itself. Only in the light of such a "project" of Nature can "facts" be discovered and "experiments" be planned. The model character of mathematical science consists not in its specific exactness or its compulsory nature, but, more fundamentally, in its primary project of the constitution of Being with which it is concerned, in what Heidegger terms the "thematisation." The "thematisation" objectivates, i.e. frees the things in such a way that they become "objects," which can be discovered, investigated and determined.

This objectivating and scientific concern with what is "vorhanden" has the temporal character of a "rendering present" in an eminent sense.

It is distinguished from the "present" of circumspection in that the discovering is "anticipating" exclusively what is "vorhanden." Existentially it is grounded in a resolve of Dasein which projects itself into the potentiality of Being in the "truth."

To make the "thematisation" of what is "vorhanden" and the scientific project of Nature possible, Dasein must "transcend" the beings that are to be thematised. "Transcendence" does not consist in the "objectivation," but the "objectivation" presupposes "transcendence." But since the thematisation of what is "vorhanden" is a modification of circumspect care, the concern with the "Zuhandene" must already be rooted in a "transcendence" of Dasein.

From this examination the analysis of the Temporality of the "world" takes its start. The phenomenon of the world is considered to be grounded in Temporality. "The existentialistic-temporal condition of the possibility of the world is that Temporality as ecstatic unity has something such as a horizon." The "ecstasies" are not without direction. Each of them has its specific "Whereto," termed the "horizontal schema." The "ecstatic horizon" is a different one in each of them.

The schema, in which Dasein moves towards itself in the mode of the future, is the "For the sake of itself."

The schema in which Dasein is disclosed to itself as thrown into the "Befindlichkeit" is termed the "Before what" of thrownness and the "To what" to which Dasein is handed over. The horizontal structure of the past is characterised thereby.

Existing for the sake of itself and left to itself as thrown, Dasein is "rendering present" as a "Being-concerned-with. . . ." The horizontal schema of the present is determined by the "In order to."

The unity of the horizontal schemata of the future, the past and the present is grounded in the ecstatic unity of Temporality. The horizon of Temporality as a whole determines in what respect the Dasein that actually exists is essentially disclosed. On the basis of the horizontal constitution of the ecstatic unity of Temporality, something such as a disclosed "world" belongs to the being which is its "There."

In the same way as the present arises out of the future and the past in the unity of Temporality, the horizon of a present arises co-original with those of the future and the past. Inasfar as Dasein produces Time (sich zeitigt), there is also a "world." Indeed, the world is neither "vorhanden" nor "zuhanden," but is there together with the "Outside-itself" of the ecstasies. If no Dasein "exists," there is also no "world" there, in the sense meant here.

Two further investigations are carried out in this connection: of the Temporality peculiar to the spatiality of Dasein, where the important point is made that only on the basis of the ecstatic-horizontal Temporality is the inroad made by Dasein into the "space" possible; and of the temporal meaning of everydayness.

(5) The next step in the enquiry is the analysis of the "historicity" of human Dasein.

So far Dasein as a "whole" has been brought into sight and analytic grasp only with regard to its "end," its "Being-towards-death." Not only the "Being-towards-one's-beginning," i.e. birth, has been left unconsidered, but also the "extension of Dasein between birth and death." If the aim of the enquiry is to answer the question about the meaning of Being and if the meaning of Being becomes accessible in the "understanding of Being" which essentially belongs to human Dasein, the phenomenon of "historicity" is of great relevance. For not only does it essentially affect and mould the Dasein of everyone, but the "understanding of Being" is grounded in "historicity" and is handed down in human "history."

This problem of "historicity" is of especial interest to the reader of the subsequent essays, since the historic nature of human Dasein is emphasised in several places, notably in "On the Essence of Truth" and in "Hölderlin and the Essence of Poetry," and since the conception of the "historicity" of Dasein forms the background for Heidegger's communication with and his interpretations of Hölderlin's poetry. Moreover, the endeavour of the "repetition" of the question of the meaning of Being could not have been undertaken in the spirit in which it is carried out, without a profound consciousness of the "historicity" of Dasein and of philosophy.

The specific mode of motion of Dasein in its Existence is different from any kind of "motion" of something that is "vorhanden"; and this kind of "motion" in which Dasein "extends" is termed its "Geschehen," i.e. the process of happening. Its structure and its existentialistic-temporal conditions are analysed to make the nature of "historicity" understood.

The analysis starts with a distinction of four concepts of "history," all of which concern human Dasein which is "historical" in its Being: (a) history as referring to the "past" as such; (b) history as referring to the origin from the "past"; (c) history as referring to the whole of beings that change "in time" and more especially, in contrast to Nature and its kind of "changes," the whole of the changes and destinies of men, of human communities and of their civilisation and culture; and (d) history as referring to whatever is handed down by way of "tradition." After pointing out in what respects a "utensil" in the widest sense of the term or the Nature of environment as a "historical soil" are "historical," Heidegger begins to analyse "historicity" itself as an essential constitution of Dasein.

The "Geschehen" (process of happening) which defines Existence as "historical" is fundamentally implied in the phenomenon of "resolve" which projects itself, in silence and in readiness for dread, into its own Being-guilty and which is "authentic" as "running forward (in thought)" to potentialities of Being.

When Dasein, concerned about its future, moves backward in "resolve" to its "thrownness," this "resolve" discloses distinct actual potentialities of authentic Existence out of the "heritage" (Erbe) which it accepts and takes over in its state of being "thrown." Made free for death as its extreme potentiality, Dasein hands itself over to an inherited, yet freely chosen potentiality of Being, thereby entering upon the simplicity of its "fate" (Schicksal). Any choice of a potentiality of Being, made from the "heritage" and binding for the future, belongs to the "historicity" of Dasein in the genuine sense.

But since the Dasein, with its choice and fate, "exists" essentially together with others, its "Geschehen" (process of happening) takes place within the greater setting of the "Geschehen" of the community, e.g. the nation, which "Geschehen" is termed "Geschick" (destiny). The choice and the fate of the individual Dasein is guided from the start by the Dasein being together with that of others in the same world, in and with its own "generation," and by the resolve concerned with some definite and preferential potentialities.

Only when death, guilt, conscience, freedom and finiteness dwell together in the Being of a being, as they do in the Care of Dasein, can such a being "exist" in the mode of a fate, i.e. can it be "historical" in its essence. Historicity

90

in this sense presupposes authentic Temporality. It presupposes that Dasein, in its Being, is essentially of the future so that it can "run forward (in thought)" to death as its extreme potentiality and, free for its death, is thrown back upon its actual "There." It presupposes that Dasein, being of the future, is co-original of the past so that it can hand over to itself the inherited, i.e. traditional, potentiality and can accept and take upon itself its own "thrownness." It presupposes that Dasein, being of the future and of the past, is of the present and, by adopting the inherited potentiality, lives in the moment in the fulfilled sense (Augenblick) and for its own age.

Resolve may not know expressly the origin of the potentialities into which it projects itself. But if it does know it expressly, the "repetition" of a potentiality of Existence handed down becomes the express mode of tradition, i.e. the return to potentialities which once had been. The authentic "repetition" of an existential potentiality of the past is thus grounded in the resolve which is "running forward (in thought)." Only in such a resolve does Dasein take the choice which makes it free for the faithful succession to what it considers worth repeating. Such a "repetition" is not a misguided inducement to adhere to the "past," but, on the contrary, it is the resolute and express "response" to a potentiality of past Existence, understood in its genuine originality.

Authentic historicity, thus interpreted and

comprehended, has its essential weight not in the "past" nor in the "today" and its "connection" with the "past," but in the authentic "Geschehen" (process of happening) of Existence which originates from the "future" of Dasein, namely the "Being-towards-death" which directs Dasein back to its actual "thrownness." Both the phenomenon of the handing over of tradition to oneself and that of repetition are ultimately rooted in the future. But these very phenomena of the handing over of tradition to oneself and of repetition explain, too, why the process of happening of actual history has its weight and import in the "past," to which both the heritage of tradition and the repetition, irrespective of their deeper roots, point.

Dasein is "Being-in-the-world" and the "historicity" of Dasein implies essentially the "historicity" of the "world" which belongs to it on the ground of the ecstatic-horizontal Temporality. Thus "utensils" and works of architecture, books and institutions have their "history" and their "fates." Nature assumes a historical significance, e.g. as the territory of settlement and exploitation, as battlefield and place of cult. This "Zuhandene" and "Vorhandene" of the "world," involved and comprised in the "historicity" of Dasein, is termed "world-historical" (Welt-Geschichtlich).

Because actual Dasein is mostly occupied with the world of its care, it understands its own history primarily in this "world-historical" sense. And as the common "understanding of Being" identifies "Being" with "Vorhandenheit" without qualification, the Being of what is "world-historical" is commonly experienced and interpreted as if it were something "Vorhandenes" that comes to pass, is happening and disappears. The kind of motion, peculiar to the process of happening in authentic historicity as well as in what is "world-historical" is usually left unconsidered.

This attitude characterises the "unauthentic" historicity of Dasein which is lost in the "one like many" and which never brought itself into the state of "resolve," in the sense described above. It lives in a mode of inner dispersal and whatever happens to it lacks inner connection. The original "extension" of the "fate" into which the individual Dasein has entered remains concealed. Without a firm stand, the "oneself" renders present the "today," forgetful of what had been and blind for genuine potentialities. Choice is evaded. And since nothing of what had been is being "repeated" in this "unauthentic" mode of Dasein, only the "reality" of what had been "world-historical," its remnants and the knowledge of it, are retained.

In contrast to this, the "resolve" of "authentic" Dasein brings about an "extension" of the whole Existence, a constant and permanent sameness, such that Dasein as "a fate" comprises in its Existence birth and death and their "in between." It is open for the "moment" and for the "world-historical" of its situation. In the repetition of potentialities of the past, Dasein brings itself directly back to what had been before. With the assimilation of the "heritage" even one's own birth has been encompassed in the realm of one's Existence. "Resolve" constitutes the loyalty of Existence to one's own self. As the "resolve," ready for dread, this loyalty is at the same time potential reverence paid to the one authority which can be recognised by a free Existence: to the potentialities of Existence which are worth "repeating."

After the characterisation of the fundamental constitution of "historicity" and of what is "world-historical," together with the attitude of unauthentic and authentic Dasein towards it, the problem of the "existentialistic" origin of history as a kind of scholarly study from the "historicity" of Dasein is outlined.

It is Heidegger's main contention that the scholarly disclosure of history is ontologically rooted in the "historicity" of Dasein and that the "idea" of history must be conceived in this light and not by way of an abstraction made from the contemporary studies of history or in an artificial adaptation to them.

History as a branch of knowledge makes it its own task expressly to disclose what is "historical." The thematisation defines its realm; the approach to it receives its methodical direction; the concepts applied in its interpretation gain their specific character. But if any historical "object" of the past is truly investigated, it must be of the constitution of a Dasein which had once been; and it presupposes the "historicity" of the Existence of the historian.

Remnants of any kind, monuments and reports are a potential "material" for such a concrete disclosure of Dasein which had once been. But their study, examination and assessment can be meaningfully carried out only on the basis of the historicity of contemporary Dasein.

In Heidegger's view, it is the "object" of history to understand the Dasein which had once been in its authentic "existential" potentiality. Such "potentiality" of the Dasein of the past is the primary and central theme of history and the "facts" which are studied are only related to it. The true historian, who treats his theme not in an "aesthetic," but in a "historical" way, can disclose the history of the past in its potentiality with such forcefulness that even its implications for the future are realised. Fundamentally, history takes its start not from "the present" nor from what is "real" only today, but from the future. The "selection" of what is to be an object of history is made by the actual, "existential" choice of the historicity of Dasein, i.e. of the historian, in which history arises.

Such an unveiling of the past in the "repetition" of a genuine historian must not be considered to be "subjective" in the bad sense; on the contrary, it alone guarantees the "objectivity" of history. For the "objectivity" of a science or any other branch of knowledge is thought to depend on whether the thematic object can be brought home to the "understanding" in its true Being and without disguise. With regard to a historic theme, the "historicity" of the Dasein of the historian makes such an "objectivity" possible.

The orientation by "facts" is required because the central theme of history is the potentiality of an Existence of the past and because such an Existence is always related to phenomena of the "world-historical" kind. Therefore the actual historical research concerns itself with the history of "utensils," of works, of civilisation and culture, of intellectual and spiritual life and of ideas. But the touchstone remains its proximity to its original and central theme and its treatment not in an "aesthetic," but in a genuinely "historical" manner.

An express reference is made to Nietzsche's well-known essay on "Use and Abuse of History" and to his distinction of the three kinds of history which are serving "Life": the "monumental," the "antiquarian" and the "critical" one, which Heidegger relates in a very elucidating way to the "future," the "past" and the "present" in his sense. Authentic historicity is indicated as the basis of the possible unity of these three kinds of history.

A discussion of the investigations of W. Dilthey, Heidegger's predecessor in this field of philosophic studies, and of the ideas of Count Paul Yorck von Wartenburg, Dilthey's friend, closes this stage of the enquiry.

(6) One set of problems has been left unconsidered up to this point. Dasein counts on "Time" and is guided by "Time," even long before any scientific or scholarly research has begun. But the factor of "Time" plays also a part in the study of both history and Nature and, besides, there is the common concept of "Time" as the "sequence of nows" which deviates fundamentally from Heidegger's exposition of the nature of Temporality. If this exposition is correct, it must be shown that and how the more common concept of "Time" arises from the Temporality of Dasein itself. With this set of problems the last stage of the enquiry is concerned; and it is Heidegger's main contention that the actual Dasein counts on "Time," without understanding Temporality existentialistically, which same objection could be raised against the common concept of "Time," as developed in European philosophy. This analysis of the origin of the common concept of "Time" from Temporality is thought to be an implicit and indirect proof and justification of the interpretation given before, which characterises Temporality as the fundamental and original (ursprünglich) Time.

The investigation proceeds in three stages: (a) the way in which Dasein, grounded in Temporality, takes care of "Time" is analysed; (b) the "world-Time," concerned with what is "zuhanden" and "vorhanden" and measured by the sun and by the clock, is analysed; and (c) the common concept of Time, as first formulated by Aristotle, is analysed.

All planning, taking of precautions, preventing or calculating of Dasein in its Care says, audibly or inaudibly: "then" this is to be done, "before" that work has to be finished; "now" this has to be tried once more; after I failed in it "at that time." In the "then" the Care speaks in "anticipation," relating to the future; in the "now" in the mode of "rendering present"; in the "at that time" in the mode of "bearing in mind," relating to the past. The horizon of these three modes of everyday Care is the "later" (späterhin), the "today" (heute) and the "earlier" (früher). This common structure of the "now," "then" and "at that time" is termed the "datableness" (Datierbarkeit); and the problem arises how such "datableness," common as it is, is possible at all. The reason given is that the "rendering present," which is "anticipating" and "bearing in mind" at the same time, interprets itself in this way. It is this "rendering present" which interprets itself that we call "Time" and the "datableness" of the "now," "then" and "at that time" is considered to be the reflection of the ecstatic constitution of Temporality.

Another trait of this "taking care of Time" is indicated by the "until then" or "during which. . . ." Time is conceived here as a "span of time," a reflection of the "ecstatic extension of historical Temporality." In this sense an extended "span" of time is also meant by the "now," "then" and "at that time," e.g. at meal-time, in the evening, in the summer, at breakfast, during the ascent, etc.

Being occupied with the world of its care, Dasein "takes its time" over it and this is the primary and genuine mode in which "Time" is experienced, independent of and before all specific measuring of Time as the continual sequence of pure "nows." Being very busy and possibly without the attitude of genuine resolve, one "loses" one's time. Authentic Existence, on the other hand, gives to its "present" the significance of the "moment" in the fulfilled sense. Not the "rendering present" of a situation is here guiding, but the Existence is guided by its future, implying its past. The momentary Existence is embedded in a "fatefully" whole "extension," in which the self has become constant and permanent in an authentic and historical manner.

Dasein can "take" its time or "lose" its time and authentic Dasein can make use of its time in its own mode, because in the disclosed nature of the "There," grounded in the ecstatically extended Temporality, a "Time" is granted to it.

The next problem is: what is meant by the "public Time," i.e. the "Time" of which one Dasein partakes together with that of others, and what are its characteristics?

Though time is primarily dated by way of events that occur in the environment, this takes place within the horizon of a care of time known

99

as "chronology" in the sense of astronomy and of the calendar. This "public Time" is not the only kind of time, but that kind of time in which "Zuhandenes" and "Vorhandenes," all that is not of the kind of being such as Dasein, are encountered. This qualified definition is of the utmost import, for it points to the essential limitation involved in our common concept of Time thought to have originated from this "public Time."

The sun and its light "date" time in the first instance and the day is the first, most natural measure of Time.

The reason for this lies in the fact that the everyday circumspect "Being-in-the-world" requires the possibility of sight, i.e. light, to take care of the "Zuhandene" on the background of the "Vorhandene" and that Dasein, in its thrownness, is submitted to the change of day and night. The dawn of the day makes it possible to resume one's daily work; and similarly significant incisions of time are the sunset and the midday.

This "dating" by the sun is an indication of "Time" for "everyone." What is "dating" is at everyone's disposal and yet it is not restricted to the realm of utensils; for in it the environment of Nature and the public environment are disclosed as well. Everyone can count on this kind of "Time." But for its more precise calculation a "measure" of it, at the disposal of the public, is required: the clock-time. It is a "Zuhandenes" which, with its regular return, has become accessible in the "rendering present" which, at the same time, is in a state of "anticipation."

Three questions arise: (a) what is implied in the "dating"; (b) what is implied in the reading of the clock; and (c) what is the nature of the "public Time."

The "dating" implies that "then" when it dawns it will be "time for" one's daily work. Time interpreted in Care is always already understood as "time for. . . ." The "now that this or that has to be done" points through the "now that" to "this" or "that" as suitable or unsuitable. In short, the "rendering present" of Care, with its "anticipation" and its "bearing in mind," understands "Time" essentially as related to some purpose or other, which itself is related to the "for the sake of what" of the potentiality of Being. In other words: the public Time unveils the "significance" of "this" or "that" by way of its purposive relations and ultimately constitutes the "worldliness" of the world. Public Time as "time for . . ." has thus essentially a character referring to the "world" and is termed "world-time." This is not to say that the "world-time" is "vorhanden," which it never can be, but to indicate that Public Time belongs to the "world" in its existentialistic-ontological sense.

In using a clock or a watch, we say expressly or inexpressively: "now" it is "time for . . ." or "now" I have still time "until. . . ." We take our time over this or that; and the reading of the clock is grounded in it and guided by it. Such an orientation in time is essentially a "saying: now" (Jetzt-sagen); and this "saying: now" is the articulation in speech of a "rendering present," on the basis of its unity with "anticipation" and "bearing in mind."

The dating by way of the clock-time is a "measuring" of time, which implies both an unalterable measure-rule (Masstab), with its permanent sameness for everyone, and the measured length on the dial provided with numbers, over which the hands move. This does in no way mean that the clock-time is determined by spatial lengths and the change in place of a spatial thing nor is this kind of "dating" a rendering spatial of time. It is a specific "rendering present" that makes the "measuring of time" by way of the clock possible. But with the help of the clock Time gains a publicity in a specific sense, such that it is encountered always and by everyone as "now and now and now." Thus the time made accessible through the use of clocks appears to be like a "multitude of nows," seemingly "vorhanden," though the measuring of time is never thematically concerned with Time as such.

The public time in this sense, developed by the measuring of time on the clock, is what is commonly called "the time." In Care everything is ascribed its time; and it can have its time, because anything that is is "in time." This "world-time," grounded in the ecstatic-horizontal constitution of Temporality, is of the same "transcendence" as the world itself. It is prior to any subjectivity or objectivity. "The world-time is 'more objective' than any possible object, because it is 'objectified' (objiciert) in its ecstatic-horizontal dimensions as the condition of the possibility of anything that is when the world becomes disclosed." "But the world-time is also 'more subjective' than any possible subject, because, if Care is the Being of Dasein, it contributes to making the Being of the actually existing self possible." Yet, fundamental as is this world-time which constitutes the being "in time" (Innerzeitigkeit) of what is "zuhanden" and "vorhanden," it arises from the Temporality of Dasein, as Heidegger has tried to show in this earlier part of the investigation.

The genesis of the common concept of Time, as Heidegger points out, arises from the clock-time. Aristotle, in his "Physics," defines Time as follows. "For the time is this: what is counted in the movement in accordance with (or: in the horizon of) what is earlier and what is later." All subsequent discussion of the concept of Time is thought to keep fundamentally within the framework of the Aristotelian definition, i.e. it makes Time the theme in the way in which it shows itself in the circumspect care of what is "zuhanden" on the background of what is "vorhanden." The time is what is "counted"; and what is counted are the "nows." The common concept of Time is the "now-time," i.e. Time as the "sequence of nows."

In this interpretation of Time two fundamental characteristics are obscured: the "datableness," grounded in the ecstatic constitution of Temporality; and the "significance," opened up by the "time for. . . ." The common interpretation of "world-time" as "now-time" has not at its disposal the "horizon" to make something such as "world," "significance," "datableness" accessible. It treats the "nows," though inexpressively, as if they were "vorhanden" like things: some pass and they form the "past"; some arrive and they define the "future." Similarly the "sequence of nows" is conceived as if it were somehow "vorhanden."

Furthermore, the sequence of nows is characterised as "uninterrupted" and "without a gap," where the extended "span" of time and the "extension" of historicity are obscured; as "endless" or "infinite," where the Temporality of Dasein is ignored and the sequence of nows is treated as if it were self-dependent and absolute, obscuring especially the finite nature of Dasein and its "Being-towards-the-end"; as "passing," but not to the same extent as "arising," which, in Heidegger's view, is the faint public reflection of the Temporality of Dasein anticipating its finite future; and as an "irreversible succession," which again points to its origin from Temporality and its primary mode, that of the future.

This common characterisation of Time as an endless, passing, irreversible sequence of nows arises from the Temporality of Dasein in its mode of "Verfallen." Within its limits, it has its natural right. For it belongs to the Being of Dasein in its everydayness and to the "understanding of Being" which prevails. Thus history, too, is mostly understood in public as a process of happening "in time" in the restricted sense.

But this interpretation of Time loses its exclusive right, if it claims to indicate the "true" concept of Time and to outline the only possible horizon for the exposition of Time. It can be understood from the Temporality of Dasein and from its time-producing function why and in what way "world-time" belongs to it. But from the horizon of the common concept of Time Temporality remains inaccessible in its nature and on principle.

A last aspect emphasised in this common experience of time is the distinct relationship of time to the "soul" or the "spirit," as found in Aristotle, in St. Augustine, in Kant and in Hegel. This gives rise to an exposition of Hegel's conception of the relationship between Time and Spirit, which, together with a clarifying note on Bergson's conception of Time, brings the whole of the European tradition since Aristotle into perspective.

It was the task of the enquiry in this second Section to interpret the original whole of actual Dasein, with its potentialities of authentic and unauthentic Existence, from its ground, i.e. from Temporality. The aim is the elaboration of the problem of Being as such. If the whole of the constitution of Dasein is found to be grounded in Temporality, then Temporality, as the ecstatic "Outside-itself," is most likely to render the ecstatic "project" of Being as such possible. In the very last sentence of the published fragment, Time is hinted at as the horizon of Being.

It is hoped that from the somewhat more detailed account given of the second Section the reader will gain an impression not only of the content and its originality, but also of the great power of analysis which with its sure grasp and profound consistency lays bare aspect by aspect a problem never approached before in this way.

4

SOME REFLECTIONS ON THE SIGNIFICANCE OF THE WORK

The question which would seem the most important of all, if it could be answered by any one individual at present, is: what is the actual "significance" of Heidegger's "Being and Time" as a "contribution" to European philosophy? This question can only very gradually be decided by way of the reactions of trained philosophers to the work in the future: it would become truly relevant, once a thinker of very high rank would be stimulated to the depth of his philosophic mind by the approach attempted and the problems treated in this work, so as either to develop his own problems in a kindred spirit or to criticise the work fundamentally and yet to advance his own constructive views on the basis of this criticism, as Locke may be said to have done with regard to Descartes or Kant with regard to Leibnitz and Hume. The only statement that may be ventured here is the suggestion that

Heidegger's "Being and Time" is of that rank and kind that it may stimulate profoundly the thought of another original thinker in times to come. In conclusion of the account of "Being and Time" given above, only a very few points may be made as to its possible "significance."

The work seems to have been misunderstood and misinterpreted in mainly two ways: it was taken to be either a *"Philosophical Anthropology"* or a *"Philosophy of Existence."*

(1) A "Philosophical Anthropology" would be a philosophical analysis of what is essential to the "nature" of human life, possibly in express comparison and contrast to that of the higher animals. It would be a "regional" ontology, inasmuch as it is concerned with one kind of beings to the exclusion of other kinds. Such a "Philosophical Anthropology" might be more especially felt to be a philosophic desideratum in an age in which the "critical" faculty of philosophy and an insight into the "limitations" of human comprehension have been highly developed, as may be said to have taken place since Locke, Hume and Kant, and in which human life is considered to be the "basis" of all kinds of thought and research concerning the great variety of things that exist or are conceived. In this sense, following Kant, the German philosopher W. Dilthey developed a Philosophy of Human Life, especially with a view to its historicity, from the basis of which all institutions and outlooks, as in religion, art and philosophy, would be more adequately understood and interpreted. Indeed,

one important trend in the whole of modern thought may be said to have a direct tendency towards such a "Philosophical Anthropology"; and it is understandable that Heidegger's work, when published, was first seen in this light. For it purported to analyse human Dasein in its structural constitution.

But while Heidegger analysed relevant phenomena and traits of human Dasein, his aim was to give in no way a "regional," but a "fundamental" ontology and not to analyse "all" that is essential to the "nature" of man (if this could be analysed convincingly), but to develop the problem of the constitution of Dasein in such a way that thereby the meaning of "Being" could find its elucidation once more. The historical perspective: that what the Greek thinkers from Parmenides and Hericlitus to Plato and Aristotle had attempted, taking the things that were "vorhanden" as their starting-point and enquiring into the essence of all that is, was to be attempted once more, but this time by making human Dasein as an outstanding kind of being its starting-point and clarifying the meaning of "Being," gives an indication of Heidegger's problem and approach if the comparison is rightly understood. Therefore not the "nature" of man as such, but Dasein as "Being-in-the-world" was analysed, this "Being-in-the-world" shown, among other points, in its relationship to the realm of "utensils" and, at a later stage, to all that is "vorhanden." The most important turn in the enquiry, however, is taken with the analysis of "Temporality." For here, with Heidegger's analysis of "future," "past" and "present" and of their "ecstatic" unity, the inner possibility of the structual whole of Care is laid bare, so as to describe it as the "transcendental horizon" of the question about "Being"—an investigation which, by its trend of thought, transcends any study of the "nature" of man in the sense of a "Philosophical Anthropology." *

(2) With the publication of "Being and Time" and more especially with that of K. Jaspers' "Philosophy" (1932) a "Philosophy of Existence" had come into being—a term applied by Jaspers himself to his own way of philosophic approach and outlook—and most of what links itself up nowadays with the movement of "Existentialism" took, either directly or indirectly, its start from either of these two German thinkers, even though the original impetus and insight goes back to the Danish thinker S. Kierkegaard.†

* For the problem of a "Philosophical Anthropology," and its difference from a fundamental ontology, cf. Heidegger's "Kant and the Problem of Metaphysics," pp. 193/236, where the "finiteness" in man and its relationship to the problem of the understanding of Being is placed in the centre.

† For a general characterisation of Heidegger's and Jaspers' philosophic thought, on the background of the philosophy of Nietzsche and especially Kierkegaard as well as of Husserl, Dilthey and Max Weber and within the larger framework of a variety of other eminent figures and prominent schools in Germany, cf. my own book "An Introduction to Contemporary German Philosophy," 1935. There it was expressly emphasised that the problem of "Being" is the one main concern of Heidegger's philosophy and that the existentialistic exposition of human Dasein is only of a "preparatory" nature.

In view of the import attached to "existentialia," in contrast to and as a complement of the traditional "categories," to "Existence" as the "substance" of Dasein, to the distinction between "unauthentic" and "authentic" Dasein and to phenomena, such as dread, care, death, conscience, guilt and resolve, it was almost inevitable that Heidegger was thought to be primarily concerned with the problem of "Existence" and with "Existentialism."

In this respect it should be borne in mind, first of all, that Heidegger draws a sharp distinction between "Existence," which concerns the individual human being and is something "ontic," like the physiological functions of a plant or the atomic structure of a piece of matter, and "Existentiality," which is meant to be an "ontological" characteristic of human Dasein. If, e.g. the analysis of "Care" as the "Being" of Dasein is considered, the reflection is meant to dwell on the formal ontological structure in the first place and not to confuse it at once with the well-known "ontic" phenomenon.

Furthermore, if I myself were asked to explain why Heidegger places "Existentiality" so much in the foreground of his exposition of Dasein, while he purports to be primarily interested in the problem of "Being," I would give as one reason what follows.

The "Existentiality" of Dasein would seem to correspond to the "οὐσία" (substance) of what is "vorhanden," the first and most fundamental of the "categories" in Aristotle's sense; and this "οὐσία" is taken to mean the same as "παρουσία" (Anwesenheit, presence). Now, the "Existentiality" of Dasein is concerned, as we have seen, with the "potentiality of Being" (Seinkönnen), with "understanding" and with "project"; and with regard to the "Temporality" of Dasein, it is concerned with its dominant and guiding "mode," the "future." The "Faktizität" or "Befindlichkeit," with its "thrownness" into the "There" and, in regard to Temporality, with its primary relationship to the "past"; and the "Verfallen," with its concern for the world of one's care and with its primary relationship to the "present," are not independent of the "Existentiality," but closely interwoven with it. Without it, "Faktizität" and "Verfallen" could not come into sight and grasp of Dasein. "Existentiality" is the one "guiding" characteristic of Dasein, just as the "future" of Dasein is the one dominant and "guiding" mode of Temporality.

From this the statement that "Existence is the 'substance' of man" may gain some clarification. For just as "substance" in Aristotle's sense is the primary "category" of the kind of beings that are "vorhanden," "Existentiality" in Heidegger's sense is the primary characteristic of the kind of beings that are Dasein. Therefore these characteristics are termed "existentialia" and the analysis of Dasein is primarily concerned with them.

(3) Whereas I do not think that "Being and Time, Part I" should be regarded either as a "Philosophical Anthropology" or as a "Philos-

ophy of Existence," the *analysis of the "existentialia" of Dasein,* in contrast to and as a complement of the "categories" of "Vorhandenheit,"
seems to me a great contribution to philosophic
studies and to philosophic insight, if it is seen
on the background and in the light of the Greek
ontology from Anaximander, Parmenides and
Heraclitus to Aristotle and the *transcendental*
philosophy of Kant. The problem, as posed by
Heidegger, is altogether novel and the philosophically-minded reader will have to grasp the
problem in its novelty first of all. The claim to
the universality of the analysis, a claim implicit
in any ontological analysis, will have to be
scrutinised. Man is not "ontically" to be considered in his "nature," in his "social" and
consequently also "historical " associations and in
his "mind" and "spirit," which, at best, would
lead to a "Philosophical Anthropology." But
man, as Dasein, partakes of "Being" and is
"Being-in-the-world." This opens up a far wider
horizon. The structural constituents: (a) the
realm of utensils, on the background of the
things of Nature, and the worldliness of the
world, (b) the self as the "one like many" with
its publicity and in its primarily unauthentic
Existence, (c) the in-Being with its modes of
"understanding," "Befindlichkeit," "Verfallen"
and "speech" and (d) the Being of Dasein, Care—
(a) characterising the "world" of the "Being-in-
the-world," (b) the "who," (c) the "in" and (d)
the "Being"—and the unity of the analysed
structure may one day be considered fundamen-

tal in a way not altogether dissimilar to Aristotle's doctrine of "categories."

(4) Apart from the ontological analysis of the structure of Dasein and beyond it, the exposition of the *"Temporality of Dasein"* as the "inner possibility" of this ontological structure seems to me to be the most relevant "contribution" made by Heidegger in the published fragmentary portion of "Being and Time." Kant, with his analysis of "Time" in the "Critique of Pure Reason," undertaken from the standpoint of the "subjectivity" of man, is in this respect his immediate predecessor; and beyond it, it would seem to be the most fundamental and profound analysis of the nature of "Time" made as a "compliment" to Aristotle's analysis in his "Physics," implying a radical criticism of it. It is this exposition of the "Temporality of Dasein" that I would think is of the utmost interest to the trained philosopher, challenging all the traditional views on the problem of Time. It would have to be examined as to the correctness of insight into the "temporal" structure of future, past and present as well as to the way in which the common conception of "time," i.e. the time of what is "vorhanden" and "zuhanden," is shown to "originate" from the basic "Temporality" of Dasein. Only then would Heidegger's philosophic thought seem to be comprehended and assimilated at least in one relevant respect.

(5) The fundamental problem with which Heidegger is concerned is that of the *"meaning of Being."* For it "Temporality," in the way in

which it is analysed, is said to be the "transcendental horizon." If "meaning" is to be understood here in the same sense as when Temporality is characterised as the ontological "meaning" of Care, i.e. as what makes the structural whole of "Care" in the unity of its articulated characteristics intrinsically "possible" (Ermöglichung), the exposition of "Being," with Temporality as its "transcendental horizon," would consist in analysing in what way "Being" is the "ground" and the "inner possibility" of Dasein, as well as of "Vorhandenheit," in their ontological structure. Naturally, such an analysis of the "meaning" of "Being" would have to comprise in itself a variety of detailed analyses, e.g. concerning the concept of the beings that are "in the whole" (das Seiende im Ganzen), of those of "Nature," implying on principle the constitution of those kinds of being that are not Dasein, and perhaps of "History," beyond the exposition given in the analysis of "historicity"; but especially concerning the "understanding" of "Being" itself, as it arises within the "horizon" of Temporality, as the "Outside-itself" (Ausser-sich), i.e. as "ecstatic" unity. What it meant and means that "Being" opened out in the horizon of "Time" so that all that is, with its different kinds of being, could become apparent would have to be demonstrated. The beginnings of Greek philosophy before Plato would thus be elucidated in their fundamental, and lasting, significance. Possibly the way in which the interpretation of the nature of "God" found its theoretical and theological exposition on the basis of the metaphysical tradition from Anaximander to Aristotle and Plotinus was to be clarified, on principle at least, in some context of the analysis. Man in his "Ex-sistence," which means an "ex-position" into "truth," i.e. into the discovering or unveiling of the things as they "are," belongs most definitely into the "realm of horizon" of the analysis of the "meaning" of "Being." The relatedness of "nothingness" to "Being" is likely to be another aspect of it; its import for Greek thought, e.g. for Parmenides, is apparent. It may be that the problem of "poetry" and of its relevance for the discovering and naming of the things that are was at first not included in the problem of the "meaning" of "Being"; but it may well be thought necessary to consider it in this "horizon of project," too. The tradition of "Ontology" would receive a fundamental reorientation, in the "Metaphysica generalis," concerned with the nature of "Being," and in the "Metaphysica specialis" traditionally subdivided in a Cosmology, Rational Psychology and Natural Theology.

I myself do not know the text of the original version of the third Section of "Being and Time." Thus it may not be thought right for me to dwell in this Introduction on the problem of the "meaning of Being." But it seems to me that something had to be said about this problem at this stage, in order not have it deteriorate into a mere empty word as well as in view of the content of the four essays. I can only hope that the indications made are not wrong and that the problem itself can be envisaged, however faintly and inappropriately. This is of import even for the understanding of the foregoing account, since the exposition of the structure of Dasein, and that of Temporality, does not stand on its own ground, but is undertaken from the "ground" of the truth of Being.

AN ACCOUNT OF
"THE FOUR ESSAYS"

1

A BRIEF GENERAL CHARACTERISATION
OF THE FOUR ESSAYS

The four essays selected for this edition differ from "Being and Time" very considerably in form, theme, treatment and tone.

Each of them is brief, originally a public Lecture or a formal Address, not a long drawn out systematic analysis where one subtle phenomenon after another passes in review in order to elucidate, step by step, one outstanding problem.

Each theme is self-contained. The philosophical essays are concerned with two fundamental problems: that of the nature of metaphysics and that of the essence of truth, while one of those on the German poet Hölderlin discussing the essence of poetry, is of a similarly fundamental character and the other, expounding one late elegy, demonstrates concretely what a poet, such as Hölderlin, endeavours to convey to his fellowmen. Each of the essays seems, at first sight, to have barely any relation to the problems of "Being and Time."

The treatment is entirely different. In "Being and Time" a whole chapter is devoted to the analysis of one relevant aspect of a "structure" and a sub-section, to the elucidation of one new phenomenon or of important links in the chain of the argument. In each of the essays only a few sentences or at the very utmost a couple of paragraphs are allowed for the discussion of the most important aspects of the theme and more than once a wholly novel perspective, for which the reader is unprepared, is opened up by only one or two propositions introducing a number of new and highly significant concepts. The treatment is not analytic and demonstrative, but condensed to the utmost and, though strictly conceptual, largely in the way of brief character-ising statements. We may be sure that the thought behind any formula ventured is as acute and penetrating as in the earlier main work. But the treatment takes this for granted and implicitly expects the same amount of analytic grasp from the reader as was implied in the preparation of the extremely concentrated exposition.

The tone of the analysis in "Being and Time" is that of a thinker who is, as it were, at one with his more intelligent readers, however novel the problem and his approach to it are. On principle every reader who is philosophically trained ought to be able to follow and assimilate the consistent and carefully progressing argumentation; and this kind of community in thought tunes the earlier work. The tone in the essays is that of a solitary thinker who communicates to others what he has meditated upon in prolonged and silent thought, but who leaves it to them what they are able or ready to grasp and to assimilate. It may well be said that the tone, and the treat-ment, in the essays is more mature and essentially philosophical, in the grand sense, while it is more remote not only from everyday life, but also from the atmosphere of scientific or scholarly presentation in the ordinary sense and profoundly akin to the realm of the poet, from which it is yet deeply separated both by its problems and by its conceptual thought.

Some of the critics seem to think that there has been a considerable change in Heidegger's outlook, if not immediately after the publication of "Being and Time," at least since the first essay on Hölderlin (1936). I for one do not share in this opinion. In my view, the themes of all the four essays, but especially of the two philosophical ones, are directly and most intimately related to "Being and Time," but not so much to the first two published Sections as rather to the third one on "Time and Being."

This may become clearer from two instances small in themselves. In the essays, man is referred to as being placed "amidst" (inmitten) the multitude of beings within the whole. In "Being and Time" the "utensil," and the concern of Care with what is "zuhanden," is primarily analysed and only relatively late in the second Section is the genesis of the discovery of what is "vorhanden" from the circumspection of Care pointed out. The perspective of man being placed "amidst" the vast multitude of beings in the whole, however, is different. It refers not to the concern of Care nor to the ontological difference between Dasein and what is "vorhanden," but to the Being of man as together with, and amidst of, a multitude of other beings, whether men or not men, whether "zuhanden" or "vorhanden," in their Being. The perspective here is thus not of Dasein, but of "Being." Similarly, the fundamental concept of "das Seiende im Ganzen," the beings that are "in the whole" did not, and could not, receive its analysis even in the second Section of "Being and Time." For here again, as with regard to the "amidst," the "horizon" is of "Being," where man is one kind among other kinds. Both concepts, that of the "amidst" as well as that of "das Seiende im Ganzen," envisage man in an essentially more "ex-centric" way than in the first two Sections of "Being and Time" where Dasein is, as it were, in the "centre."

As to "On the Essence of Truth," Heidegger himself has pointed out in the meantime that this essay offers some kind of insight into the thought required for, and the "region of the dimension" aimed at in, an exposition of "Time and Being," the third Section of the main work.*
But already in the concluding Note to the essay, the express statement can be found that the "realm of the horizon" is not only the truth of what is, but the truth of "Being," thus indicating the same greater context. The import which, in the Section "The Essence of Truth" of this essay itself, is attached to the notion of "in the whole" as well as the fact that the wide realm

* Cf. "The Letter on 'Humanism,'" 1947, p.72, and the end of the Introduction to this essay.

of erring is thought to be opened up by the oblivion of such "in the whole" points likewise to the wider "horizon" of "Being" envisaged here, as does indeed for the reader of insight every portion of this essay.

"What is Metaphysics?" moves in the same "realm of horizon," as is evident not only from the "Postscript," but already from the text itself, when "nothingness" is characterised as essentially belonging to the "Being" of whatever is and not merely as the counter-conception of what is. If it were different, the phenomenon of "nothingness" would hardly have been chosen to elucidate the question "What is Metaphysics?" "Dread" with its "nothing" is analysed in "Being and Time" in preparation for the exposition of Care as the Being of Dasein; and "guilt" with its "nullity," in preparation for that of "resolve" as "authentic" Care and for the essence of Temporality itself. But the "nothingness" in the essay on metaphysics would seem to be of wider compass and farther reach than the two similar ones described in the main work.

The fact that Heidegger does not treat "philosophical" problems exclusively, but is seriously engaged in the expounding of poems, such as those of Hölderlin, and considers this task to be a "necessity of thought" is of an elucidating interest in this respect. A poet, such as Hölderlin, is very far removed from Dasein in its "everydayness" with which at any rate the first Section of "Being and Time" was largely concerned. According to Heidegger, he meditates upon what is "Holy," just as the true philosopher meditates upon "Being." Essentially different as the aim and the work of the poet is from that of the thinker, the fact remains that Hölderlin's poetry has entered into the orbit of Heidegger's expositions when the problem of "Being" itself and that of "Time and Being" was uppermost in his mind. And it is likely that in the light of these problems both essays would be studied, understood and assimilated more appropriately.

In "Hölderlin and the Essence of Poetry," the moment in which "ravenous Time" is riven into present, past and future, i.e. when Time once and for all opened up in its "dimensions," is explicitly referred to, as is, in "On the Essence of Truth," the moment when the first thinker asks the all-decisive question: what is the essence of all that is? In the essay on Poetry it is pointed out that, only when Time has been made to "stand" (zum Stehen gebracht), can man truly expose himself to change, to all that comes and goes; and only then comes what is "permanent" into sight and into word, the gods, the world and "Being" itself which likewise is opening out so that what is may become apparent. The problem of "Time and Being," Time as the indispensable and conditioning "horizon" for Being is discussed here in nuce and indeed in the simplest possible way. And if some readers may wonder at the fact that what is ascribed in one essay to the poet is considered in the other essay to be primarily the work of the thinker, they may do well to reflect upon the singularly close relationship between literature and philosophic thought in Greece, more concretely: upon the way in which the Pre-Socratic thinkers from Thales and Anaximander to Anaxagoras were fundamentally related to Homer and other early poets and upon that in which Plato was related to them as well as to Aeschylus and Sophocles—a problem which still waits for its scholarly elucidation, if not for its appropriate posing.

In the essay on the elegy "Homecoming" the great theme "Being and Time" is likewise apparent, if more veiled. Here I wish to remind the reader only of the commentary, early in the essay, upon the "angel of the house," with its reference to the earth, and the spatiality which it affords, upon the "angel of the year," with its reference to the light and its seasons, and upon "the High one," with his dwelling-place the "Ether," the source of serenification and of joy. How the "Being" has "opened out" and how such "opening out" was interpreted by one great modern poet, Heidegger endeavours to make us realise; and the important term "in the whole" may receive an elucidation from the way in which the things that are were envisaged by the poet, namely not in the spirit of separation, but "in the whole," and in which they are likewise interpreted in the essay.

But it would be wrong and altogether one-sided exclusively to emphasise that the essays on Truth and on Metaphysics, on Poetry and on the content of the elegy move, each in its way, in the "horizon" of "Being." The part which the meditation upon human Dasein plays in them is very considerable as well. However, both, man and Being, cannot be separated from each other fundamentally. For, as Heidegger phrased it more recently, man is the "guardian" of "Being" and dwells in its proximity. Otherwise he could not "enter" into "Dasein," the only one of all kinds of being to do so. In "Being and Time," too, Dasein, it is true, is only the starting-point; yet, it is the one starting-point from which the problem of Time and of Being is to be unfolded.

The light which is shed in these essays on man's position "in the whole" will be obvious to the reader and need hardly detain us here. The moment in which man has entered into that all-decisive "ex-position" in which he treats and discovers the things as what they are, i.e. the moment in which "truth" has come into being, is the revolutionary incision in the development of mankind and the beginning of its history and of genuine civilisation. "Poetry" establishes what is "permanent" in human Dasein and, beyond this, man himself is thought to "dwell poetically" on earth.* In "What is Metaphysics?" the mood of dread is discerned as the state in which a thinker may authentically find

* Here an analysis of the nature of the power of "imagination" and of its significance for poetry, for philosophy, and for human Dasein may be required to substantiate the suggestion. For the time being, cf. in this respect the analysis of the "transcendental power of imagination" interpreted as the "formative centre" and "ground" of ontological knowledge in the first edition of the "Critique of Pure Reason," in Heidegger's "Kant and the Problem of Metaphysics," pp.119/194.

124

himself exposed to "nothingness" and "transcendence" and, beyond this, metaphysics is characterised as belonging essentially to the "nature of man" and as the "fundamental happening" (Grundgeschehen) in Dasein. In the expounding of the elegy, the "There" in the Dasein of the poet, "homeland" and "homecoming," is envisaged in its concreteness and, through and beyond the poem, the poet himself in his solitariness between the "Holy" and his fellow-men, with his joy, sorrow, and cares, is the one actual focussing point.

One more aspect should be briefly mentioned here, especially as it concerns also Heidegger's own consciousness of the historical position of his philosphic work and relates to all the four essays. "Being and Time, Part I" has been characterised as a "transcendental ontology" and much is to be said in favour of this characterisation. At the same time, the analysis is guided by a "Seinsverständnis" (understanding of Being) and carried out with a view to the problem of Being. The intention to overcome the "subjectivity" of approach, in which modern philosophy since Descartes became rooted, is implicit already in this work and becomes more outspoken in his later essays. In this respect, it is a foremost contention of Heidegger that man must be envisaged "amidst" what is, human or non-human, "in the whole," i.e. as belonging to "das Seiende im Ganzen," though it is man alone that is in this "ex-centric" position of "Ex-sistence" from which he is able to envisage himself together with other beings in this way. Indeed Heidegger claims to have abandoned such "subjectivity" of man on principle and to philosophise from a different "ground," that of the truth of "Being." If so (and much may be said in its favour), he is likely to be the first thinker of very high rank to have carried out his philosophic thought from a historic position which has changed fundamentally from that of his predecessors and of most, if not all, his contemporaries; and this, undoubtedly, increases very much the difficulty for the appropriate comprehension and assimilation of his thought.

The atmosphere and the "orbit of thought" in the essays, their difference from the analysis of "Being and Time, Part I" and their profound relationship to the problem of "Being" itself, had, it was felt, to be characterised in general at first before each of them, in some of their aspects, is discussed in a preliminary and, it is hoped, preparatory way.

2

ON THE ESSENCE OF TRUTH

It seems best to start the introductory commentary with a discussion of the essay which is published in the third place in this edition: "On the Essence of Truth." The essays about Hölderlin may be more easily accessible to the intuitive understanding of a sensitive reader. The discussion of "Nothingness" in the essay on the nature of Metaphysics may seem more striking at first sight by its novelty as well as by its brilliance of treatment. But the problem of the Essence of Truth seems to me to be the most comprehensive of all. It is deeply rooted in the hardly discoverable beginnings of European thought, hidden in more statements of the greatest pre-Socratic philosophers, and though mostly disguised, it accompanies the philosophic tradition throughout the centuries with a leading and directing force. Being philosophical, it cannot help embracing the special problems of all kinds of truth, not only that of science and that of religion, but just as much those of technical productivity, of economic calculation, of political statecraft and of artistic creation. For the problem of truth is envisaged as philosophical only when it is contemplated both in its deeply founded unity and in its comprehensive breadth through which it affects all kinds of human civilisation in their historic tradition and in their present state.

The novelty of philosophic thought which marks Heidegger's "Being and Time" and the variety of his publications for the last twenty years can therefore be felt most strongly in his study of this central philosophic problem. Especially for the trained philosopher it is likely to prove the most interesting and thought-provoking essay of the four, at any rate in the longer run. But it is probably also the most difficult essay to understand. It requires to be studied slowly sentence by sentence and it may well have to be re-read several times until the main trend of thought is grasped and assimilated, the new philosophic language has lost its initial strangeness and the underlying ideas have gained their peculiar significance and forcefulness in the reader's mind.

It would seem only fitting that, in view of the rank of the essay, the difficulties which the reader has to face in its study and gradual comprehension should be stated frankly at the start.

(a) The essay, originally a public lecture, is written in a very condensed form. It contains a number of most elucidating notions, partly new, partly a rendering of the ancient Greek tradition, such as those of "overtness" and of "letting-be," of truth (ἀλήθεια) as an "uncovering" and of "ex-sistence" as an "ex-position" into an "uncovering" as well as of "being" (τὸ ὄν, ens), "being as such" (τὸ ὄν ᾗ ὄν), "being in the whole" (καθόλου), "essence" (οὐσία, essentia, substantia) and "Being" (το εἶναι, οὐσία, τὸ ὄντως ὄν). But these notions are mostly introduced in passing and often discussed in no more than a very few sentences, hardly in such detail that the reader can gain an entirely clear and well-defined idea of them and of their fundamental significance from this context alone. This first difficulty of brevity is due to the vastness and the intrinsic complexity of the problem and to Heidegger's entirely novel approach to it as well as to his intention of encompassing it within a reasonably short space. The more the reader has penetrated into the formidable thought-content, the more

128

is he likely to be amazed how much ground connected with the problem has been covered in this one essay and how far the thinker has advanced into a territory not thought out before.

(b) Another difficulty arises from Heidegger's attitude towards philosophic language. On the one hand, he is deeply interested in the concepts and terms moulded by former great thinkers and handed down in the philosophic tradition and he is keenly intent on recapturing their original meaning. One example of this in our essay is his interpretation of the terms "Vorstellen" (representation) and "Gegenstand" (object), while another even more important and thought-provoking example is his new rendering of the concept of truth where he insists that the Greek term "ἀ-λήθεια" alone, derived from λανθάνειν (to remain concealed), is indicative of its original and most telling meaning.* On the other hand and in connection with the first-mentioned tendency, he is prone to coin new philosophic terms which in themselves are descriptive of meaning. In this way he renders, e.g. truth as "Ent-ber-gung" (dis-covery, un-covering, re-velation, un-veiling) and makes it linguistically correspond to "Verbergung" (concealment), which is one important kind of untruth. This attitude of his to language makes considerable claims on the

---

* Cf. "Being and Time," German edition, p. 219 f., with its most valuable reference to the first fragment of Heraclitus where the words "to remain concealed" and "to forget" (ἐπιλανθάνεσθαι) are used in direct contrast to bring out more forcefully and clearly the meaning of the philosophic conception "λόγος."

reader; but it should be emphasised that Heidegger chooses his concepts, especially if he has to coin them afresh, not arbitrarily, and only after long searching reflection and that it is the phenomena and the problems themselves which he envisages that compel him to do so.

(c) But the greatest difficulty for understanding and appreciating the whole trend of thought in this essay—far more than that of its condensed brevity or that of its new concepts—is of course a philosophic one: the vastness and intricate nature of the problem of truth itself, as visualised and contemplated by Heidegger, and more particularly his new philosophic approach based on the conviction that the problem of truth is inseparably bound up with what is meant by "Being." Of this more will be said later. It is the way of thought, the standpoint from which, and the perspective in which, everything is viewed that are novel, solitary and difficult to grasp at first, as they always are with original thinkers. That the linguistic rendering may appear hard, forced and out of the ordinary is ultimately a result of this new approach.

These kinds of difficulty with which everyone has to cope in the earlier stages of his study of the essay are mentioned here in the belief and the expectation that, once the thoughtful reader has overcome them, he will feel richly recompensed by the originality of the philosophic treatment of the problem and the new vista which it opens up. In this connection his attention may be drawn to a distinction made by Heidegger himself in the concluding note. The new ideas and concepts which he advances, important as they are, are not so much his primary concern as rather the sequence of the problems to which he moves on step by step, and the direction and ultimate orientation of his "way of thought" of which they are revelatory. This "way of thought," he suggests, arises from and leads to an "essential experience," namely that "only out of the Dasein, into which man may enter (but which is not identical with human life), a proximity to the truth of Being prepares itself," i.e. for those that live with a historical consciousness.

It is Heidegger's conviction that the historic era in which philosophic problems were approached from the standpoint of "any subjectivity of man as a subject"—a standpoint very often taken in modern times—has come to its close. The basis from which he approaches the problem of truth is the "Da-sein," as philosophically analysed in "Being and Time," implying among other characteristics, a "transcendence" which (if I understand Heidegger rightly) is indicated in this essay by the notion of "ex-sistence" as an "ex-position" into a "discovering" of beings, one of which is man himself. The all-important sequence of thought in this essay is guided by "a change in the relationship to Being" which Heidegger seems to think belongs fundamentally to our own present age as well as to his philosophy. It is this "change in the relationship to Being" and its relevance for the problem of truth which he for one believes can come into new and full grasp again now for the first time since the days of the Pre-Socratics, while it has become somewhat obscured during the whole of the great history of philosophy since Plato, that he is trying primarily to communicate to his readers.

In this Introduction to the essay it cannot be attempted to discuss in any greater detail the new concepts which Heidegger introduces and develops. To do so would mean to give an almost running commentary to the text, considerably longer than the essay itself. Instead I should like to restrict myself to outlining the general sequence of thought, the importance of which has been emphasised above, and to commenting only on occasion upon the novel perspective in which the problem of truth is envisaged here.

In this respect it may be helpful for a first study of the essay to see it grouped under five main headings, though after some time the reader may prefer to abandon this arrangement again: A. The formulation of the problem (Introduction). B. The starting-point: the conventional theory of truth as an "agreement" between thought (representation, proposition) and thing and its more comprehensive historical setting (Section 1). C. A reflection, on the lines of transcendental philosophy, but in a fundamentally non-subjectivistic and non-anthropocentric approach, in two stages: (a) upon the inner possibility, and (b) upon the ground of the inner possibility, of this theory. (a) "overtness" and (b) freedom in the sense of "letting-be" being the respective two key-terms of this reflection (Sections 2-4). D. The new interpretation of the nature of truth and of untruth, concerning the whole of the historic era of mankind and its civilisation, including its history of philosophy, of science and of learning prepared in Section 4, but set out substantially in Sections 5-7). E. Conclusion: The task of philosophy with a view to the nature of truth as outlined in the essay (Section 8).

The essay intends to advance the philosophic meditation upon the nature of truth one stage further beyond the distinctly subjectivistic approach, prepared by Descartes and manifestly followed up by Kant and his successors. Thus it aims at, and carries with it the force of, a fundamental change in the whole realm of philosophic thought. It starts with the conventional view that truth is propositional truth and it leads on to the outlook that truth is inseparably and essentially bound up with the whole of human Dasein in its historic era, with the way in which man finds himself placed amidst other beings in the world and especially with man's unique and close relatedness to "Being." * In our essay Heidegger uses the

---

* In a more recent publication of the year 1947, in a "Letter on 'Humanism' " addressed to M. Jean Beaufret, Heidegger speaks of man as of the "shepherd" of Being, of the "neighbour" of Being and of himself in his philosophic thought as of a "wanderer on his way into the neighbourhood of Being." He ascribes to human Dasein the task of the "guardianship" of, and in this sense the "care" for, Being. I am quoting these phrases here only

phrase "way of thought" in a sense as if his thought was walking on a path in some definite direction. To some readers, however, his "way of thought" may well seem to resemble either that other "way" which Plato said he had found out of the cave or else a fast non-stop flight in an aeroplane where only the main places of the globe can dimly be seen in farther than bird-perspective for a little while.

The great importance which Heidegger attaches to the problem of truth can be gathered from the fact, to my knowledge most unusual in his philosophic productivity, that this problem was discussed by him in some greater detail already in "Being and Time," at an outstanding place of the work, namely at the end of the "preparatory fundamental analysis of Dasein" (§ 44, pp. 212/230).* Readers well versed in German may wish to compare the two versions. The way of procedure is similar, starting from propositional truth and leading, in the earlier version, up to the interpretation that truth means "being discovering" (entdeckendsein) and "being discovered" (entdecktsein) and that Dasein is both in truth and in untruth. It goes without saying that the discussion of the problem in "Being and Time" is much more closely

---

to substantiate the vague characterisation given above of "man's unique and close relatedness to Being."

* An interpretation of Plato's theory of truth (1942, reprinted 1947) has also been published. But it came too late into my hands to make any special reference to it.

bound up with the preceding analysis of Dasein. The earlier exposition differs from the later one in that it contains a number of most valuable references to utterances of philosophic authors, such as Parmenides, Heraclitus, especially Aristotle, Thomas Aquinas, Kant, Brentano and Husserl; there can also be found an analysis of the way in which the traditional view could arise that truth is "seated" in a proposition and its agreement with a fact, and a discussion of the fundamental problem why we are compelled to presuppose truth. Otherwise, the earlier treatment is less self-contained and more in the form of a sketch than is the subsequent essay.

Now I propose to comment, partly very briefly, upon a number of questions that may arise under the five main headings indicated above.

A. Introduction. The problem with which the thinker is concerned is not any one kind of truth, but truth as such. It may be argued that, in the essay, Heidegger discusses only "intellectual" truth. His reply, if I understand him rightly, would be that only when truth, as conceived in early philosophic thought, has entered into human life and has transformed it profoundly in such a way that it thereby is "Dasein" is it possible to speak of truth in the full sense; that truth, arising with the first thinker's question: what is the essence of all that is? is of a far greater incisive and revolutionary significance for man and his civilisation than is commonly supposed; and that truth, once it has come into being, is fundamentally one and indivisible.

B. Section 1; *The starting-point.* Here Heidegger discusses not only the "current" theory that truth is thought to consist in the approximation between thing and meaning and between proposition and fact, in accordance with the traditional formula: "veritas est adaequatio intellectus et rei." But he traces at once this theory back to its historic setting in Christian theological and modern secularised thought, i.e. to the relationship between God, the created things and man and the relationship between reason and the world-order of existing things. This seems to me a noteworthy point to be borne in mind. The reason for this reference to the more comprehensive setting of the problem of truth would appear to be that Heidegger is convinced that the conception of truth is always essentially related to the interpretation of the nature of all that exists, attempted in any age or in any greater historic era. In this sense he speaks, in the beginning of Section 8, of "the well-preserved system of the truth of beings within the whole." In other words, the reference to the historic setting is the first, if implicit, refutation of the theory that the seat of truth is in the proposition and its agreement with a fact or a thing.—The reference shows, too, that Heidegger's apparently purely systematic expositions are accompanied by an acute historical consciousness; in this case it is also to prepare for the greater historic perspective which is to open up later in the essay.

C. Sections 2-4: *The preparatory exposition.* The comparison with Kant's transcendental method, here suggested, requires qualification in two respects. Firstly, it is only the *direction* in which the thought tends that can be compared, i.e. the questions about the *inner possibility* of "agreement" and about the *ground of the inner possibility* of "rightness," but not the *execution* which is as brief, allusive and open to further questioning as Kant's treatment is detailed and full of close-reasoned argumentation. Secondly—this has already been mentioned, but cannot be emphasised too strongly—Heidegger's solution is professedly, and I think in fact, not subjectivistic or "anthropological" (in the philosophical sense of this term), as is Kant's. Provided the comparison is strictly confined to the direction in which Heidegger's analysis is moving, its first stage (in Section 2) may be thought to resemble Kant's analysis of the forms of space and time and of the categories, its second stage (in Sections 3 and 4), Kant's analysis of the much more hidden operations of transcendental intuition, apperception and especially imagination.* At the same time, the comparison

---

* Cf. Heidegger's interpretation of the "Critique of Pure Reason" and in particular of the function of imagination in it in "Kant and the Problem of Metaphysics." There, e.g. the term "Entgegenstehenlassen" (letting a thing stand opposite to oneself) finds a somewhat detailed discussion, pp.63/82 and later. The key-term "letting-be," in Section 4 and later, is also referred to and briefly discussed in that work.

would be most misleading if the reader were not to keep his thought carefully away from the idea of any spontaneous activity on the part of the subject or of any a priori forms or the like. With this Heidegger has nothing to do. Even Hegel's philosophy, as could be shown from his "Logic," is fundamentally subjectivistic in a sense in which Heidegger's philosophy is not. I have ventured to make this comparison with Kant for two reasons. Without it, the titles of Sections 2 and 3 "The inner possibility of . . ." and "The ground of the inner possibility of . . ." could not be properly understood. Furthermore, many readers, and among them perhaps even some trained philosophers, may otherwise overlook the profundity of reflection which lies behind the condensed statements of those few pages.

C.1. Section 2: *The first stage.* In the first stage of Heidegger's, as it were, "transcendental" reflection, the problem is: how is an "agreement" between a proposition, based on a "representation," and the thing which is "represented" possible? He develops his view, while at the same time giving an explanation of the two philosophical terms "Vorstellen" (representation; or, according to the meaning of the German word, letting something stand in front of oneself) and "Gegenstand" (object; or, according to the word-meaning, a thing standing opposite to oneself). "Representation," then, means: "letting a thing stand opposite to oneself as an object." One important notion, however, should

138

be added. If I represent a thing in my mind in such a way as it is, the thing must, somehow, have "come" to me, be it a coin or a star or a fact of remote history. Heidegger describes this by the phrase: "that the thing, though it remains in its place and remains generally what it is, 'traverses' an 'overtness' towards oneself." Now, in whatever way this "overtness" may have come about, it is not produced by any human representation, but it is only accepted and related as a "realm of relations" of its own. All human activities, all man's calculations and workings go on within such "overtness"; and all his dealings with other things or with his fellow-men are, Heidegger suggests, possible only by reason of this "overtness."

This concept of "overtness" may become a little clearer if the great difference between the way in which the highest animals live in their "environment" and the way in which man knows, plans and acts in the "world" is reflected upon for a moment. A mammal or a bird may have its definite relation to its food, its sex-partners and offspring, its enemies and its surroundings and it may have some sense-perceptions of them. But they are not to the animal as what they actually are, but merely the aims of desires and instinctive care or the cause of fears. No animal lives in "overtness" and none of the things to which it is related is for it in "overtness" either. In contrast to this, if a carpenter plans to make a table, he knows the qualities of the wood for what they are, the tools, how he is best going to use them, and the purpose, size and design of the table to be made. He has an image of the finished table before his mind, while he is working, he takes this image for his guidance and the finished table is in the end to "agree" with his "representation" of it at the start. This is possible only because, Heidegger would assert, the wood, the tools, the design of the table and the carpenter with his craft are in "overtness." It is as if at some time in the early history of mankind the huge realm in which men with their practical—technical, economic, political—mastery of the things around them and with their varied knowledge of them live and act, had been widely flung open, whereas it had been, as it were, "closed" before; and it is to this tremendous and little thought of event of the huge realm of the "world" widely flung open that the concept of "overtness" *seems* to point. For this characterisation of the "overtness" in which the wide realm of beings is "opened up" and no longer "closed," cf. the various references of the "Erschlossenheit," i.e. the "disclosed" state, of Dasein in the account given of "Being and Time." The present essay would seem to deal with the problem: how is such "Erschlossenheit" of Dasein possible? This "overtness," then, is thought to be the permanent and indispensable condition for all human civilisation, for all human knowledge and for all human purposive activities. It is found to be in particular the permanent and indispensable condition of all propositional truth. For only if the things about which some statements are made "traverse," the "overtness" towards man and only if he is able to take the things themselves for his guidance when he makes his statements about them, i.e. only if he is, together with things, in "overtness," is an approximation between a thing and a statement possible at all.

C.2. Sections 3 and 4: The second stage. In the second stage of Heidegger's "transcendental" reflection the problem is: what is the ground of the possibility of a correct proposition, where the binding standards are taken from the object in an "overtness" of human attitude and activity? This ground is found in "freedom" in a very specific sense, namely in the sense of "letting-be." This term means that man concerns himself with the things around him as they *are* and treats them, and among them himself and his fellow-men, as "beings"; an attitude and behaviour which may seem at first sight only too common, but which, Heidegger insists, is pre-eminent in its significance and which has brought about the most incisive and most revolutionary transformation in the life of mankind. To this importance attached to the "letting-be" it is due that Heidegger, following the Greek terminology, speaks of "beings" instead of things; that human life, inasfar as it has entered into the treatment of things as they "are," is characterised as "Da-sein" (being there) and that "Being" (Sein) is the one phenomenon of outstanding significance.* Or

---

* Cf. "The Letter on 'Humanism,'" 1947, p. 76: "Being —this is not God nor the ground of the world. Being is

reversely, because he was steeped in Greek thought and had meditated long upon "Dasein," beings and Being Heidegger found out the incisive relevance of what he terms "letting-be." Or again differently, both his insight into the significance of "letting-be" and his philosophic concern with "Dasein," beings and Being belong inseparably together.

Now this concept of "letting-be" is intimately connected not only with that of "overtness," but with two other fundamental interpretations: that of "truth" as an "un-covering" of what is and that of "ex-sistence" as an "ex-position" into such an "un-covering." Only in the light of these two interpretations can the meaning of "letting-be" (as well as of "overtness") be properly understood and educidated.

(a. Truth as an "un-covering" of what is.) In order to make clear to oneself why Heidegger insists on the re-interpretation of truth in the sense of the Greek concept ἀλήθεια, it may be helpful to start from two well-known English words with which everyone is entirely familiar: discovery and revelation. Both words seem to have been coined in a spirit not very different from that which is inherent in the Greek term. Both words have a positive meaning; but in form and in the underlying and accompanying thought-content they are compounds of a root

---

farther than all that is and yet it is nearer to man than any one being, be this a rock, an animal, a work of art, a machine, be it an angel or God. Being is what is nearest But the proximity itself remains farthest from man."

of a likewise positive, though opposite, meaning and of a privative prefix.

To "dis-cover" means to separate and to take off a "cover" from a thing underneath over which it was spread and which it had hidden until that moment. The thing, fact or principle, e.g. a mine, America, a crime, the law of gravity, is made accessible to sight, insight, use or treatment by removing the "cover," of whatever nature it may have been. The word applies to one circumscribed thing, fact or principle and it is therefore particularly well suited as a term in science. And if we think of the multitude of scientific discoveries made during the last two or three thousand years, it would seem as if at a great number of points and in a variety of respects "covers" had been taken away. But whether we do so or not, the word itself conveys a complexity which is necessarily absent from a word, such as "truth."

The meaning of the word "re-velation" is similar and yet different. Here a "veil," as before a "cover," is thought to be taken away. But the "cover" is meant to be more closely connected with the thing underneath, therefore the prefix indicative of separation "dis-"; whereas the "veil," in itself more transparent than a "cover" and by its nature obscuring the things that lie behind, is thought to be removed much more suddenly and its vanishing makes what is behind at once apparent and perhaps lucid, whether it is a thing, a great perspective or life and the Godhead itself. Whereas the word "discovery" is applied especially in science, the word "revelation" has a specific religious and theological connotation, though it is used in other contexts as well.

There is no similar word of this more complex type, comparable to "dis-covery" and "re-velation," covering the whole range of possible kinds of truth, in either English or Latin, Italian, French and German. Only the Greek term for truth in the philosophical and, hence, in any other sense, ἀλήθεια, is of the kind.* But when we now come to consider Heidegger's re-interpretation of truth, we have not only and not even in the first place to think of the linguistic expression, but of the philosophical significance implied as well as of the historic tradition which began to become obscured, once "ἀλήθεια" was identified with "ἰδέα" by Plato and still more so when it was rendered as "veritas" in the post-Greek tradition (though the last-mentioned aspect of the historic tradition since Plato is not expressly discussed in this essay).

"ἀλήθεια" means an "uncovering" (or "unveiling") of the things as they are, but neither in the scientific and scholarly nor in the theological sense, i.e. neither in the sense of a multitude of "discoveries" made with regard to many particular facts or things nor in the sense of a "revelation" by God. That all things, in what

* Cf. Aristotle's interpretation of five ways in which the soul is in truth (ἀληθεύειν) in the "Nicomachean Ethics," Book VI, among them any kind of purposive productivity (τέχνη) and any kind of prudent thoughtfulness in practical conduct (φρόνησις).

they are, were in a state of permanent concealment, were embedded in a primary mystery
which, as it were, shrouded them belongs to the
background against which all "uncovering," i.e.
all arriving at and establishing of "truth" has
taken and is taking place—a background which
is not irrelevant and which should not fall into
oblivion, for it is inseparably bound up with
"truth" itself. But "truth" as an "un-covering"
and an "unconcealment" was, in Heidegger's
view, originally experienced for the first time in
human history when the first thinker raised in
profound astonishment the question: what is
all that is? It was then that the things within
the whole (das Seiende im Ganzen, $\kappa\alpha\theta\delta\lambda o\nu$)
were released from their initial and long-lasting
state of "concealment"; and according to Heidegger this was the most incisive and most
revolutionary moment of all in the development
of the human race: history and civilisation in
the deeper and great sense began with it. This
change was brought about by "thought" or by
what was afterwards called "philosophy."

(b. "Ex-sistence" as the "ex-position" into an
"un-covering" of what is, i.e. into "truth.") If all
things, and with them man himself, were embedded in a long-lasting mystery and if the "un-
covering" of what is took place by the power
of thought, i.e. by a thinker raising the question:
what is all that is? what is its essence?—hereby
Heidegger's great problem "Time and Being" is
formulated—then the state in which the thinker
was, and which enabled him to advance his

145

question, should be reflected upon and characterised more closely.

Here Heidegger re-introduces, but with an entirely new connotation, the concept of "Existence" which had been of considerable import in the first two published Sections of "Being and Time." It is sharply distinguished from two other meanings of the term, prevalent in the philosophic tradition and today: (a) from existence in the common sense of an "existing" thing, i.e. from the fact that a thing can be found to be there and that it continues in being; and (b) from "Existence" in the modern sense of the term as introduced by Kierkegaard and made a fundamental conception of all philosophy especially by Jaspers, a term which Heidegger here defines as "the ethical endeavour of man, based upon his bodily and inner constitution, on behalf of his self." This, obviously, would be insufficient to characterise the state of mind of Anaximander, Parmenides, Heraclitus or Plato when they, face to face with "un-concealment," felt compelled to ask: what is the innermost essence of all that is? It would be insufficient to characterise the state of mind of any true thinker.

"Ex-sistence" means an "ex-position" of the thinker. He is placed outside the huge realm in which "concealment"—concealment of what the things actually are and concealment which shrouds human life—rules. He is transformed into an altogether different "position." It is in this different "position" and in it alone that he is able to ask his all-important and all-embracing question about all that is within the whole, human and non-human. He has withdrawn from the common everyday contact with things and men in a way, similar to that in which Plato describes the liberation from the fetters in the "cave" in order to ascend into the light of the "sun"; in the solitude of his "ex-position" he is closer to "Being" and to men and things as "beings" than he had been before, in the "cave"; here he meditates upon his question; but when, according to Plato's myth, he descends again, he conveys to his fellow-men the insight which he has gained, a matter which we shall have to contemplate when we come to consider the "letting-be" itself and the "overtness" of human activity and knowledge.

For such an "ex-position" the concept "transcendence," i.e. the ascent above or beyond anything that is and that may become "uncovered" for human Dasein, has also been used both in the philosophic tradition and by Heidegger himself.* But the concept of which the term "ex-position," and "Ex-sistence" as an "ex-position," seems most strongly reminiscent is that of "ecstasy," provided that this concept is cleared of any falsifying mystical or religious connotation and is taken in that sense in which Plato, before Plotinus, describes, in the "Phaedrus" ch. 27, the "ex-position" of the soul before

* Cf. the second Section of "The Essence of Ground": "Transcendence as the realm of the question about the essence of ground," pp. 10/30.

birth, above all of the soul of the philosopher, into that "superheavenly place" where it envisages "Being" and all that is "un-concealed" (τἀληθῆ), including justice, moderation and knowledge, in its essence. This comparison, however, must not mislead the reader. The "exposition" of early great thinkers into the "un-covering" of what is took place in their actual Da-sein and not in a "superheavenly place" before their birth. When I ventured to refer to this great passage in the "Phaedrus" (ch. 24/29), I did so to remind the reader of the profound astonishment with which Plato contemplated the "ex-position" into the "un-covering" of all that is: the intense sense of wonder at the fact that the things can be envisaged as and known for, what they are and the great difficulty in comprehending this fact inform and permeate the myth in every detail of its content.

The "exposition" of a thinker into the "un-covering" of what is induces him to reflect not upon the nature of any special beings, but upon the nature of beings *within the whole,* i.e. of beings, human and non-human, in the world. It is the radical consistency and comprehensiveness by which his reflections and his questioning are distinguished. But "Ex-sistence" as an "ex-position" into the "un-covering" of what is is not restricted to the philosopher. Men may not be conscious of it, but it is fundamentally and essentially bound up with human civilisation, especially in the way in which it has developed in the Occident since the early days of Greece.

148

Only as an "ex-position" into the "un-covering" of what is can the term of "letting-be" and that of "freedom" as "letting-be" be properly understood.

(c. Freedom as "letting-be.") As Heidegger points out, the expression "to let something be" means in common language not to interfere with it and not to have anything to do with it. This is not meant here. It means that men concern themselves with a thing in the way in which it is. As has been emphasised before, no animal is able to treat a thing as it is. But any artisan and engineer, any doctor and teacher, any scientist treats the things with which they are concerned as what they are. Each in his own way partakes of the "ex-position" into the "un-covering" of what is. That is to say, he allows it to be what it is, as a doctor, e.g. he takes the ill person who consults him as a patient, examines the parts of his body in special ways to find out from what kind of illness he is suffering and considers what kind of medicaments and what kind of treatment is likely best to cure his illness. To act properly and usefully, he takes the symptoms of the body of the ill man for his guidance in the diagnosis and the well-known medicaments and ways of treatment of a particular illness for his guidance in his advice. To him the patient *is*, the special kind of illness *is*, the medicaments and ways of treatment to be applied *are*. Otherwise he would not *be* a doctor. The same is the case with all other human activities and with all knowledge. "Letting-be" means thus to take a thing for what it is. And "freedom," rightly understood, consists, in Heidegger's view, in this human attitude that men bring themselves into the inner "position," consciously or mostly unconsciously, that they concern themselves with the things, whether they are human or non-human, such as they are. This, Heidegger suggests, is meant when we think of "truth." "Truth" is not restricted to knowledge, scientific, scholarly or philosophic, but every human being who lives in a historic civilisation is, in his own way, concerned with "truth."

Nevertheless, the philosophers had a very special and distinguished task and function in this "ex-position" into the "un-covering" of what is. They reflected upon the multitude of beings as beings within the whole, in totality; they experienced what "being un-covered" means in contrast to the preceding state of an all-embracing mystery; and with their insistence on "Being" and "beings," which they realised was not an arbitrary concept, but the most fundamental, elucidating and civilisational of all, they were the first to offer a meaningful and well thought-out foundation, out of their theoretical insight, for human Dasein and for the historic future of human civilisation. Rising against the flux of Time which had swallowed up innumerable generations when things had remained concealed to men as what they are, they became aware, Heraclitus most consciously so, that mankind had lived up to that moment as if they had been in a sleeping and dreaming state. The "un-covering" of what *is* would mean that men would *be,* together with a great multitude of other beings in one world, in a whole and that only when men learnt to take and treat things as they were would the world in which they potentially were actually "open up" and would men emerge from a long-lasting enclosure into an "overtness" of a very wide range. For here it should now be added that, when in our earlier discussion of the term "overtness" it was said that "the huge realm of the world seemed widely flung open for man," it was, in Heidegger's view, this one fact that men learnt to take things for, and treat things as, what they *are* and it was, above all, the insight of the philosophers into the import of what "Being" and "beings" mean that brought about the "overtness."

Three important points of insight result from the foregoing discussions, inasfar as "truth," human Dasein and philosophy are concerned.

Truth consists in the "uncovering" of what is. Its "seat" is therefore not in a correct proposition and its approximation to a fact or a thing, but it concerns the whole of the "overtness" in which the things are when man has come to let them be what they are. Truth, therefore, affects essentially every kind of human activity, all human behaviour and attitude. Furthermore, truth is inseparable from all that is and from Being. The moment the things are taken for, and treated as, what they are, man is "un-covering" them and thereby he exposes himself to truth.

The opening up of the huge realm of beings,

the treatment of things as what they are is the greatest transformation which human life has undergone. To be there amidst a multitude of other beings and to experience oneself as being there in this way is meant by "Da-sein." This transformation is hinted at, too, by the term "Ex-sistence" as an "ex-position." Man, by his nature, is not yet "Da-sein." He only may enter into "Da-sein." And he enters into it, not so much when he performs his own activity, unaware of what he is doing, but rather when he realises the full significance of being there amidst a multitude of other beings and of truth as the second newer realm which has opened up for man during the last three milleniums. The "ex-position" of man into the realm of what is, which he is "un-covering," makes civilisation and history possible and with them all the potentialities of historic humanity. "Freedom" consists in Heidegger's view essentially in this "ex-position" into the "uncovering" of what is. But this exposition of man into truth holds such sway over man and his destiny that it would be wrong to say that "freedom" was a quality of his Being. Rather the reverse. As Heidegger puts it: "Freedom, i.e. the ex-sistent, un-covering Da-sein, owns man and owns him in such an original way that this freedom alone grants to humanity the distinguishing relationship to what is within the whole, the relationship which makes all history possible." These assertions that truth is the "un-covering" of what is and that man's entering into it means for him the most incisive change that has taken place, the beginning of all history and civilisation, are likely to occupy the controversial discussion of the technical philosophers.

As for the philosophers, or as Heidegger prefers to call them: the thinkers, they seem to be no less than the ultimate inaugurators and guarantors of this tremendous transformation. Even though artisans and some other people may have begun to treat the things with which they were concerned as what they are, before the first thinker raised his crucial question, not only did they not know what they were doing, but the new attitude towards things had no name, no sure foundation and no justification. Only the reflection of the early Greek thinkers upon "beings" and "Being" and their deeply puzzled questioning brought into clearer sight and grasp, into word and recognition the new state of men and of things, once they had emerged from concealment and oblivion and had entered upon their "uncovering." Moreover, they were concerned not with any special things as they are, but with all that is in totality. Concentrating with singlemindedness on the problem of "Being," they asked what a "being" was as such, i.e. as "being" (τό ὂν ᾗ ὄν), and what the "beings" were as "beings" within the whole, related to "Being" itself. Thereby they brought to conceptual relief and to a well-reasoned argumentative foundation the new attitude towards men and things, the principle of which had never before been understood: they formulated for mankind for the first time what it means to be "in truth."

The Sections 2-4 in Heidegger's essay deal only with the preparatory analysis. In the Sections 5-7 the problem of the essence of truth and of untruth is expressly discussed.

D.1. Section 5: The interpretation of the essence of truth. The interpretation is based on the preceding exposition and employs all its main concepts, such as "overtness," "letting-be," "freedom," "Ex-sistence," "ex-position" and "uncovering." But one key-term, formerly introduced as well, is now placed in the foreground and assumes a significance not emphasised so clearly before: "das Seiende *im Ganzen*" (the things that are *within the whole.*) And one other key-term of Heidegger's philosophy, analysed in "Being and Time," but not introduced in this essay so far, gains a fundamental importance as well: the *"Gestimmtheit"* of man and of his attitude and behaviour in his relationship to the things that are within the whole. In the preceding Sections Heidegger discussed the problem of the ground of the inner possibility of any approximation between a true proposition and a fact or a thing; and he found this ground in "freedom" as the "letting-be." Here the problem of the essence of truth itself is envisaged. Therefore it seems especially noteworthy that the exposition focusses on these two aspects: the "Gestimmtheit" and the "within the whole."

"The things that are *within the whole*" implies the varied relationship of human **Dasein** with the things of Nature that form its background, with the manifold kinds of utensils produced and used in civilised life, with one's fellow-men and with the historic tradition in which Dasein is carried on; but it applies likewise the varied connection of the things one among the others, e.g. the possible hierarchy among beings, such as that of matter, living beings, man and anything higher than man. The things that are "within the whole" and the relationship of human Dasein to them is thus something much more comprehensive than the human contact with beings as beings, though the latter is fundamentally inseparable from the former.

How this "whole" is termed, whether "world" or "universe" or left unnamed, is of comparatively little import. (A Christian who believes that the world is created by God would be reluctant to call the whole "world"; for God would be within the whole as well.) But it would seem important that the "whole" is not just the abstract sum-total of the things that are, but that the "in-Being" of Dasein and of all things within the whole is emphasised.* And it seems even more important that "truth" is interpreted as the "uncovering of the things that are *within the whole*." This means that, if there is truth

---

* Cf. not only the detailed analysis of "in-Being" in "Being and Time," pp. 130/180, but also the explicit contrast, in "What is Metaphysics?" between the whole of the things that are which cannot be comprehended and our being placed amidst things which are somehow uncovered within the whole.

at all, it is of necessity and at once related to the "within the whole." Truth cannot be without it, however much any specialised knowledge or any particular mastery of things may pretend and falsely imagine itself to be so and though the "within the whole," in contrast to any special set of things, remains always and of necessity "incalculable" and "incomprehensible."

It is a famous saying of Hegel that "the true is the whole." * This conviction which is inherent in the philosophic European tradition, though rarely so outspokenly stated as by Hegel, can be traced back to many great thinkers of the modern period as well as to Thomas Aquinas, Aristotle, Plato and the Pre-Socratics. The conception of a systematic philosophy concerned with the totality of problems was rooted in it.

Heidegger, like all of us, is separated from these thinkers by the deep gulf that has opened up through the vastly increased specialised knowledge in all branches of learning and life, claiming exclusively for itself the title of truth. But against this tendency with which many may be prone to agree today Heidegger firmly insists that truth is the ex-position of human life into the overtness of the things around him "in the whole"; and that, if we ignore or dispute this relationship, we ignore or dispute the way in which we are placed amidst other beings and are bound to fall a prey to "error," one essential kind of un-truth.

* Cf. Hegel, "Phenomenology of the Mind," Preface, p. 16.

This emphasis by Heidegger on the "within the whole" seems to me to deserve in particular the attention and reflection of the reader.

The relationship of human Dasein to the things that are within the whole is characterised by the term *"Gestimmtheit."* This term is untranslatable. "Gestimmtheit" means: to be in a mood," "humour," "frame of mind." But Heidegger expressly states that "Gestimmtheit"—literally, the way in which man is "tuned"—is not to be taken either psychologically or with a view merely to the individual's personal life, as, incidentally, was done by Dilthey, the first in more recent philosophy to emphasise the great import of "Stimmung," e.g. of optimism or pessimism, for the development of a "Weltanschauung." For "Gestimmtheit" is to Heidegger inseparably bound up with the "ex-sistent exposition into the things that are within the whole." And the "Gestimmtheit" of a human Dasein has a distinctive function of somehow revealing the things within the whole to man, the individual may be consciously aware of it or not. What, e.g. the "Gestimmtheit" of a poet, his "joy" tinged with sadness, reveals of the things within the whole may be seen from Heidegger's interpretation of the poem "Homecoming"; what the "Stimmung" of dread in a philosophic mind, from the discussion of "nothingness" in "What is Metaphysics?"

A "mood," such as joy or dread or boredom, does not relate a human Dasein strictly to one thing or a few things. It colours or "tunes" the relationship to the things that are within the whole and it implicitly discloses in what way a human Dasein is placed within the whole, a phenomenon termed by Heidegger "Befindlichkeit." The "Befindlichkeit," and its "Gestimmtheit," is one fundamental aspect of man's "in-Being" in the whole.* The "Gestimmtheit," thus understood, is an elementary, but important link of man with all other beings as beings, vague as to its special content, but far-embracing and generalising. And as Heidegger holds the view that "truth" as the "uncovering of the things that are within the whole" relates human Dasein to the "whole," he finds that this relationship to the things within the whole is embedded in a tuning atmosphere, with which every special behaviour of man directed towards truth is in harmony. Owing to this "Gestimmtheit" man not only "feels" or "experiences" himself to be connected with the vast multitude of other beings within the whole. The concepts of "feeling" and of "personal experience" are rejected by Heidegger as inadequate derivatives. But his Dasein itself has become embedded in a "Gestimmtheit" which is uncovering the things in the whole, once freedom, as the exposition into truth, has taken place. Thus Heidegger states: "Every kind of behaviour of historical man, whether of especial relevance or not, whether comprehended or not, is tuned and by this attunement raised to the plane of the things

* Cf. "Being and Time," pp. 134/140, and the reference to the phenomenon in my account of the work.

that are within the whole." In other words: the "Gestimmtheit" strengthens and reveals the connectedness of human Dasein with the things within the whole, once they are brought into the overtness of truth. As he suggests, it is the "within the whole" itself, incalculable and incomprehensible as it is and remains, that is "tuning" everything.

The "within the whole" and the "Gestimmtheit" which vaguely reveals it are, as it were, the two conceptual "signposts" to which Heidegger pursued the problem of the essence of truth in this essay.

D.2. Sections 6-7: The interpretation of the essence of untruth. The problem of untruth is inseparably connected with that of truth, in the current theory of propositional truth as well as in Heidegger's meditations. But their characterisation is wholly different.

In the current theory, untruth is the "negative" of a true proposition, a proposition where the preceding judgment was wrong and where, for a demonstrable reason, there is no agreement between "representation" and fact or thing. For the current theory, the untrue proposition is the corresponding and precise counterpart to the true one.

For Heidegger the problem of untruth is more fundamental and far-reaching in that it is concerned with the whole of human Dasein and the things that are within the whole; it is more intimately bound up with the problem of truth itself in that the "within the whole" is revelatory and concealing at the same time; and it comprises two entirely different aspects: the not-yet-truth of concealment, the mystery that precedes and outlasts all uncovering and revealment; and the vast realm of human erring.

If truth has arisen only with the "exposition" of man when he began to take the things for, and treat the things as, what they are, a long period of Time must have preceded this historic era, in which there was not-yet-truth. Truth, as the Greek term ἀλήθεια suggests by way of its privative ἀ—, is an inroad made—an inroad of the most tremendous kind—into the realm of what is now named "being," but what was not known as "being," before the inroad was made. By this "inroad" of "uncovering" or "revealment" man has broken into a mystery which not only preceded this "un-covering," i.e. truth, but persists prior to it and side by side with it, notwithstanding all "un-covering." The "letting-be" brings not only into "overtness" the multitude of things in the whole as what they are, on account of which knowledge is acquired and accumulates and practical activities go on; but the "letting-be" also preserves the older state of the concealment of the things that are in the whole. Heidegger emphasises that the mystery does not concern this thing or that, but that there is only one mystery which pervades the whole of human Dasein and all the things that are, just as there is one "overtness" of truth in which the things that are stand out.

According to Heidegger, this is the legitimate

and authentic nature of "untruth," i.e. of the not-yet- and never-wholly-truth. It is mainly in this sense, but not only in this sense that Heidegger stated in "Being- and Time" that "Dasein was equally original in truth and in untruth." *

The adequate conceptual characterisation of this first kind of untruth: the concealment prior to truth and persisting side by side with truth is extremely difficult, because prior to truth there is no essence, nor a distinction between "universal" and "particular," between possibility and actuality, between cause and effect, reason and inference, ground and what is based on the ground. In his preceding investigations Heidegger could enquire into the "ground" of the "possibility" of a correct proposition. Some fundamental traits both of the essence of "freedom" and of the essence of "truth" he could positively characterise. But this is not possible with the mystery prior to, and pervading, truth. In that case the mystery would be falsely forced into the comprehending grasp of truth applying its concepts and distinctions. For the "dis-essence" of concealment is, as Heidegger puts it pregnantly and most precisely, the "pre-essential essence" (das vor-wesende Wesen). The second paragraph in Section 6 seems to me masterly in its conceptual forcefulness and profundity, formulating the uniqueness of the mystery in an only seemingly paradoxical way, while it could be formulated adequately in no other way at all.

If I understand the author rightly, the exposi-

* Cf. "Being and Time," p. 223.

tion reaches in the preceding and in the present Sections (5 and 6) the closest proximity to what he calls in the concluding note "the truth of Being," implying also its remaining mysterious concealment. The concept of "Being" itself, however, is expressly named at the end of Section 7 and in the last Section.

The great danger in the human pursuit of truth, arising from "freedom" as the "letting-be" of the things that are, is that, like the incalculable and incomprehensible "in the whole," the relationship of freedom to the "uncovering" or "revealment" as well as the fundamental concealment of Dasein and of the things that are in the whole are liable to fall into "oblivion." The oblivion of much that is fundamental to the problem of the nature of truth seems to have closely accompanied the history not only of human Dasein and its civilisation throughout the last three milleniums, not only the history of science and of learning itself, but even the history of philosophy soon after the truth of Being and of what is within the whole rose from concealment for the first time, though some other fundamental traits were faithfully adhered to in that great tradition. However, only if the whole complexity of the problem of truth, including the kinds of untruth which belong to it, is borne in mind, may it be hoped for that this state of oblivion is broken into once more; and this is what Heidegger endeavours to do in the essay.

This oblivion paves the way to the other great realm of un-truth, that of erring. It is true, man relates himself usually in his activity to some set of beings such as they are; but he is prone to restrict himself to what is practicable and what can be controlled and mastered. Thus he tends to take either himself or some aspects of the things that are, which he can calculate, as the measure of all things. He insists that the attitude which he takes is right; and the oblivion of Dasein amid the multitude of beings within the whole and of its mystery encourages him to do so. With this insistence he begins to move in the realm of erring, of which there are many modes.

In contrast to the "mystery" which precedes and which accompanies truth, the realm of erring is characterised as the "essential counter-essence" of the original essence of truth. Errors of judgment and of knowledge are, in this respect, only one and in fact the most superficial mode of erring. The characterisation of this second kind of un-truth is so clear and so impressive that it does not seem to require any comment.

"Mystery" and "erring" are thus the two great forms of "untruth," co-existent with truth as the exposition of man into the uncovering or revealment of the things that are in the whole; and both are hemming in Dasein and its being in truth and endanger it from either side. As Heidegger phrases it: "The mystery rules and the erring oppresses; and man, in the Ex-sistence of his Dasein, is subject to both of them." It is these three great entities of human Dasein: mystery, truth and erring that Heidegger wishes to bring home to the thoughtful reflection of his readers.

E. Section 8: *Conclusion.* In the first few sentences of the concluding Section, Heidegger's outlook and innermost creed finds its formulation. "In the thinking of Being the liberation of man for Ex-sistence, a liberation which is the ground of all history comes to word." This beginning of philosophy is termed a "world-moment" (Weltaugenblick), i.e. a moment decisive not only for human life, but also for the world, since truth, which is a matter concerning not only man, but all other things as well, thereby comes into being. It is this high evaluation of the "thinking of Being" that Heidegger submits to discussion in this essay.

What is meant by "the well-preserved system of the truth of the things that are in the whole" has been briefly referred to in the first section by the indications made about such a "system" in medieval philosophy and in that of earlier modern times.

Heidegger holds the view, voiced here as well as in the beginning of the essay "What is Metaphysics?" that genuine philosophy and the outlook of "common sense" are opposed to each other by their very nature. The nature of philosophy can be comprehended and defined only out of its relationship to the original truth of what is as such in the whole. "Common sense" clings to the facts, i.e. to what is palpably and unquestionably there, forbidding any more profound search and questioning.

Heidegger expressly contrasts his approach to

the problem of truth with that of Kant who, with "his metaphysical position grounded in subjectivity," brought about the last hitherto fundamental change in European metaphysics. The difference between Heidegger's own approach and that of Kant and his successors is indicated by the questioning of Kant's statement that "philosophy is to prove its integrity as the keeper of its own laws" and by his own implicit suggestion that philosophy itself "is kept to the laws and is induced to keep to the laws by the truth of that of which its laws are laws"; in other words: that philosophy is obedient to, and serving, the truth of Being. From the early statement (in Section 2) onwards that, on account of the "overtness" of human behaviour and activity, man lets himself be guided in his judgment and his propositions by the objects and the standards which they imply can this non-subjectivistic and fundamentally non-anthropocentric approach be traced.

What is most pertinent in the essay is perhaps best summarised in three main propositions:

(1) Truth is primarily not seated in a concept or a proposition and its relation to a fact or a thing. But truth is a phenomenon of a most comprehensive kind and of the greatest consequence for human Dasein and European civilisation, since the beginnings of Greek philosophy.

(2) Truth is inseparably bound up, and is actually one, with the philosophic thought of Being. Such thought of Being is not primarily a matter of the "intellect" nor restricted to it,

but it introduces and brings about an altogether new attitude of man towards his own life and all the things around him in the universe, owing to which he can know himself and the things in an "objective" way and can build up a historic world of civilisation, guided by a sense of his position "in the whole."

(3) Co-existent with truth in this comprehensive sense are the mystery which preceded it and persists and the manifold ways of erring, corresponding to the kinds of truth.

The essay is kept in the utmost possible "nearness to Being." It is moving in the direction towards it as its goal, as the end of the Sections 7 and 8 show as clearly as does the concluding note. But no premature statement is made about the truth of Being. When the reader comes to study the interpretation of Hölderlin's poem "Homecoming" and of the poet's speaking with the god whom he yet cannot name, he may well feel reminded of Heidegger's "nearness to Being," the question about which, deeply confusing and multifarious in its meaning as it is, he confesses, is not yet mastered.

Inasfar as the whole of Heidegger's work is concerned, the essay holds a unique position, at any rate for the time being. As has been pointed out above, "Being and Time" breaks off after the end of the second main Section, before the exposition of "Time and Being." In the "Letter on 'Humanism,'" 1947, the author points out that in this third Section of Part I of the main work, the whole of the thought had to be reversed and that this Section was held back, because the thought failed to find the adequate words for this "reversal" and did not succeed with the assistance of the language of (traditional) metaphysics. The essay "On the Essence of Truth," the author continues, was to give some insight into the thought of the reversal implied. Here, and apparently only here and not yet in the first two main Sections hitherto published, did the endeavour of thought arrive in the "region of the dimension," in which the whole of "Being and Time" was experienced and conceived. It arose from "the basic experience of the oblivion of Being."

3

THE ESSAYS ON FRIEDRICH HÖLDERLIN

Throughout the nineteenth century, Friedrich Hölderlin (1770/1843)* was known mainly as a solitary, somewhat remote poet of an idealistic and elegiac temperament, the author of odes and elegies, written in Greek metres which he was thought to have mastered to an unparalleled extent, of hymns in free rhythms, and of one completed novel, "Hyperion." Even the great fragmentary versions of a tragedy, "Empedocles on Etna," as well as his later poems, especially many of the hymns, were little known and their full value little appreciated. An essay on his whole work and outlook of great penetration

* His period of literary productivity was confined to the 1790's and the first few years of the new century.

167

by W. Dilthey, published in 1867, stood alone and exerted hardly any influence on public appreciation at the time.

The actual discovery of Hölderlin's outstanding rank as a spirit and as a poet, and his subsequent recognition by a wider public, may be said to belong to this century only and more particularly to the decade before the outbreak of the First World War. Dilthey's essay, in the collection "Das Erlebnis und die Dichtung" (1905), was republished, and now met with understanding and success; and, from 1913 onwards, the new, and since authoritative, edition of his collected works appeared, prefaced by most valuable essays by Norbert v. Hellingrath, a young scholar killed in the First World War, and a friend and follower of the eminent German poet Stefan George, to whose memory Heidegger's essay on "Hölderlin and the Essence of Poetry" is dedicated.

Stefan George, in a memorable, comparatively little known, short essay, praised Hölderlin as "the great seer" of the German nation and, with his later poems, which only then were beginning to attract public attention, as the "founder" and ancestor of a line of poets to come; as "the rejuvenator of language and thereby the rejuvenator of soul"; as the "corner-stone of the next German future" and, a point to be borne in mind for Heidegger's treatment, as one who called for the New God. Hölderlin, Dostoevsky, Kierkegaard and Nietzsche—apart from Nietzsche all of them only very recently discovered in their greatness at that time—were the four illustrious figures in literature and thought who stood out like new stars in the days immediately before the outbreak of the First World War.

To Heidegger Hölderlin's poems are "a temple without a shrine" or "a chiming bell hanging in the free air" which the slightest wrong touch from without will jangle; and he holds the view that, despite the many interpretations hitherto given, none of us today knows what these poems are and mean in truth. He is to him a poet, not of the past, but of the present and even more of the future. Hölderlin, above all the other great figures of the far removed or the more recent past, Homer and Sophocles, Virgil and Dante, Shakespeare, Goethe and Rilke, is the poet with whom Heidegger, as a philosopher, holds prolonged discourses of thought, living as they do—to use a favourite quotation by Heidegger from Hölderlin's great hymn "Patmos"—"near to one another on mountains farthest apart," the thinker whose task it is to proclaim "Being" and the poet who has the mission to name what is "holy." It may be said that what Kierkegaard was to both Jaspers and Heidegger on the way of ascent to their philosophic outlook, stimulating and reassuring them in their ideas and claim, Hölderlin is for Heidegger now that he has arrived in his own realm of thought.

A genuine appreciation of a great poet, and an interpretation of his works by a true thinker is a rare phenomenon, even though the relationship between literature and philosophy has been very much closer in Germany since the days of Kant and Schiller than in many other countries. Our first question, therefore, is: what is it in Hölderlin that attracts Heidegger so strongly? In order to answer it, three points may be emphasised.

(1) In Heidegger's view, Hölderlin differs from all earlier great poets by being "the poet of the poet," i.e. the poet who, meditating throughout his work upon the very nature of poetry, was destined to put it into words. This deep thoughtfulness and reflectiveness on the part of Hölderlin creates a bridge between him and the philosopher. Heidegger thus advances his own interpretation of the nature of poetry by commenting upon some well-selected utterances of Hölderlin in poetry and prose, taking them as words of guidance, even though, in doing so, he is giving an exposition of his own views.

(2) Hölderlin felt himself, as a poet, to be in an entirely solitary position, a messenger between "the gods" and the people; and in his poetry the poet is envisaged as being, by his nature, the one who has the mission to communicate to men what he has learnt of "the gods" in his meditative intercourse with them. Thus Hölderlin's figure and poetry has kindled in Heidegger a new interpretation of the nature of poetry and literature in the great sense. Hitherto it has been thought that the message which poets, like other genuine artists, convey is one of "beauty," even though this conception has been growing increasingly vague of late. Heidegger's

view is different. He is of the conviction that the poet's mission is to "name" what he has found to be "holy," whatever the relation between "what is holy" and "beauty" may be.

A final test of the truth of this new conception of the nature of poetry, stimulated by Hölderlin and suggested by Heidegger, cannot be sought for in these essays. It would require a re-examination of the greatest works of literature in this light, of Homer, Virgil and Dante, of the tragedies of Aeschylus, Sophocles and Shakespeare, of Goethe's works, centering in some of his poems as well as "Iphigenie," "Faust" and "Wilhelm Meister." For this new formula that the poet names what is "holy" is an "idea" in the strict sense of Kant's Transcendental Doctrine of Methods;* and as such it requires investigation of the appropriate material, inspiring and guiding the scholarly work of interpretation, to manifest its fruitfulness or to show its restrictions. In the abstract, or with the application to Hölderlin's poems alone, it cannot be properly discussed, accepted, rejected or judged in its possibly far-reaching significance. Even if some, perhaps essential, qualities of great poetry and literature remain unelucidated by the application of this principle, it seems a relevant and stimulating approach to the work of a poet and writer to ask: what actually did he find to be "holy," worthy of communication to his fellow-men. For whether or not such a genuine message is contained in the work of an author, and is its main-

* "Critique of Pure Reason," B.862.

spring, may well decide his rank and his claim to the serious consideration of a cultured public.

The approach to poetry and literature has been changing for some time, together with the social changes, and those in the intellectual and spiritual life, that conditioned it. Thus the question: what is it that makes poetry and literature profoundly relevant to man, and when and why is it relevant, has been asked by more than one thinker and literary historian in Germany since the days of Nietzsche. Heidegger's answer, onesided as it may appear at first and as it may remain, points in a direction of very great import for poetry and literature of the highest rank. And his interpretation of the mission of the poet, in an age in which the spiritual foundations are deeply questioned, seems supported, within the German orbit, not by the poetry and literary work of Hölderlin alone, but by that of the two most outstanding German poets of recent days, Stefan George and Rainer Maria Rilke. Though George wrote many of his most beautiful poems earlier in his life, he remained dissatisfied until, in "Der Teppich des Lebens" (The Tapestry of Life), he was able to discover the great spiritual mission of poetry, introducing it by a sustained kind of dialogue, in a number of poems, between angel and poet; and he rose to the height of his outlook only after having passed through an experience of a divine and absolutely binding character, of what he found to be "holy," and which forms the centre of his later works. Rilke produced the volumes containing his greatest poetry in the span between "Das Stundenbuch" (The Book of Hours), the work of actual initiation, where he aimed with single-mindedness at one thing only: the "naming" of God out of his own experience and thought, and the late "Elegies" and "Sonnets." In the Elegies he endeavoured to envisage the essentials of human life, with its frailty, before the forum of powers greater than man, the "angels"; in the Sonnets he presents as the model figure of a poet to be emulated Orpheus who, with his song, was believed to range widely through the realm of the living and as far as that of the dead, though there with tragically less vivifying power.

(3) Besides Hölderlin's reflectiveness, which made him the poet who gave expression in his work to what the nature of poetry itself is, and besides his striving more intently and zealously than many other modern poets to name what he found was "holy," there is yet a third important aspect, whereby Hölderlin stands out and with regard to which Heidegger must feel a profound affinity with him.

Although Hölderlin was primarily interested in Greek humanity and civilisation and thus prominently in the Greek myths—only towards the end of his literary production did he write a very few great hymns about Christ—he lived with the consciousness that "the gods" in whom men could, and should, believe and whose nature and ruling power the poet is to "name" and to praise, were no longer, as in earlier times, actu-

173

ally present in his own age, i.e. that man even with his most exalted thought could hardly penetrate to their Being, even though, with the same grandeur as at all time, they were somehow there. It is from this angle that the singular rank and significance of Hölderlin's poetry can best be seen. His work marks a turning-point in history. In Heidegger's view, a new era was ushered in: the era when "the old gods" had gone and "the new god" had not yet come and been revealed. It is the era to which our own age belongs: the era for which Nietzsche, speaking of the Christian creed which in his own age and country found fewer and fewer true believers among the cultured and the intelligentsia, recoined the unforgettable word of "God's death" * —the symbol for the new spiritual situation, against the background of which he strove hard, but almost in vain, to develop constructive philosophic ideas—and for which Heidegger, adopting a word from a poem of Hölderlin, uses the more cautious phrase of "God's fail," i.e. God's withholding His presence and His being as known by man hitherto, despite the fact that, somehow, He is there.

There is one especially penetrating passage in Heidegger's essay on the elegy "Homecoming," stimulated by the words: ". . . es fehlen heilige Namen"—holy names are lacking. It refers to a

* This expression, used in a different sense as characterising a special state of mind manifest in the Roman world before the appearance of Christ, can also be found in Hegel's "Phenomenology of the Mind." Nietzsche was apparently unaware of its former use.

very serious limitation, for which even the word "tragic" would appear inappropriate and too light, both in the era and in Hölderlin as a poet. Though Hölderlin confesses that he has often conversed with "the God," he is unable to "name" Him and, by "naming" Him, to make Him appear in his Being and Glory before the thought of men. As Heidegger phrases it: Hölderlin's poem, it is true, makes "what is holy appear"; but "the God remains afar." It is the era in which God "remains afar"—both Hölderlin's and our own age. This creates between him and us a contemporaneous situation. There are, in Heidegger's view, two false ways arising from this tremendous, deeply disquieting situation: people may try to invent a "god" in some cunning way to overcome the emptiness so hard to bear—it is as if here Heidegger was turning against a creed, such as that of Nazism; or they may be content to acclaim God in the traditional way, unconcerned whether they truly believe in Him, shunning a scrutiny of their own soul, mind and professed faith. What is avoided in both these ways is the actual Presence of this "God's self-withholding," which must be endured until the present era of trial is over. The mere appearance of "godlessness" should not be feared. Hölderlin thought "the one thing needful," on which to concentrate all his Care, was: to hold out and persevere in the utmost proximity of "God's self-withholding," until out of such proximity the word that could reverently and convincingly "name" the High one was granted.

175

With this attitude, Hölderlin would seem to Heidegger to be a model to be emulated. For Heidegger, too, who, in his youth, could not convince himself of the existence of God according to St. Thomas' proofs, lives with the ever-present consciousness of what he, following Hölderlin, calls "God's self-withholding."

Thus Hölderlin is to Heidegger, as he was to Stefan George, "one who calls for the new God," but "calling" only, without succeeding in making Him appear, as no one has succeeded hitherto.

There is, however, one word more to be said about the discourse that has been going on between Heidegger and Hölderlin "on mountains farthest apart." Despite the difference in their vocations, a similarity in Hölderlin's and in Heidegger's own position should not be overlooked. In a similar way as Hölderlin strove to "name" what is "holy," endeavouring to penetrate into it to the presence of God Himself, did Heidegger strive to describe the fundamental unchanging features of human Dasein and its temporality, to arouse once more, in a new way, the quest for "Being." As we know from the essay "On the Essence of Truth," it is Heidegger's conviction that out of the "Da-sein," into which man can enter, a "proximity to the truth of Being is preparing itself"—a "proximity," different from and yet akin to the other "proximity" of Hölderlin, the nearness to "God remaining afar." The spirit in which the problem of the nature of Truth is approached in that essay and in which the problem "What is Metaphysics?" is treated can, perhaps, gain some elucidation when this similarity in position and endeavour and the resulting affinity is observed.

The unity of the three aspects here considered in advance will, I hope, help to explain the singular attraction exerted by Hölderlin and his poetry on Heidegger's thought.

In a prefatory note, Heidegger explicitly states that his "commentaries"—Erläuterungen—on Hölderlin's poems do not claim to be contributions either to the history of literature or to æsthetics. They have arisen, he explains, from a "necessity of thought."

The reader will do well to bear this qualification in mind. The essays are of a genre of their own, being rooted in the "dialogue" between a thinker of distinct originality and a great, singularly solitary poet. Very often Hölderlin's visionary statements and Heidegger's thought can be felt to have merged into one. But, of course, almost inevitably does the ethereal atmosphere of the elegy "Homecoming" suffer once the thought tries to grasp and fix its myth, though the exposition compensates richly for this only momentary loss, by drawing attention to the depth of thought, the grandeur of approach and many a detail which otherwise easily escapes the notice of the reader. Above all, the seriousness with which every word of the poem is cared for is praiseworthy and promising for the future of the interpretation of Hölderlin, as well as for the appreciation of poetry and literature in general. For the profound reverential respect which Heidegger shows in his treatment arises from his insight that true poetry is one of the greatest treasures of mankind, the vessel of something "holy"; and this spirit, deeply felt to be the appropriate one, seeks to spread beyond the single application, published here. Conversely, one cannot help feeling, especially in the essay on the "Essence of Poetry," at some points as if Hölderlin's words and atmosphere were leading Heidegger farther than he might have gone without them. But the moment one tries to imagine a strictly systematic exposition of the nature of poetry, one realises how much is here gained by the constant translucent presence of the great poet with his sanctioning authority.

It would be idle and, more than that, senseless to try and analyse what is Hölderlin's and what Heidegger's in this dual unity. Yet, in a repeated reading one feels sometimes the one, sometimes the other stepping forth. With regard to the essay on the "Essence of Poetry," e.g. one may at first read it as an exposition of the meaning of five key-passages from Hölderlin; and if this aspect should be ignored completely at a later stage, something that is essential to the essay is being lost. At the same time, the essay contains many ideas and concepts fundamental to Heidegger's philosophy. To name but a few, the "overtness" in which man stands amidst other beings—a trait well known from the essay "On the Essence of Truth"; the essence of language as conversation—a fundamental existentialistic of human Dasein; man living in the "world" and being "historical"; the significance of Time, against the changes of which something constant and abiding, "the gods" and "Being" are discovered. In short, the reader cannot fail to feel the prominence of Heidegger's outlook in the essay, at some stage of his study of it. And yet again, the exposition is so entirely guided by the selection of the key-passages—whatever is pointed out bears an obvious special reference to them, other passages chosen might have provoked utterances that would have thrown light on yet different aspects of poetry not touched upon—that once more the pendulum swings back to the point of balance.

The situation in the essay on the elegy "Homecoming" is somewhat, but not altogether, different. It is an interpretation; and, as Heidegger points out in the introductory remark on the occasion of the repetition of the "Address," originally delivered in celebration of the centenary of the poet's death, the last, but most difficult step of the interpreter is to disappear again with his comment after having done his service, so that the poem may stand out and be read and enjoyed in itself. Thus here Hölderlin stands in the forefront. Yet, when we are studying the exposition more closely, the individuality and the outlook of the thinker make themselves, inevitably, felt, page by page. The Care—the Being of every human Dasein, and so also of that of the poet, is contemplated, the joy of the poet,

179

his innermost essence and basic "mood," through which he rises to greet the "holy," and the sadness, arising both from the incapability of "naming" the God and from his solitariness among his countrymen. The outlook of a mythical kind, on Earth and Light and on the God on High, one feels is shared by the thinker. The concern for the right kind of love of one's homeland, difficult to attain, with its hidden and "reserved" treasures of tradition and the actual attachment to Swabia are, no doubt, felt as intensely by Heidegger as they were by the poet. Hölderlin's position, facing the crucial situation of "God's self-withholding"—this we have already seen—is very similar to Heidegger's own position. Thus the interpretation of the poem, undoubtedly in the first instance only serving the poet, cannot fail to be regarded as a contribution formulating, up to a point, the author's own thought. The dual unity of poet and thinker, strongly established, cannot be dissolved.

One reservation should, in fairness, be made. It concerns the essay on "Hölderlin and the Essence of Poetry." The essay contains a number of very far-reaching, and, some readers may think, over-bold, propositions. E.g. that the nature of language must be understood from the nature of poetry; and, that poetry is the original language of a historic people. This is a view, held in the eighteenth century by the German thinker Hamann who, through his disciple Herder and the latter's influence on Goethe in his youth, greatly contributed to the revival of German lyrical poetry in modern times; but it is largely, if not wholly, discredited among scholars nowadays. Here, obviously it is advanced, in the first instance, in support of a most comprehensive statement of Hölderlin, concerning the very great significance of poetry for human life as a whole. But beyond the chain of philosophic argument implied in the exposition, it is, unfortunately, in no way substantiated. It would seem to require not only a representation of the theory and of the arguments in its favour, but also a detailed analysis of a considerable number of words, likely to belong to the very early stages of language, to make the view acceptable; and it must be hoped that either Heidegger himself or a member of his school will offer such an analysis in future. For the time being, the judgment on these propositions and on similar ones is best kept in abeyance.

Hölderlin and the Essence of Poetry

The essay seems to me to possess a beauty of its own, owing to the careful selection of the five key-passages and its resulting almost dramatic composition. It starts briefly and unassumingly with the statement that poetry is "the most innocent of all human activities" and it leads up to the thought-provoking and comprehensive reflection that, whereas all the other activities of man are "greatly meritorious," the actual dwelling of man on earth, his Dasein, is "poetic." But I will not follow Heidegger's

181

exposition strictly, as has been done in the afore-going discussion of the problem of truth—every reader will soon realise that the sequence of thought is of considerable relevance in each of the essays—and I will concentrate on the two main problems: what is the nature of language, which offers the material to poetry? and what is the nature of poetry itself?

(About the nature of language.) As has been pointed out in the general part of this Introduction, Heidegger considers "speech," i.e. the use of language, to be one of the few fundamental characteristics which constitute human Dasein as Dasein. The reader well versed in German may wish to study this brief, but important section in "Being and Time" (German edition, § 34, pp. 160/166).

One very interesting, and indeed provocative, statement which requires comment is made in connection with the problem: why is language a "good" for man. Heidegger does not accept the common definition that language is a means of communication as one indicating its essence. In his view, only a consequence of the essence of language is mentioned thereby. More funda-mental than this is that language, as such, enables man to stand in the "overtness" of all that is. The nature of "overtness," in which man meets and treats things as what they are within the immensely wide horizon of the whole, and its great import for Dasein, civilisation and truth, have been discussed above. Without the use of

words for things that are, such "overtness,"
Heidegger realises, could not have arisen. And
though it is true that language serves the purpose
of communication and of information, its actual
function seems to be to name anything that is,
non-human or human, and its characteristics.
Because language brings about "overtness," man
can be in the "world." Therefore the statement:
"Only where is language, there is world."
"World" in this sense is the "world" of human
Dasein, as analysed in "Being and Time"; and
this means, as Heidegger puts it here: "the ever
changing realm of decision and work, of deed and
responsibility, but also of arbitrariness and noise,
decay and confusion," that is, of all the authentic
and the inauthentic ways of Existence. Therefore Heidegger infers: "Only where is world,
there is history." Thus language is the essential
pre-requisite of man being in the world and
living in the historical atmosphere of tradition.
Compared with this fundamental fact, whereby
language is "that event which has the highest
potentialities of humanity at its disposal," information by way of language seems to Heidegger
but an incidental and consequential trait, much
as he emphasises at all times, and so also in this
essay, that the actual life of the language consists
in conversation and that the sum-total of words
and the rules of grammar as such are but the
"foreground" of language. The relation to the
things around him, which language enables man
to have and constantly to intensify, and the

183

tremendous transformation brought about in man's Being in this way, is Heidegger's primary concern at this point.

The other aspect mainly discussed is the actuality of language in conversation, or, more precisely, as conversation, just mentioned. Conversation implies both speech and listening, and it means: one person speaking with another about something, which helps to bring the participants in the conversation in closer touch one with the other.

In Heidegger's view, language is essential only as conversation. And the sense in which this view is entertained here becomes clear when Heidegger, following the wording of the key-passage from a poem of Hölderlin, considers not only the manifold conversations of a single individual during his life-time as one long conversation in which he is engaged, but all the linguistic utterances of men in the many languages that are as but *one* conversation going on through the last few millenniums.

Heidegger's question, then, following again the key-passage of the section, is: since when is man engaged in this conversation? and how did it come to begin? Whenever a man discusses a matter with another one, both consider one and the same thing about which they come to agree or to disagree. This relatedness to one and the same thing is therefore essential to any kind of conversation. And it is here that Heidegger introduces the fundamental notions of "Time" and later, of "Being," the key-concepts of his own philosophy; and this passage is for the study of Heidegger's outlook the more noteworthy, since the third huge Section about "Being" in his main work has not yet been published.

Something "that remains and is constant" must have been experienced by man, before conversation was possible and could come into its own. And this, Heidegger suggests, took place in that very moment that "Time" opened itself up for man in its "dimensions" of present, past and future. Up to that moment the life of the race, like that of other species, went on in a flux where no consciousness could fix on anything. Only when the present was experienced as present and the present of something remaining and constant was realised, against the background of which all the changes that went on could be visualised, could words, and thus the one conversation, originate. This point: the experience of Time in present, past, and future, as the indispensable condition for the experiencing and wording of things is a suggestion which Heidegger herewith submits to discussion.

In this one great unended "conversation," the gods experienced as present and the things in the world have been named. Again in following the key-passage under consideration, but undoubtedly voicing his own view as well, Heidegger separates the naming of "the gods" from the wording of the things that are. But—and this is worth emphasising and remembering because Heidegger's view on "Being" greatly resembles in this respect that on the gods—"the

185

gods" are named only when they actually speak to men, manifesting themselves in their Being and power. Heidegger is far removed from the view, entertained by many in modern times, that "the gods" are only an imagining of human thought. He takes them to be "real," i.e. of their own kind of Being, and the difference between them and the things in the world is only: that, because of human shortcomings, they are visualised only by some and not by all. But if it is the experience of something remaining and constant that brings about language and speech, it is "the gods" very much more than the things of common life that have initiated language in man's Dasein.

Hereby Heidegger has prepared the ground for his discussion of the nature of poetry.

(About the nature of poetry.) Here the essential position of the poet between the gods and the people, bound in his work to both of them, and the era of "barrenness" with its twofold lack: the no more of the gods of the past and the not yet of the god of the future, historically ushered in by Hölderlin's poetry, are discussed. But before doing this, Heidegger points out the great mission which, in his view, poetry from the beginning has had. It is the establishing, through the word and in the word, of what is lasting and significant for man's Dasein. Heidegger ascribes to the poet, and not to the philosopher or to the founders of religion, the deed of having made man aware of the simple, of the measure by which things are to be judged, and of "Being,"

186

the ground of the appearance of the things, itself. It is, according to him, the poet that names the gods and the things which they signify, thereby making man realise for the first time in his history how he is placed in the world, related to the things around and before the gods, and thus establishing firmly, through the medium of well-chosen words, the ground, scale and standards for human Dasein.

In the "Postscript" to the essay "What is Metaphysics?" a fundamental distinction is drawn between science directed in its calculations by the "will to will" and philosophy, a free response to the "Voice of Being." A similar distinction can be found in this essay, concerning the whole of human Dasein, but this time with its emphasis on what is "poetic." Most of what man works and produces may be considered as rightly acquired and he "deserves" to own it. But, beyond this, he dwells in his life on earth "in the Presence of the gods and encountering the essential nearness of the things"; and this "poetic" endowment is not a "merit" of man of which he may be proud, but a "gift" of higher powers owed in the first instance to the devoted response of the poets.

Thus Heidegger attaches a very much greater importance to poetry than is done commonly. Poetry is, in his view, not an accompanying adornment of Dasein nor one of the various phenomena of culture nor the mere expression of the "soul" of a civilisation, as Spengler once suggested. His interpretation is that poetry is

187

the "ground of history," guiding and inspiring men by its words and visions.

In this essay Heidegger has opened up a new vista. Hardly could more be hoped for from one Lecture concerned with both Hölderlin and the nature of poetry. Yet, the statements made are so new and so challenging that one wishes in more than one place the exposition would have gone into further detail. How poetry is related to magic, myths and religion, to early institutions, law and political life, above all to philosophy is left untouched. And that the nature of language, about which relevant points are made in the essay, should be "understood," and this may mean explained, from the nature of poetry, this is in itself such an unusual proposition that a much more explicit elucidation of it would seem urgently desirable.

However this may be, the essay as such, the first written by Heidegger on Hölderlin and on the problem of poetry, is most interesting and enriching inasfar as the outlook of the thinker itself is concerned. Beside the philosopher stands the poet, reminding man, who, with his practical day-to-day endeavours, is so much the servant of Time which drives on relentlessly, of what is truly great and significant, awakening in him, temporarily at least, a sense of tranquillity and a concentration of what is abiding. It characterises, often decisively, the philosophy of an original thinker; which kind of spiritual or intellectual activity he considers to be most akin to his own. In the middle ages, this position was held by religion and theology, in the earlier modern times mainly by mathematics and physics. For Schelling it was poetry and the arts and, later in his life, mythology and religion. For Hegel it was religion and the arts. And for Schopenhauer, the arts and saintliness. In the second half of the nineteenth century it was practically universally science and scholarly studies. Though Heidegger, as can be seen from the essay "What is Metaphysics?" feels himself intimately bound up with science and scholarship, he regards the poet, and the poet alone, as his actual peer. This evaluation arises from his theme, the transcendent nature of "Being." Science and scholarly studies do not rise to that height. Religion, which does, seems to Heidegger too doubtful in its nature and, recognised by its representatives or not, nowadays to be involved in a crisis. Of the arts only poetry and literature speak through words; and here he finds among its greatest representatives a call and a striving, similar to that in true philosophy. One is inevitably reminded of Greece, where Homer and Hesiod and the early lyrical poets preceded the great pre-Socratics and the tragedies of Aeschylus and Sophocles, the philosophy of Socrates, Plato and Aristotle. A relationship of an exalted kind, as this in Greece, is being envisaged when Heidegger ascribes to the poet the task of naming, and thereby bringing into the realm of the known, what had been going on before in the undistinguished flux of Time of the pre-historical ages. The philosopher asks his question about "Being" only if and when gods and things have been brought, as such, into sight and "conversation" by the poet.

Remembrance of the Poet. An Interpretation of Hölderlin's Elegy "Homecoming"

What a poet achieves cannot be stated in the abstract. It can be found in the poems alone; and it can be pointed out only by faithfully commenting upon them word by word and vision by vision. It is therefore most fortunate that, side by side with the Lecture of 1936, containing Heidegger's statement about the nature of poetry on principle, the commentary on one great poem of Hölderlin, written in 1943, is published in this collection. What is meant by the "holy" with which the poet is concerned, what by a poet "naming" that which thereby, and thereby only, is brought into the realm of the known, and what is meant by the poet concentrating upon the "simple," upon what is opened up by "Being" itself and upon standards for human Dasein, all this can be tested by the study of this interpretation. Kant's famous saying: "concepts without intuition are empty; intuition without concepts is blind," holds good. The reader is therefore requested to consider both essays together, bearing in mind what is suggested in the one, while reading the other. What is said, e.g. about the "naming" of the gods, or of "Angels," in the essay now under review, can be fully appreciated only if and when the poet's response to powers greater than man, emphasised in the earlier essay, is understood in its rare, serious and thought-provoking significance.

One example, referred to in the middle of Heidegger's interpretation, may be singled out at the start, to show in what sense the poet confronts us with the true reality of things. Hölderlin describes his crossing over the Lake Constance on his journey from the Alps, which to him are "the divinely built castle of the heavenly ones," to his homeland by saying: "Far on the Lake's expanse there was a joyful undulation Beneath the sails." Heidegger comments: if we consider the Lake Constance geographically or in connection with traffic, we mean thereby the lake situated between the Alps and the upper Danube, through which the Rhine flows. The presupposition here, Heidegger suggests, is: there is Nature in itself, the globe with the Alps, the upper reaches of the Danube, the Rhine and the Lake; there is then what we generally experience as the "landscape" of Lake Constance; and there are, thirdly, separated from both, the special experiences of the poet whereby the landscape assumes a "mythical" colouring. This is a common sense and rational framework, bound up with our predominantly practical approach to life, by which we actually degrade and ruin for ourselves what the poet is to communicate to us. We should realise that this framework, to which we are deeply accustomed by our habits and practical needs, conceals from us the actual

191

reality, the things as they are. When the poet speaks of "the lake's expanse" and of "a joyful undulation beneath the sails," he is wording what is actual; and when we then think of the Lake Constance in the geographical sense, we step outside the realm of poetry, making it a mere "adornment" (as Heidegger calls it in the essay on the "Essence of Poetry") of everyday life and keeping the poet's insight away from us, instead of realising that here, for once, we come face to face with the things as they are.

I have chosen this simple example from the essay at the start, because what interferes here with our readiness of reception—the strongly fixed habits of thought of our ordinary everyday life—is likely to interfere the more with the grand and rare vision advanced in the poem itself. As long as we do not consider the notions produced in daily life, to which we tend to cling, to be the result of our life in the "cave," in Plato's sense, fettered as we are by our practical concerns, so long we are not free really to hear and to assimilate what the poet wishes to convey.

But it is also, partly, the consequences of scientific and rational thought developed during the last centuries and spread, levelled, in public opinion that makes us think that we know much about Matter, Organisms and Men, so that we have grown increasingly chary in thought of powers higher than man. Here, too, we have to try and put our acquired prejudices and presuppositions aside. For otherwise the poet's vision will be to us not more than a fable.

The general atmosphere of the things, visualised in the poem, Heidegger emphasises early in his interpretation, is "joyous," a word, significantly, already used in the second line, and frequently afterwards, and "serene." This joyful serenity is not thought to emanate primarily from the "mood" of the poet, but to be a feature of the things in themselves. Such a serene atmosphere, manifest in the people as well as in mountains and trees, "greets" the poet who is coming home. Intensely felt by the poet and all-pervading as it is, though unobtrusive, it seems to come from powers greater than man; and thus Hölderlin "names" the "Angels" of the house and the "Angels" of the year. The Earth with its spaciousness, granting homes to men and the field of history to the peoples, and the Light with its change of seasons and the time allotted to men for their sojourn are greeted by the poet as the serenifying "Angels."

This term—"Angels"—should be taken literally. It is a right and a mission of the poet to remind men of powers greater than they. And this is needed at all times, but more than usually in days when the scientific and rational thought, legitimate in its own sphere, tends to bar man from the things above him. The thought of what "Angels" are or may be has grown exceedingly vague. The Greeks knew intensely that "war" or "love" was a power far greater than man, which could take hold of him at any time; and so was "prudence" and the healing power of sight and vision; thus he "named" Ares and Aphrodite, Athene and Apollo. And if the Greeks thought these were "gods," they recognised a power, even greater than the gods, to which all of them submit: μοῖρα, destiny. The order is, fundamentally, similar to that of the "Angels" under "God." It is as if man, whenever his soul and spirit is open for the things greater and higher than man, visualises first and nearest to him powers (he may call them "gods," "angels" or a man truly God) great and mighty enough to affect deeply his own whole "Being" and beyond them, unfathomably and incomprehensibly, an even greater power under which they rule or of which they are messengers.

By "naming" Earth and Light as "Angels," as Heidegger, I think, rightly, infers from other poems such as "Der Wanderer" (The Wanderer). Hölderlin gives a new concrete significance to this notion, provided we ourselves are open to their serenifying power and visualise what they are spending moment for moment.

But before "naming" the "Angels of the year" and the "Angels of the house," Hölderlin speaks (line 21 ff.) of God Himself, who dwells high in Heaven, higher than even the Light. Heidegger suggests—and there is good reason for such a suggestion in the poem—that the God's dwelling-place is the realm of the most joyful, "the Serene" itself, as Heidegger puts it: clarity, majesty and joyfulness in one. From it the serenification, with healing power even for the sad ones, proceeds; and while the nature of God Himself remains unknown in this era of "barrenness," of "God's self-withholding," his dwelling-place is thought to be the "Ether."

In two places of the poem it is stated that Hölderlin has been much in discourse with God, "the great Father," speaking to Him and learning from Him; and the confession, highly relevant to the nature of poetry, is made: "whatever poets meditate upon or sing is mostly concerned with the Angels and with Him."

One more point is to be emphasised. The general atmosphere of "joyfulness" is felt and the "holy," God and the Angels, is evoked in the state of "Homecoming" of the poet. Homecoming, Heidegger interprets, is "the return to the proximity of origin." "Origin," as I understand it, includes many things: one's own origin and childhood, the land of one's fathers and its customs and traditions, the great and lasting experiences that one has had as well as the true greatness, with Angels and God being present or near, with which every stretch of country which is one's homeland cannot fail to be imbued. It is this nearness to one's "origin" in every sense that, inevitably and rightly, provokes loyalty and devotion. And thus the sense of "joyfulness" is aroused and intensified if, after a prolonged absence, the wanderer returns home. He feels and realises the more strongly and clearly what "treasure" is held by the landscape and forests, rivers and meadows, towns and villages, weather and sunshine, ways of life and customs of his home district. A "treasure" which has been there and, possibly, in the form of venerable places and institutions, has accumulated through generations, especially "under the arc of sacred peace," and which points with a similarly lasting force to the nearer and farther future. Such "treasure" cannot be worded by the poet. It is there, "reserved" for the young and the old, offering them strength and succour, if and when and to the extent that they are aware of it. The true poet, such as Hölderlin, is aware of it with an intensity and a depth of realisation not shared by anyone else—one of the reasons why he is, essentially, solitary—and such awareness is the more acute when he has been away for a while and returns seeing all that is cherished in his homeland afresh. It is now, in this home-coming mood, that Hölderlin conjures up in his poem the mountain range of the Alps, the "divinely built castle of the heavenly ones," which he has just left, and the God on High with whom, being alone, he held many a discourse, to be greeted by the unobtrusive "joyfulness" of city, river and hills, oak, birch and beech, gardens and birds, and of the passing country-men.

What is it, Heidegger asks, that makes a poet a poet? What is it that allows and that compels him to meditate upon Angels and God and to be more deeply aware than all the others of the "treasure" held by the homeland? What is it that

196

singles him out among other mortals? It is his own pure and unmitigated "joyfulness." Here, I think, a profound observation is made by Heidegger, deserving attention and reflection on the part of his readers.

The Angels—Earth and Light—and God, "the great Father" in the Ether, are there, no matter whether men recognise them or not. But they by themselves, even though they spend joy, fruitfulness and blessing day by day, are not capable of reaching men and communicating their Being and working for them unaided. It is the poet who, owing to his inner "joyfulness," is "open" for them, encounters them and, while singing of them, rises into the utmost proximity to them; as Heidegger suggests: "coming home" in a primary sense. "Joy" is not a by-product of the endowment of the poet or of his writing a poem. It is his very essence. And in writing a poem, this "joy" which essentially belongs to him rises into actuality.

It seems a noteworthy contention that the writing of a poem does not merely cause joy to the poet, but that it *is* itself "Joy," the serenification brought about through the mystery of being in proximity to the "Origin." This is not to say, I repeat, that the "joy" of the poet is the source of his vision. The powers greater than man are there, and their "serenification" of the cosmos is at work, whether a poet rises to praise and "name" them or not. But the open-mindedness of the poet for them and the winging power of "joy," enabling him to such rare open-mindedness, is required if he is to "name" what is "holy."

Heidegger, in "Being and Time," has pointed out that "Care" is the "Being" of man, whatever his station and his vocation. Care is the poet's concern, too, when choosing the appropriate words. A word chosen too high or too low, a word too much or too little, a word "unfitting" in any way; and he is offending against his vocation. But Care as such would never induce the poet to sing a hymn or an elegy. Something more powerful and more positive makes him evoke the "holy." And this is hinted at by Heidegger's reference to the "joy" of the poet.

The serenification of the poet in his proximity to the "origin" and the care with which to "name the holy" in the right way is the contrapuntal equipment of the true poet. But, in an "elegy," the "holy" is named in sadness, despite the joy and serenification of the poet. An elegy is, by its nature, a song of "sadness." What, we ask, arouses the "sadness"?

There are some elegies of Hölderlin, in which poignantly the cause of sadness steps forth: in "Menon's Laments about Diotima" the separation from his love, that love through which, as he had confessed in an earlier poem, he and Diotima, "only known by the gods, had created their more secret world"; in "The Archipelagus" the fall of Athens and Greece with all their glory; in "The Celebration of Autumn" the autumnal farewell and the nearness of Night and of Death; and in "Bread and Wine," from which Heidegger quotes one great stanza at the end of his essay on "Hölderlin and the Essence of Poetry," the remoteness of the gods in our era. In fact, in none of the other great elegies of Hölderlin is the cause of sadness so little conspicuous as in "Homecoming."

Yet, sadness pervades, almost imperceptibly, this poem naming the "holy." Even when it speaks of the "Joyous," this is calmed and restrained to serenity. A quietude, often noticeable in Hölderlin's poems, spreads through the whole of "Homecoming." An equanimity, as it were, longing for a greater proximity to God than can be attained, and accepted with an undertone of resignation, can be felt, particularly towards the end. It is the solitariness of the poet between the Heavenly ones and the people that provokes this deep-founded sadness, tuning the poem and determining its character. The care for praising and honouring God "of whom he has been silent so long," the concern whether his song does not remain far behind what he ought to reveal, the remote kinship with his countrymen whom he yet deeply loves, even the imploring invocation of the Angels—all of them contain a note of subdued sadness, which does not speak direct, but has entered into his "joyous" naming and thought of the "holy."

Heidegger's interpretation seems to me distinguished by the way in which from the start, from the first paragraph on, he takes this "elegiac" tone of the poem into account, while

discussing it expressly only towards the end,
tentatively, with great shyness and respect.
Rightly does he refer to that beautiful epigram
about Sophocles, who in and through his tragedies gives vent to what is most Joyous, while
he, Hölderlin, in his essentially hymnic poetry
embodies, unintentionally, but without disguise,
genuine sorrow, the sorrow of lonely worship.

If we look back on Heidegger's essays about
Hölderlin, what stands out foremost is the exalted position and mission of the poet. It may
seem to many readers unduly heightened and
intensified owing to the fact that Heidegger takes
no account of the debt which, it may be supposed, a poet such as Hölderlin owed to Greek
mythical thinking; or of the religious tradition
in which "Angels" or "God" are thought of,
however vaguely; or of the spiritual and intellectual life of Germany, particularly great and
stimulating in that period, of which Hölderlin
with his work, despite his isolated position, was
a part. This is alien to Heidegger's thought.
However much his outlook differs from that of
Schopenhauer, who most definitely had no influence on him, there is this similarity that the
poet, in Heidegger's case the poet alone, is
thought to stand on his own and to penetrate
to what is actually relevant, beyond the range of
other men except the philosopher, to what
Heidegger calls "the holy." It is an interpretation of the nature of poetry which, inasfar as I

can see, has hardly any forerunner; and challenging and, undoubtedly, one-sided as it is, it cannot fail to arouse dispute and criticism; but, being of a profoundly stimulating nature, it may, it is hoped, also induce scholars and other readers to contemplate the great poetry and literature of Hölderlin and of the ages in this light, testing to what extent Heidegger's suggestions contain substantial truth.

Apart from this main aspect, it seems to me most noteworthy that, in Heidegger's view, the "holy" which, he insists, calls the poet to his office and work is of the same "reality" as men and things, and thus of a far greater kind of "reality" than these are. Thus the outlook on the nature of the poet has undergone a fundamental change. He is no more considered to be "creative," in the sense that he is thought to produce a world of his own imaginings, but to be a messenger in response to greater powers. The cult of "the man of genius," a heritage from the eighteenth century, is given up, even though the singular rank of the poet is emphatically insisted on. Moreover—and this may be of help in understanding Heidegger's interpretation—the subjectivistic and "humanistic" approach common in the last centuries and largely also today, is abandoned in the essays on Hölderlin as much as in those on philosophical topics: man is visualised as standing "in the open" amid all that is, with things below him and powers above him.

4

WHAT IS METAPHYSICS?

This essay, in time the first published of those collected in this volume, is Heidegger's Inaugural Lecture, when he was appointed to the Chair of Philosophy as the successor to his own teacher Edmund Husserl. A pronouncement on principle could be expected on such an occasion, and a pronouncement of this kind it was. It deals with the problem of "nothingness," conceived as a metaphysical problem; and it addresses itself to the scientists and scholars of his audience who, by the subject matter of their respective studies, radically exclude the "nothing" from their considerations.

The problem chosen by Heidegger for the discussion of the nature of metaphysics is surprising and provocative indeed. And the first question which a thoughtful reader may well put to himself is: why did the author, whose main purpose it is at all times to re-awaken a sense of the seriousness, utmost relevance and urgency of the problem of Being, discuss the apparently very odd, enigmatic and unusual problem of "nothingness" as the representative problem selected for elucidating the question "What is Metaphysics?"

When we speak of "Being," it is very rare that we bring the problem entailed really home to ourselves in thought. "Being" is not identical with any special kind of being, such as that of a star or the earth or a plant or an animal or a man. It is in all that is; and while we live amidst all that is, we think practically always of some kind of being or other, but rise hardly at all to the transcendent conception of Being itself. In metaphysics, if there should be metaphysics, we go in thought beyond, i.e. transcend, the sphere not only of everyday life, but also of the objects of science and learning. Metaphysics is, in accordance with Hegel's saying in the "Phenomenology of the Mind," which Heidegger quotes, from the standpoint of common sense "the world turned upside down." Heidegger suggests that the problem of "nothingness," really understood, is intimately and inseparably connected with the problem of "Being"; and actually, that we rise to the problem of "Being" only if we have faced the problem of "nothingness." In discussing the problem of "nothingness," he thus shows how rare it is that we truly meditate upon "Being." And in order to stimulate such meditation and to direct it to the line of approach, which he thinks is the proper and only one in this field of thought, he embarks upon the analysis of a problem which to many of his readers will, at first sight, seem no problem at all.

Towards the end of the essay such a doubter, provided he is intimately acquainted with the history of philosophy and metaphysics, may grow pensive. Here Heidegger explicitly hints (unfortunately, only hints) at the great significance of the conception of the "nothing" for the interpretation of all things both in Greek metaphysics and in Christian dogmatics. The conception of "nothingness" is, in these two greatest types of European metaphysics, intimately linked with what essentially is, and assumes its colouring and special characteristics from the interpretation of the nature of all things, whether they are regarded fundamentally as formed matter or as created out of "nothing." Inasfar as the problem of "Being" is not philosophically analysed, the problem of "nothingness" remains unelucidated, too. In that case, the "nothing," as Heidegger points out, is the vague counter-conception to the things that are. But once the metaphysical problem of "Being" is again consciously faced, the "nothing" is seen to belong intimately together with the "Being" fundamental to the things. Thus, e.g. Hegel asserts that "pure Being and pure Nothing are the same."

I have been drawing the attention of the reader right at the start to these brief, but well-founded and penetrating historic allusions, because to us who have been living for the last century in an atmosphere and a tradition of an assumed autonomy of science and scholarly studies, which are progressing in their own spheres without meditation upon fundamental metaphysical questions—a tendency, once ushered in and supported by the ideas of Comte's Cours de philosophie positive and of Mill's theory of induction—the problem of "Being" as well as that of "nothingness" are alien; and we are thus on the whole unconcerned about, and ignorant of, the place which "nothingness" holds in the realm of metaphysical thought.

In short, Heidegger's posing of the problem of "nothingness" as an elucidation of the question "What is Metaphysics?" is, in my view, a sign—and, more than that, another proof—of the fact that he is genuinely meditating upon "Being," feeling that it is his task and responsibility to awaken his contemporaries once more to reflection upon this greatest of all philosophic concepts, by bringing before their mind its very opposite, the conception of "nothingness." No one but a thinker to whom the problem of "Being" is of actual relevance could have conceived of this undertaking. And not one of his readers who once grasps the metaphysical range of the problem of "nothingness," i.e. its preparatory character for the conceiving and unfolding of the problem of "Being," could ever come to interpret Heidegger's approach as "nihilistic."

In what way, then, does Heidegger give an exposition of the problem of "nothingness"? In his elaboration of the question as to how the "nothing" is "given" to us, if "given" at all (Section 2 of the Inaugural Lecture) he has one negative and one positive answer.

The "nothing" may be thought, and in fact has very often been thought, to be a specific mode of negation, derived from it and from the idea and linguistic expression "not," and thus to belong to the realm of formal "Logic." Heidegger insists that, as long as the "nothing" is sought for in this field of purely intellectual and abstract thought, it cannot be encountered in its genuine and primary nature. In his view, the "nothing" is not a derivative of logical negation, but, on the contrary, the logical form of negation and the various kinds of "not" that may be found and cognised are the outcome and relatively remote derivatives of the "nothing" given in an actual, if rare, fundamental experience.

A distinction of great significance, which also contains a weighty reason why the first Section of "Being and Time" is concerned with an exposition of the nature of human Dasein, separates this negative answer from the positive one. The totality of all that is can never be comprehended in its absolute sense. This, Heidegger admits, is impossible on principle.* But in contrast to this impossibility stands the fact that we, as men, are placed amidst a great multitude of beings within the "whole." This is, indeed, our fundamental position, which constantly repeats itself throughout our life; and this being placed amidst beings within the "whole" (the "Befindlichkeit" of Dasein, as analysed in "Being and Time") opens up the realm of metaphysics; we are thus, potentially, face to face with metaphysics already

* Therefore, inasfar as this was the aim of metaphysics in former times, Heidegger disagrees with it. This is a noteworthy point, as in his "Postscript," published fourteen years after the lecture, Heidegger claims, and I think rightly, that his whole exposition of the question "What is Metaphysics?" arises from a way of thought, which has also entered into the overcoming of metaphysics, by reflecting upon the ground of all metaphysics and upon its, the ground's, incomprehensibility.

in our actual Dasein, however little many of us may be aware of this fact.

One term requires comment: within the "whole"—for without this, Heidegger's interpretation of how the "nothing" is genuinely encountered cannot be understood. The "within the 'whole'" is, as it were, the pivot of Heidegger's subsequent argument and analysis.

Many readers may be prepared to accept that man is placed amidst a great multitude of beings. But they may fail to see and refuse to acknowledge that this multitude of beings is met with within the whole. This is not an irrelevant or arbitrary addition; nor is it a product of abstract thought, but an expression of demonstrable experience. Heidegger himself refers to a "unitariness" of the "whole" experienced in everyday life, even if we are occupied with matters which attract our full attention so that we may think it is these matters alone that are there. No experience, be it of a landscape or of friends or of our own professional activity, is without this width of horizon within which the especial things or persons are met and activities performed, to which, from an early time onwards, the name of the "world" or the "universe" was attached, and which produces a familiar, though usually unnoticed atmosphere of unitariness. The "mood," the specific "Gestimmtsein," as we know from earlier discussions, evoked in the individual, is the outcome of his being placed concretely amidst the variety of beings within the whole; and Heidegger refers explicitly to the mood of boredom to show that it is not aroused when something special is boring, but only when we are under the impact of the "whole"; in such a state of mind everything, things, persons and oneself, as it were, gather and are one in a "mood." Whereas, usually, the "whole" remains in the background and at the horizon of our experience, it is then that it gains fuller force and becomes prominent; and it is then that "what is within the whole" (das Seiende im Ganzen), as the author calls it, actually manifests itself in personal experience. Heidegger also draws the attention to another example, very different from boredom, the joy aroused by the presence of the existence of a beloved person, in which, he suggests, "being within the whole" may likewise reveal itself. These examples are used to point to the great variety of "moods," in which "what is within the whole" can be genuinely experienced, but also to prepare, by way of contrast, for the altogether different and far more fundamental experience of "nothingness." I feel that I should remark that, in my view, Heidegger has not made the meaning of the notion "within the whole" fully clear, and this is probably impossible to do in passing; a much more detailed phenomenological description would be required for this purpose. But the notion as such, it seems to me, is a genuine and very important one. Without it, "transcending" thought, such as the realisation of "nothingness" or the visualisation of "Being," would be impossible. And the implicit emphasis that the "totality" of things (das Ganze des Seienden) is not only incomprehensible, but not even experienced, yet that the things are experienced *within* something total, within the "whole," in other words: that in-being is the only approach to the whole open to us, seems to me most appropriate and formulated in a felicitous philosophic conception. Perhaps I should add that the description of boredom as of a mood disclosing "what is within the whole" satisfies me more than the brief reference to joy in the given example, even though I think I can imagine why it is of a similarly revealing kind.

The "moods," fundamentally enough understood, bring us before "what is within the whole" and bring its impact home to us. Heidegger's question as to the genuine, primary and adequate experience of "nothingness," if this is not a mere derivative of the logical form of negation, therefore is: is there any one specific "mood" which brings the individual face to face with "nothingness," thereby revealing to him its nature? His answer is: "dread" is this one basic "mood," however rarely it may be experienced.* The

* It may be remembered that, in "Being and Time," "dread," as distinct from fear, is described as the dread not of anything in particular, but of something most comprehensive and total, namely dread of "being in the world"; but such "dread," according to Heidegger's analysis, implies also an intense desire of the individual to be able to "be in the world" in an authentic way. It would therefore be wrong to emphasise unduly the "negative" aspect of such a phenomenon. Moreover, the analysis of "dread" immediately precedes, and in some way prepares for, that of "Care," interpreted as the "Being" of human

descriptive characterisation of "dread" as disclosing "nothingness" is given in such a masterly, elucidating and impressive way that, in this respect, no further introductory remark seems required.

Having pointed out that "nothingness" is actually being experienced by man in the rare state of "dread"—a discovery to which Kierkegaard seems to have been the only forerunner*—Heidegger has so far done nothing more than opened up the approach to the problem: what

---

Dasein. What is pointed out, in "Being and Time," with regard to the structure of human Dasein, is followed up in a similar way in the Inaugural Lecture, in view of the problem of the nature of metaphysics. Here, too, the realisation of "nothingness," experienced in "dread," precedes, and prepares for, the genuine meditation on "Being." A similar, somewhat dialectic sequence can be observed in the analysis, in "Being and Time," of, on the one hand, an individual's Being-towards-his-own-death and, on the other, the resulting resolve and the acquired authenticity of existence. If any inference of a more general nature should be drawn from Heidegger's insistence on, and analysis of, so-called "negative" experiences, it would, in my view, be that he has gained the insight, and some may even say, wisdom, that such experiences, truly endured, bear a fruition, not to be had in any other way.

* S. Kierkegaard, "The Concept of Dread," e.g. "Nothing! But what effect has—nothing? It evokes dread." (German edition, p. 36) Or: ". . . the relationship of dread to its object, the something which is nothing. . . ." (p. 3?) Or: ". . . the nothing which is the object of dread. . . ." (p. 57) Kierkegaard uses several times the term: "the nothingness of dread" (pp. 57/58). But it seems fair to emphasise that the reference to the relationship of dread and "nothing" made by Kierkegaard is but occasional and does not play a major part in his exposition of the nature of "dread." Serious students of Kierkegaard's thought may well have read it, without realising its profound significance.

210

is the significance of the experience of "nothingness," humanly and metaphysically; and in what way can it be shown that the experience of "nothingness" in the state of dread is prior to any logical form of negation and any other form of "not," linguistically used? (Section 3.)

In order to elucidate the human and more especially the metaphysical significance, Heidegger concentrates no more, as before (towards the end of Section 2), on "dread" as revealing "nothingness," but on the phenomenon of "nothingness" itself. This is a turn of thought which the reader would do well to watch; otherwise he misses something essential in the essay. Whatever the nature and functions of "nothingness" may be, the phenomenon of "nothingness" is discussed, as if it were something like a thing, something quasi objective, though avowedly it is stated at once that it is not anything that "is" and that it is not an "object." But "dread," if I understand the subsequent exposition rightly, may now be likened in some way, to a sense-perception which makes it possible for us to perceive an object, or to the mind when it meditates upon Being; and the emphasis lies here on that which is comparable to the object or to Being, i.e. on "nothingness." If I may exaggerate for a moment, "dread" is here nothing more than what makes "nothingness" accessible. But again Heidegger, quite rightly, states: "dread" is not an "apprehending" of "nothingness." In other words: from now onwards Heidegger actually treats "nothingness" as a metaphysical phenomenon, as a strange and bewildering, but very important kind of "entity," if the term "entity" be used for a moment inappropriately and metaphorically. Were he not to do so, he would not be dealing with a metaphysical problem. "Nothingness" belongs to what we commonly call the ultimate "reality" of things. It is not just a matter of human thought or of a special kind of "feelings" or "emotions" (dread) which makes things look different from what they actually are. As in "Being and Time" and in the "Essence of Truth," Heidegger attempts to overcome here, if, as I say, I understand him rightly, the "anthropological" and "subjective" approach to philosophical problems, favoured and even predominant in philosophy since Locke, Hume and Kant. The thought in this Section is very original and most daring; and my task can only be to help, if possible, a little in the understanding of it.

What, then, is the phenomenon of "nothingness," as visualised by Heidegger? "Nothingness" is encountered in the state of dread, not as something isolated, apart from the things in the world,* but as one with them. The first essential trait emphasised is that, in the state of dread, things seem to slide away, sink away, that the control over things strangely loosens and weakens. This is taken to be a functioning of the

* I am using these more familiar expressions here for the reason that they may be more easily understood, though Heidegger's own term "das Seiende im Ganzen," or "the multitude of beings in the whole," or "what is in the whole," or "what is in totality," is more appropriate.

"nothing." It is "one" with the things in the world, yet, owing to its functioning, the things somehow change. The second essential trait is described as a withdrawal, a retreat from the things, but so that eyes and thought, as it were, still spellbound, rest on them. This indicates more the effect upon man, but is likewise thought to be an attitude enforced by the "nothing." This trait is characterised in somewhat more detail. The "nothing" is said essentially not to attract, but to repel, thereby bringing about the withdrawal or retreat on the part of the individual. But while the repelling force is thought to emanate from the "nothing," experienced in the state of dread, the attention of the individual is drawn and fixed to the things in the world, as they slide away and sink; it is as if the "nothing," in repelling the individual, was pointing to them, inducing him to get proper hold of them, impossible as this is in the very state of dread. Heidegger concludes: it is the nature, the essence of "nothingness" to press, through dread, upon the Dasein of the individual in the described way, by repelling and enforcing a withdrawal, by making the things in the world slide away out of reach and yet by directing and fixing the attention of the powerless man on them. It is not merely the "feelings" of the individual that are aroused; this would be a misleading understatement; the whole of his "Dasein," i.e. his actual relationship with the things and persons around him, as they are, and even with himself, is profoundly affected. This Heidegger calls: the "nothing" is at work, the "nothing" is function-ing, coining for it the new terms "nichten" and "Nichtung" (as it were, literally, "to nothing" and "the nothinging"). This is the first step in the exposition of the phenomenon of "nothing-ness." It may be mentioned that in its descrip-tion Heidegger contrasts its functioning with two apparently similar, but fundamentally different phenomena, annihilation and negation. It is obvious that neither of them play any part in the test experience of "dread."

The second step of the exposition (as such at least I would regard it) goes beyond the very subtle phenomeno-logical description given so far, by attaching a unique importance to the, admit-tedly rare, experience of dread and the function-ing of the "nothing." It takes its start from the fact that the "nothing," directing and fixing the at-tention of the individual on to the things out of his reach, somehow fills him with the sense of its strange nature and—so Heidegger suggests—makes him turn the more decidedly to the things that are, which he now, and only now, begins to discover in their true nature and in their funda-mental otherness, compared with the "nothing." In other words: threatened and utterly disquieted as man is by the engulfing force of "nothingness," he approaches the things in the world after such an experience in a spirit and attitude altogether different from that before. Against the back-ground of "nothingness," a background of horror and awe, the things in the world begin to stand out as what they actually are. And with this experience of the "nothing" behind him, he is endowed with the power and made ready to grasp reality itself. So far the "mood" of dread had seemed to be one among many, if of a peculiar character of its own. And whatever the effects of the functioning of "nothingness," the question of its relevance to man's Dasein as a whole has not been raised. This is done now. And Heidegger's suggestion and contention is: that "nothingness," and its experience by man, is the indispensable pre-requisite for the things in the world to come into their own and to be known and treated for what they are. It is obvious that this vision and outlook of Heidegger, once grasped, is likely to arouse dispute. In its favour reference may be made to early myths, such as the Greek one of Chaos preceding all Titans and Olympian gods, to early philosophy and to the beginning of Genesis. Here it is merely a matter of noting the import and originality of Heidegger's interpretation.

One weighty reason for the assumed relevance of this experience to man's Dasein is given afterwards. While being under the impact of "nothingness," which manifests itself, being inseparably bound up with the things in the world, by which man is surrounded, man *transcends* all the things. That "nothingness," rightly understood, is "beyond" the things that are, and that man's exposure to it in the state of dread is of a transcending nature, is a notion worth considering. For transcend we must, too, and transcend

215

we do when thinking, authentically, of Being. And thus "nothingness," in its metaphysical sense seems, as Heidegger points out, not to be merely the counter-conception to anything that is, but, more fundamentally, to belong together with "Being," the essence and ground of what is.

On these last pages I have been commenting, largely by way of paraphrasing, upon only the first part of Section 3 of the essay. But this part seems to me to require a particularly careful study. Once the reader has grasped the ideas advanced in it and has thought them out for himself, the later part should not offer substantial difficulties, inasfar as the actual understanding is concerned. Therefore I will select only a very few points from it for a preliminary discussion.

Those who hold the view that negation, as applied in rational thought, is the source of all forms of "not" may find it interesting to see the reference to other specific ways of behaviour met in actual life, such as opposition to others or the loathing of their actions, refusal or interdict, or renunciation. In all of them, according to Heidegger's interpretation, "nothingness" is functioning in one way or another, though not so purely and genuinely as in the experience of dread. Outspoken negation, in the form of words, may be added to all of them, but is not required by these ways of behaviour as such. This reference to ways of behaviour, other than the experience of dread and rational negation, seems to me—apart from the analysis of "dread" and of "nothingness" itself—the weightiest argument advanced by Heidegger in support of the view that "nothingness" is primarily encountered somewhere in life itself and not in logical thought. If I see the problem rightly, critics would have to analyse ways of behaviour, such as in the examples mentioned, showing that no "negative" force—Heidegger would say: no functioning of "nothingness"—is at work in them, which, it seems to me, would be difficult to assert and to demonstrate; or that "negation," as applied in rational and logical thought, is a phenomenon so much of its own that the other forms of "nothingness," as experienced in the state of dread or as manifest in specific ways of behaviour, are not only of a fundamentally different type (a line of reasoning which may well be taken up and is, I think, implicitly admitted by Heidegger), but that "negation" shows no resemblance to them whatever and is not dependent on them. A problem of a very interesting kind has thus been posed by Heidegger's analysis.

As for "negation" itself, which Heidegger considers to be one form of the functioning of "nothingness," he argues (a) that the "not" cannot be a "derivative" of negation. To negate something, the something to be negated must first be "given." And something of the "not" character can be envisaged only if and when we, in all our thought, anticipate that there is the "not." Thus negation is thought to be "dependent"on a somehow "given" "not," and not vice versa. (b) This argument, basing negation on the "not," is followed up by the other one, tracing the

217

"not" back to its origin from the functioning of "nothingness," as the manifestation of which in the realm of thought the "not," and thus negation, is interpreted. It is obvious that by this way of argumentation the idea of an autonomous "Logic" is profoundly challenged.

In the last part of the Section, the problem of "nothingness" is explicitly taken to elucidate the nature of "Metaphysics." Here a definition of "Metaphysics" is given. "Metaphysics is the *questioning beyond* the things that are, in order to regain them *as such* and *in the whole* for the purpose of comprehension."

The import of the characterisation that, in the state of dread, we are "transcending" the realm of things when exposed to "nothingness" and of the other trait that, faced with "nothingness," man turns to the things in the world with a keener interest to find out what they actually are is hereby shown to the full. That we, together with the multitude of beings, human and non-human, are *"in the whole"* or *"in the universe"* can be realised only if we are able to transcend in thought the realms of things. Otherwise concepts such as "world," "universe," "whole," "totality" would remain dead, non-understood words handed down by tradition. And in order to study and to comprehend, if possible, something that is *as such,* to investigate it in its very nature, to do this, Heidegger insists, a "transcending" is likewise required. Otherwise, science and learning would degenerate into a mere accumulation and classification of knowledge, instead of the scientist or scholar knowing and in his own work demonstrating that he is pursuing his own discoveries and investigations within the one vast realm of truth opened up in Nature and History.

To have clearly pointed out the significance which "Metaphysics," rightly understood, possesses for all of us, but in particular for the scientist and the scholar who today, for the most part, think that it is of no use to them whatever, is not the least valuable part in Heidegger's essay.

There are, in Heidegger's view, two main criteria that a problem is of the metaphysical range: (a) though but one, it embraces and permeates the whole realm of metaphysics; and (b) the thinking being who advances the question and who thinks it out for himself—here therefore author and reader alike—is himself questioned in his very being.

These two aspects are gone through by Heidegger with regard to the problem of "nothingness." Here the references, quoted in the beginning, to Greek metaphysics, to Christian dogmatics and to Hegel's "Logic" are made to prove that "nothingness," if not clearly conceived as a problem, is taken to be the metaphysical counter-conception to what actually and substantially is; but that, if envisaged as a problem, it is seen to belong to the "Being" itself of all that is. Referring to the old metaphysical proposition: *ex nihilo nihil fit* and giving to it, for the Christian interpretation of the creation, the different, surprisingly apt version: *ex nihilo fit—ens creatum*, he ventures to offer a new formulation for his own outlook, defining strikingly the great import of the metaphysical experience of "nothingness" for all human knowledge of beings: *ex nihilo omne ens qua ens fit.* Only through the transcending to "nothingness" does man approach the things as what they are and only thus do they come truly into their own.

As to the second aspect, the import of the experience of "nothingness" for the scientist and scholar is emphasised. Through the exposure to "nothingness" the strangeness of the things that are will be newly and deeply felt. Only when they are impressing one as strange can the genuine astonishment—the Greek θαυμάζεσθαι—be aroused, which impels us, as if we were the first to do so, to ask for reasons, for argument and to commence research.

Heidegger ends his Inaugural Lecture by drawing attention to the import of "metaphysics" for the life of mankind. Far from being one branch of specialised philosophy, it is (so Heidegger suggests) "the fundamental happening in Dasein and as Dasein." This definition is not explained here. But the reader who bears in mind Heidegger's exposition of the "Essence of Truth" will remember that the greatest incision in the history of mankind is the moment when the first thinker, facing the vast realm of things, puts to himself the question: what is the "Being" of all that is? Thereby man and all the things that are come into the open, the horizon widens immensely; knowledge, technique, action, civilisation and history gain their foundation, and the life of man, up to that time only one of the many species covering the globe, which, together with everything else, is embedded in dark unknown mystery, changes into "Dasein." It is to this momentous event, and to its renewal age by age on the part of self-dependent, original thinkers (for perpetual renewal in the past there has been, and in the present and future there must be, unless the proud edifice of knowledge becomes a Tower of Babel and man forgets the very foundations of his civilisation) that Heidegger points with his definition. And it is for the reason that "metaphysics," with all its consequences, has vastly transformed human life, a transformation carried on by tradition, that Heidegger makes the bold suggestion that, inasfar as we authentically exist, we are already and always standing and moving within the realm of "metaphysics."

Aptly does Heidegger close his Inaugural Lecture about the problem of "nothingness" by renewing the question which the aged Leibnitz once advanced in one of his last works, the essay entitled "Principes de la nature et de la grâce fondées en raison" (§ 7): "Why is there something rather than nothing?"

Postscript

The "Postscript," written many years later, which is less of a pronouncement and more reflective in tone, may—after its most valuable last portion—be called the confession that true philosophy, or what Heidegger, in contrast to the "exact" and "calculating" way of thought in science, terms "the essential thinking," is a thanksgiving and a voluntary sacrifice in response to "Being."

In "response" to "Being." The reader of "Hölderlin and the Essence of Poetry" will remember that the "naming of the gods" by the poet is, in Heidegger's interpretation, not an act of spontaneous imagination, but in "response" to the speaking of the gods to man and to the claim they thereby make on him. Similarly it is the author's deep-founded conviction that "Being," though once, in a great historic moment, discovered and revealed by a thinker, is in no way a "product" of thought. "Being," and its "truth," was long before men came into their own by thinking it. Essential thinking, i.e. true philosophy, meditating upon "Being," is an "event of Being" itself. Without "Being" being recognised as the one tremendous entity lasting through Time, while men with their short lives appear and vanish, thinkers pronouncing "Being" and poets naming "the holy," the meditation of the "Postcript," and its characterisation of the nature of science in contrast to that of philosophy, cannot be understood and appreciated.

In the beginning, as has already been mentioned, Heidegger draws attention to the fact that our age is one of transition as regards the nature of "Metaphysics." Metaphysical thinking moves, and cannot help moving, at all times "in the realm of the truth of Being"; and the "truth of Being" is to such thinking the unknown and unfounded ground, the ground beyond which thinking cannot penetrate. All things that are, non-human and human—so we are induced to think—have risen and will rise from "Being." But far more fundamental than this, prior to it, is "Being" itself embedded in its "truth." Both are inseparable. The "truth of Being" is and manifests itself as the "Being of truth." If this is so, the question must be asked: what is metaphysics in its own ground? This was the question aimed at in the Inaugural Lecture. Such questioning, as Heidegger puts it, is essentially ambiguous. It thinks metaphysically; yet, it thinks at the same time out of the ground of metaphysics, and this means, Heidegger seems to suggest, it thinks no longer metaphysically. For metaphysical thinking brings the entity of beings up to the level of comprehending concepts; and in doing so, it encounters "Being" itself. But it is unable actually to meditate upon the "truth" of "Being" as truth and to grasp it, even though it moves in the realm of this truth. This is why "What is Metaphysics?" must remain a question.

A depth of reflection is fathomed in this first part of the "Postscript," of which little can be found in express words in the Inaugural Lecture. It is the mature reflection upon what had been attempted by raising the question "What is Metaphysics?" as a question; and it is, in its way of deeply meditative thought, more akin to the later Sections of the "Essence of Truth" than to the vigour, directness and relative lucidity of the Inaugural Lecture.

In the Lecture, science and scholarly studies were taken as the starting-point and its end was devoted to a discussion of the import of metaphysics for scientific and scholarly knowledge. Heidegger rightly emphasises that the metaphysical questioning need not have taken this start. In the essay "On the Essence of Truth" reference is made in the beginning to a great variety of kinds of truth, to all of which metaphysics is thought essential. Any of the forms of life, mentioned there, could have formed the starting-point, owing to the universal significance of metaphysics.

In this connection Heidegger begins to discuss the nature of science, here understood in its precise sense, i.e. physics and chemistry in the first place. Here he makes a reference, possibly of considerable importance, to the "will to will," which is said to be a feature of all that is—a statement which I must admit I do not understand. I think what may be meant, to judge from the context, is: modern European life, and with it modern science, is characterised by this trait: the "will to will." If this were meant, it would be a very interesting interpretation of modern European life, far more penetrating than many other ones. It would mean that the European is consciously intent upon making the "will" of the individual the "essence" of his

Dasein, with all the responsibility it implies, theoretically and practically, privately and socially. What makes this reading of Heidegger's statement likely is the addition that its preliminary, present-day form is the "will to power," a passing utterance which leaves it open whether the author thinks that this tendency manifests itself in political life alone or, probably, more generally.

As for science, Heidegger suggests that it is one way of the "calculating objectivation" of a sphere of being; and that such "calculating objectivation" is imposed upon modern science by the "will to will" as a condition by which it secures its control. Such "objectivation" of a sphere of being—Matter, approached mathematically—which, keen on progress within its own setting, does not analyse its presuppositions, is then too often, mistakenly, identified with "Being" itself. To this problem Heidegger later returns, when contrasting scientific calculation with metaphysical thought.*

First he discusses two objections: (a) that his treatment of the problem of "nothingness" would imply "nihilism"; and (b) that the insistence on "dread" as the basic "mood" ignored the virtue of courage. The reply to the second objection requires no further comment. But the reply to the first objection contains a most interesting hint,

* About the problem of science and "objectivation" cf. the account given in the section "Dasein and Temporality" of "Being and Time."

more explicit than in the Lecture i*.*elf, at the "nothing" belonging profoundly together with "Being" itself.

He rightly points out that, wherever the scientist searches the things that are, he never encounters "Being," since it is only his aim to explain the things that are and since "Being" is not an existing quality to be found in the things. "Being" cannot be objectivated, neither in thought nor by being produced, like a machine. It forms an absolute contrast to, and is fundamentally different from, all that is. It is as different from the things that are as is, in its way, "nothingness." And one trait in the experience of "nothingness" is now explicitly emphasised which was only implicitly hinted at in the Lecture: in "nothingness," as bound up with the things in the whole, we experience a "vast spaciousness" which gives every single thing the warrant to be. It is, Heidegger suggests, as if "Being" itself—though then not yet recognised in its essence—was transmitting "nothingness," in the state of genuine dread, to man. It thus remains an open question whether "nothingness," as a metaphysical phenomenon, is really as "negative" as it may appear at first sight to someone who has not acquainted himself deeply with its problem.

However, the most valuable contribution made in the "Postscript," apart from the introductory part about the "ambiguity" of metaphysics, seems to me contained in the portion dealing with the "essential thinking" of philosophy and meta-

226

physics, prefaced by a brief discussion of the problem of "Logic" and that of "exact" thought, as applied in science.

"Logic," as it is commonly known, Heidegger insists, and in this the followers of the German philosopher W. Dilthey would agree, is a way of thought inherited from the Greeks and their special experience of "Being" which, moulded on the "$\varepsilon\tilde{\iota}\delta o\varsigma$," the form that could be seen, was of a peculiarly objective kind. It seems, therefore, especially applicable when we are studying the things as "objects," as in science. It may be that already in the study of human life, of individuals and groups, of literature and art as well as of religion, other ways of thought are applicable than the forms of traditional "Logic" or its present-day successor, "Logistic." In metaphysics, definitely, the phenomena and problems meditated upon are not, and can never be made "objects," in the sense of "objects" studied in science and in the scholarly pursuits concerning human life. To mention but one weighty reason that prevents this: if a metaphysical phenomenon or problem is actually and seriously approached, the whole of the Being of a thinker is involved and implied as well. Though transcending the realm of beings, he cannot step outside his own Being and outside "Being" itself, to observe it in "objective" detachment, as he can do with all things in the world, including special aspects of human life. This is also the reason why Heidegger, in the Inaugural Lecture, indicated as the second criterion of a problem being "metaphysical" the trait that the questioning thinker, as such, is "involved" in the question and is actually being questioned as well. As we are "in the whole" and as metaphysics arises from our being, together with a great multitude of other beings, "in the whole," we cannot, artificially, extract ourselves from this all-determining position and consider "Being" or "nothingness," as if we were placed in an entirely imaginary "outside," far different even from the "nothingness" we may or may not have experienced. In other words, there is a legitimate and significant way of thought, that concerns metaphysical phenomena and problems, different from that of "Logic," "Logistic" and the "exact" thought, applied in science—provided that, as Heidegger suggests, but as not all who otherwise agree with many points of his outlook may accept, "Logic" comprises only the formal traditional "Logic," its modern offspring of "Logistic" and similar types of thought, and not all the various ways of human thought that are possible.

Heidegger characterises the "exact" thought, as applied in "science," by discussing one dominant trait: that of "calculation." In his view, calculation has one important function: to bring the things so considered more into human control and under man's disposal.* The reader will be reminded of the statement made at the be-

---

* The German word "das Beistellbare," used by Heidegger to indicate that it belongs to the nature of the things cognised by science to be placed at man's disposal, seems an almost literal rendering of the original meaning of the Greek term for "knowledge": ἐπιστήμη.

ginning of the "Postscript" that in modern European life the "will to will" is functioning and that this great tendency is manifesting itself in "science." Heidegger also emphasises, in my view rightly, that all calculation, despite its vast field of application, is, fundamentally, a "whole," a "unity" of a very special kind, belonging to the very much vaster field of the "incalculable," of "Being," within which it "objectivates" and treats in its own way what it can legitimately so approach. But philosophic and metaphysical thought, in Heidegger's terminology the "essential thinking," moves, by its very nature, outside the realm of "calculation"; and it is against this background that he characterises such "essential thinking," in the way of a personal confession.

Only man can become aware of that tremendous and awe-inspiring "reality," termed "Being," which embraces, and for thought is essentially beyond, all that is. It claims him and his devotion in thought and life, even if its religious counter-part, God, may fail to do so. In response to its claim, the "thinker" dedicates his life, as if it were in a free sacrifice, to uphold the "truth of Being." For only man can be its "guardian" among all that is. Owing to "Being," all the things are. And it evokes in the "thinker" the deepfelt and all-important impulse of giving thanks to it for this its grace. This, Heidegger suggests, is prior to all philosophic thought, uttering itself in conceptual language. The impulse of giving thanks to "Being" and its grace is, as Heidegger puts it, the human response of the thinker to "the Word of the soundless Voice of Being," listened to with singular attention. The conceptual wording of thought in a philosophical work is but its subsequent and consequent manifestation. By rising to respond to "Being," its truth and dignity, in such a way, the thinker takes leave of all the individual things that are, to devote himself, with singlemindedness, to the upholding of the truth of "Being." Otherwise the truth of "Being" and the Being of "truth" would not find its place and domicile in historical humanity, as it deserves and must. Only if and when philosophic thought is carried out with such singlemindedness in the spirit of free sacrifice, in obedience to the "Voice of Being," not seeking support from the things that are, may it succeed, no matter how rarely, in kindling thought of the same kind in others.

Here the comparison, referred to at an earlier place, between the "thinker" and the poet is made. No one, beside the poet, Heidegger suggests, cares so seriously and intently for using the right word, as does the philosopher. He seeks to find the word out of which the truth of Being may be heard. Only if he zealously guards his words, dwelling for a long time in the meditation of matters that command silence and cannot be worded until their realm becomes lucid, will he be able to speak in an authentic way and communicate what he has to say in terms that remain memorable. "Dread," in the sense of horror and awe, opening up for man the abyss of "nothingness," is one of those great instances of speechless silence. For "nothingness," this is Heidegger's last word about the problem of the Inaugural Lecture, is, in its otherness to the things that are, "the veil of Being."

Nothing more can be attempted by this "Introduction," and by the subsequent essays which themselves are but an introduction to the work of thought of one outstanding contemporary German thinker, than to point to its singularity and relevance. His approach to many problems is a new one; and this, inevitably, means: it is at first sight, and perhaps for some time to come, provocative. The English-speaking reader, having grown up in a tradition vastly different from that of the thinker, will decide on his own how to react to it. There are but a very few thinkers living today, in an age of the autonomy of science and learning where, therefore, even the cultured and the intellectual public tend to shrink from the realm of philosophic thought—in Germany there is but one other outstanding thinker of very high rank, Karl Jaspers—whose thought deserves attention, study and serious discussion as much as that of Martin Heidegger.

NOTE

The thought of the address "Remembrance of the Poet," which contains a number of hints on Hölderlin's elegy "Homecoming," and of the lecture "Hölderlin and the Essence of Poetry" is of a kind which becomes plainer when compared with the questions asked in the two other lectures published at the same time—"On the Essence of Truth" and "What is Metaphysics?"

The above mentioned discourses make no claim to be contributions to research in the history of literature and to æsthetics. They arise from a necessity of thought.

The references from Hölderlin's poetry are to volume and page of the edition begun by Norbert von Hellingrath (Propyläen-Verlag, Berlin, 1914).

REMEMBRANCE OF THE POET

PREFATORY REMARK TO A REPETITION
OF THE ADDRESS

It is not permissible for us to repeat a celebration of "Remembrance of the Poet," even if we wished to. On the other hand we must always be practising thinking about the poet afresh in the only way in which it can begin. That is the attempt to think about what has been made into poetry. Such an act of remembrance arises out of a dialogue between thought and the writing of poetry, although at first the dialogue itself and what is spoken of, are not mentioned.

What has been made into poetry is preserved in the poem. As practice for "Remembrance of the Poet" let us listen to the elegy "Homecoming." All the poems of the poet who has entered into his poethood are poems of homecoming. If we are going to apply to these poems the traditional descriptions of "elegy" (song of mourning) and "hymn" (song of praise), then we may do so only if we know the essence of the sorrow which here sings songs of mourning, and if we know the essence of the holy being, which is invoked in this poem. The song "Homecoming" sings both of one and of the other, of the sorrow, and of the holy being, and of the communication between them. The poem "Homecoming" "meditates" on that which the poet in his poethood invokes ("the Holy"), and on the way in which the poet must tell of what has to be written of. On that account and only on that account the following address causes us to attend

233

to this poem, Hölderlin's last elegy. The inner-most core of the poem is concealed in line 42, which mentions the people of the country.

"To whom the holy gratitude smiling brings the fugitives." About this the address is silent.

Yet in spite of the names "elegy" and "hymn," we do not to this very hour know what these poems of Hölderlin really are. The poems appear like a shrine without a temple, where what has been made into poetry is preserved. Amid the noise of "unpoetic languages" (IV, 257), the poems are like a bell that hangs in the open air and is already becoming out of tune through a light fall of snow which is covering it. It is per-haps for this reason that among his later lines Hölderlin speaks that saying, which though it sounds like prose, is yet poetic in a way that few others are ("Entwurf zu Kolomb," IV, 395):

"Sent out of tune
  By little things, as by snow,
  Was the bell, with which
  The hour is rung
  For the evening meal."

Perhaps every explanation of this poem is a fall of snow on the bell. But whatever an expla-nation can or cannot do, this always applies: in order that what has been purely written of in the poem may stand forth a little clearer, the ex-planatory speech must break up each time both itself and what it has attempted. The final, but at the same time the most difficult step of every exposition consists in vanishing away together with its explanations in the face of the pure existence of the poem. The poem, which then stands in its own right, will itself throw light directly on the other poems. And so when we next read the poems, we feel that we had always understood them in this way. And it is well for us to feel this.

To Kindred Ones

There amid the Alps it is still bright night and
    the cloud,
Writing of the Joyous, covers the night within
    the yawning valley.
There, thither, rushes and roars the boisterous
    mountain breeze,
Steep down through the firs there gleams and
    dwindles a ray.
The joyously-shuddering chaos slowly hurries
    and struggles,
Young in appearance, yet strong, it celebrates
    loving strife
Beneath the rocks, it seethes and totters in the
    eternal lists,
For morning dawns more bacchanalian there.
For the year grows more unendingly there and
    the holy
Hours, the days, are more boldly ordered and
    mingled.
Yet the storm-bird marks the time and between
Mountains, high in the air he hovers and calls
    on the day.
Now too the village watches fearless from down
    in the depths,
And, familiar with the high, gazes up at the
    peaks from below.
With a presentiment of growth, for already, like
    lightning-streaks, the old
Cascades are falling, the ground steams under the
    tumbling,

Echo sounds all about, and the imponderable
  workshop
Moves its arm by day and night, conferring gifts.

Meanwhile the silver heights gleam peacefully
  above,
Already the luminous snow up there is full of
  roses.
And yet higher up still above the light there
  dwells the pure
Blissful god rejoicing in the play of holy beams.
Silent he dwells alone, and brightly shines his
  countenance,
The heavenly one seems disposed to give life,
To create joy, with us, as often when, conscious
  of measure,
Conscious of all that breathes, hesitant too and
  sparing, the god
Sends to cities and houses most genuine happi-
  ness, and gentle
Rain to open out the land, brooding clouds, and
  you too,
Dearest breezes, and you, soft vernal seasons,
And with slow hand makes joyful those who sor-
  row,
When he, the creative one, renews the seasons,
  and refreshes
And touches the quiet hearts of ageing people,
And works down into the depths and opens out
  and illumines,
As he loves to do, and now once again a life be-
  gins,

237

Charm flowers, as before, and an immanent spirit
   comes,
And a joyous courage swells again the pinions.

Much spoke I to him, for whatever poets medi-
   tate or sing
Is of value chiefly to the angels and to him;
I prayed much, for love of the fatherland, so that
   not
Unimplored the spirit might once suddenly com-
   mand us;
Much for you also who are beset with care in the
   fatherland,
To whom the holy gratitude smiling brings the
   fugitives,
People of the country! For you, whilst the lake
   rocked me,
And the helmsman sat calmly and praised the
   passage.
Far on the level of the lake was one joyous undulation
Beneath the sails, and now the town flowers and
   shines forth
There in the early morning, for hither from the
   shady Alps
The vessel comes escorted and rests now in the
   harbour.
Here the shore is warm, and the valleys amicably
   open,
Beautifully luminous with paths, gleam ver-
   dantly towards me.
Gardens stand in groups and already the glitter-
   ing bud is beginning,

And the song of the birds makes invitation to
  the wanderer.
All seems familiar, even the hastening greeting
Seems the greeting of friends, each face seems
  congenial.

To be sure! It is the native land, the soil of the
  homeland,
That which thou seekest is near, and already
  coming to meet thee.
And not in vain does he stand, like a son, at the
  wave-washed
Gate and gaze and seek loving names for thee
With song, a wandering man, O blissful Lin-
  dau!
This is one of the hospitable gates of the land,
Tempting one to go out into the much-promis-
  ing distance,
There, where wonders are, there, where the di-
  vine quarry runs,
High up the Rhine breaks its bold path down
  into the plains,
And forth out of the rocks the jubilant valley
  emerges,
In there, among the bright mountains, to wander
  to Como,
Or, as the day changes, down the open lake;
But me thou temptest more, O hallowed gate-
  way!
To go home, where flowering ways are known to
  me,
To visit the country there and the lovely vales of
  the Neckar,

And the woods, the green of holy trees, where
the oak

Gladly keeps company with calm birches and
beeches,

And a place in the mountains amicably capti-
vates me.

There they welcome me. O voice of the town, of
the mother!

O thou touchest, thou stirrest old teachings in
me!

Yet they are still the same! Joy and the sun still
flower with you,

O you dear ones! And almost brighter to the eye
than before.

Yes! What used to be, is still! It prospers and
ripens, yet nothing

That lives and loves there, abandons faithfulness.

But the best, the discovery, that lies beneath the
arc

Of holy peace, is reserved from youth and from
age.

Foolish is my speech. It is joy. Yet to-morrow and
in future

When we go and gaze out-of-doors upon the
living field,

Beneath the tree's blossoms, in the festive days
of spring

Much shall I hope and speak with you on this,
you dear ones!

Much have I heard of the great father and long

Kept silence about him, who refreshes the wandering season

Up there in the heights and rules over moun-
   tain-ranges,
Who presently grants to us heavenly gifts and
   calls
With brighter song and sends many good spirits.
   O tarry not,
Come, ye preserving ones! Angels of the Year!
   And ye,
Angels of the house, come! Into all the veins of
   life,
Rejoicing everything at once, let the heavenly
   share itself out!
Ennoble! Rejuvenate! So that no human good,
   no
Hour of the day may be fittingly hallowed
Without the Joyful Ones and without such joy,
   as now,
When lovers are reconciled, as it behoves them.
When we bless the meal, whom may I name and
   when we
Rest from life each day, say, how shall I give
   thanks?
Shall I name the High Ones then? No god loves
   what is unseemly;
To grasp him, our joy is scarcely large enough.
Often we must keep silence; holy names are
   lacking,
Hearts beat and yet does speech still hold back?
But lyre-music lends to each hour its sounds,
And perhaps rejoices the heavenly ones who
   draw near.
This makes ready and thus care too is almost

Placated already—the care that entered into the
  joy.
Cares like these, whether he wills or no, a singer
Must bear in his soul and often, but the others
  not.

"Little knowledge, but much joy
Is given to mortals. . . ." (IV, 240.)

According to its title, this poem of Hölderlin's tells of homecoming. That makes us think of arriving on the soil of one's homeland and meeting again the country-people of the district. The poem describes a voyage over the lake "coming from the shady Alps" to Lindau. In spring 1801, Hölderlin then a family-tutor, travelled back over the Bodensee from the Thurgau town of Hauptwyl near Konstanz to his home in Swabia. So the poem "Homecoming" might have given a poetic description of a joyous return home. Yet the last stanza, attuned to the word "care," gives no hint of the joyfulness of someone returning home completely carefree. The last word of the poem is a blunt "not." But the first stanza, which describes the Alpine range, stands forth uncompromisingly, itself a mountain-range of verse. It shows nothing of the delights of home. The "echo" of the "imponderable workshop" of what is not homely "sounds all about." Certainly, the "homecoming" which is enclosed by stanzas like these, is much more than a mere arrival on the shore of "the land of one's birth." For even the very arrival at the shore is curious enough:

"All seems familiar, even the hastening greeting
  Seems the greeting of friends, each face seems
    congenial."

243

At home the people and the things seem pleasantly familiar. But as yet they are not really so. Thus they shut away what is most their own. And therefore home at once delivers this message to the new arrival:

> "That which thou seekest is near, and already coming to meet thee."

Even with his arrival, the returning one has not yet reached home. Thus home is "difficult to win, the shut-away" ("The Voyage," IV, 170). Therefore the newcomer still remains in search of it. Only what he seeks is already coming to meet him. It is near. But what is sought is not yet found, if "find" means to receive what is found as one's own, to be able to dwell in it as a possession.

> "But the best, the discovery, that lies beneath the arc
>   Of holy peace, is reserved from youth and from age."

Hölderlin later made alterations in a second fair-copy of the poem, and instead of "But the best, the discovery . . ." wrote "But the treasure, all that is German . . . is still reserved." The innermost essence of home has indeed been long since prepared, and has already been given as their own to those who dwell in the land of their birth. The innermost essence of home is already the destiny of a Providence, or as we now call it: History. Nevertheless, in the dispensation of Providence, the essence is not yet completely

handed over. It is still being held back. Therefore too, that which is alone conformable to
Providence, that which is fitting, has not yet
been found. That then, which has already been
given and is yet at the same time being withheld,
is called the Reserved. In the guise of what is
reserved, the discovery is approaching and remains still sought-after. Why? Because they, "who
are beset with care in the fatherland," are not
yet ready for it—not yet ready to have the innermost essence of home, "all that is German," as
their own possession. Then homecoming really
consists solely in the people of the country becoming at home in the still-withheld essence of
home; previous to that, even, it consists in the
"dear ones" learning at home to become at home.
To do this it is necessary to know thoroughly
what is best and innermost in home. But how
shall we ever find it, if it is the case that for us
there is a seeker, and that the sought-for essence
of home shows itself to him?

"That which thou seekest is near, and already
coming to meet thee."

Everything of home that is openly friendly,
light, gleaming, shining and bright meets one in
a single appearance of friendliness on reaching
the confines of the land.

It is

"Tempting . . . to go out into the much-
promising distance,

. . . .

But (more tempting to the poet)

245

> To go home, where flowering ways are known
>   to me,
> To visit the country there and the lovely vales
>   of the Neckar,
> And the woods, the green of holy trees, where
>   the oak
> Gladly keeps company with calm birches and
>   beeches,
> And a place in the mountains amicably cap-
>   tivates me."

How shall we name this calm mien with which
all men and things give greeting to the seeker?
We must name this inviting disposition of a
home already approaching, with the phrase
which throws its light over the whole poem
"Homecoming," the phrase "the Joyous." In the
second stanza the lines are strewn with "the Joyous" and "joy," and it is almost the same in the
last. In the other stanzas these words occur less
often. Only in the fourth stanza, which actually
describes the aspect of "the Joyous," does the
word not appear. But in the opening of the
poem "the Joyous" is mentioned at once in its
relation to the writing of poetry:

> "There amid the Alps it is still bright night
>   and the cloud,
>   Writing of the Joyous, covers the night
>   within the yawning valley."

The Joyous is what has been made into poetry.
The Joyous is joy harmonised into poetry. So
too it is the rejoiced and therefore the enjoying.

Itself it can again delight others. Thus the Joyous is at the same time the cause of joy. The cloud "there amid the Alps" lingers above, against "the silver heights." It uncovers itself to the imperious light of Heaven, while at the same time it "covers . . . the yawning valley." The cloud can be seen from the clear brightness. The cloud writes poetry. Since it is gazing into whence it is itself gazed at, so therefore is its poetry not vainly thought out and invented. To write poetry is to make a discovery. And to do this the cloud must indeed reach out above itself to something other than itself. Not from it does the poetry spring. The poetry does not come from the cloud. It comes upon the cloud in the form of what the cloud is lingering over against. The clear brightness, in which the cloud is lingering, serenifies this lingering. The cloud is serenified into the Serene. What it writes, the "Joyous," is the Serene. We call this also "the spatially-ordered." (We are using this word both now and subsequently in a strict sense.) The spatially-ordered is, within its spatiality, freed, clarified and integrated. The Serene, the spatially-ordered, is alone able to house everything in its proper place. The Joyous has its being in the Serene, which serenifies. Even the Serene first shows itself anew in that which causes joy. While the serenification makes everything clear, the Serene allots each thing to that place of existence where by its nature it belongs, so that it may stand there in the brightness of the Serene, like a still light, proportionate to its own being. That which causes joy shines forth towards the homecoming poet,

> ". . . where the oak
>   Gladly keeps company with calm birches and
>   beeches,
>   And a place in the mountains amicably cap-
>   tivates me."

Near is the gentle spell of well-known things and the simple relations they bear to one another. Coming nearer yet and nearer, even though less evident than birches and mountains and therefore mostly overlooked and passed by, is the Serene itself, wherein both men and things now first appear. The Serene lingers over its unobtrusive appearance. It demands nothing for itself, it is no ob-ject and at the same time it is not "nothing." Yet in the Joyous, which first comes to meet the poet, there already predominates the greeting of that which serenifies. But those who announce the greeting of the Serene are the heralds, ἀγγελλοι, the "angels." Is is for this reason that the poet, when he is greeting the approaching Joyous in home, invokes in "Homecoming" the "angels of the house" and "the angels of the year."

"The house" is intended here to mean the space which for men houses that wherein alone they can be "at home" and so fulfil their destiny. This space is given by the immaculate earth. The earth houses the peoples in its historical space. The earth serenifies "the house." And the earth which thus serenifies is the first angel "of the house."

"The year" houses those times which we call the seasons. In that "mingled" play of the fiery brightness and the frosty dark which the seasons offer, things blossom out and then close up again. The seasons of "the year" give to man in the changing of the Serene that time which has been meted out for his historical sojourn in the "house." "The year" sends its greeting in the play of the light. The serenifying light is the first "angel of the year."

Both, earth and light, the "angels of the house" and the "angels of the year," are called the "preservers," because in greeting they bring to light the Serene, in whose clarity the "nature" of men and things is safely preserved. What remains safely preserved, is "homely" in its essence. The heralds send greeting from out of the Serene, which keeps everything in a state of homeliness. The granting of homeliness is the essence of home. It is already approaching—namely, in the Joyous, wherein the Serene first makes its appearance.

Yet what is now already approaching, still remains the sought-after. Since, however, the Joyous only draws near where it is met and welcomed by the composition of poetry, therefore the angels, heralds of the Serene, appear only if there are any who are composing. That is why there occurs in the poem "Homecoming" the phrase:

249

". . . For whatever poets meditate or sing
   Is of value chiefly to the angels and to him."

The song of the poetic word is of value "chiefly
to the angels," for they, as heralds of the Serene,
are the first "to draw near"; "and to him" the
poetic saying is of value. Here the "and" really
means "to him more than anybody."

Who is he? If it is "to him" that the writing
of poetry is most valuable, and poetry tells of
the Joyous, then he dwells in the Most Joyous.
But what is this and where is it?

The cloud, "writing of the Joyous," provides
the clue. The cloud hovers between the summits
of the Alps, and covers the mountain ravines,
down into whose unlighted depths the serenifying beam of light penetrates. That is why young
Chaos "celebrates" a "loving strife" there "beneath the rocks," and "celebrates" "joyously
shuddering." But the cloud, a "hill in the heav-
ens" (IV, 71), dreams between the heights towards the Joyous. The cloud, as it composes,
points upward into the Serene.

"Meanwhile the silver heights gleam peace-
   fully above,
   Already the luminous snow up there is full
      of roses.
   And yet higher up still above the light there
      dwells the pure
   Blissful god rejoicing in the play of holy
      beams."

In the Alps there occurs that increasingly still
self-surmounting of the high right up to the very

250

highest. The peaks of that mountain chain, which is the furthest embassy of earth, arise into the light to meet the "angel of the year." Therefore they are the "peaks of time." But further up yet above the light, the Serene first clarifies itself into the pure serenification, without which even the light would not have its brightness allotted to it. The highest "above the light" is the streaming lighting itself. This pure lighting, which for each "space" and each "temporal space" houses (i.e. grants, here) a vacant place—this we call the Serene,[1] after an older word of our mother-tongue. At one and the same time it is the clarity (*claritas*) in whose brightness everything clear remains, and the highness (*serenitas*) by whose strength everything high stands firm, and the joyfulness (*hilaritas*) in whose play every liberated thing hovers. The Serene preserves and holds everything in tranquillity and wholeness. The Serene is fundamentally healing. It is the holy. For the poet, the "highest" and the "holy" are one and the same: the Serene. As the origin of all that is joyous, it remains the Most Joyous. Here there occurs the pure serenification. Here in the "highest" dwells the "high one," who is who he is, as having en-joyed "the play of holy beams": the Joyous *One*. If he is a person, then he seems inclined "to create joy, with us." Since his essence is serenification, so "he loves" to "open out" and to "illumine." Through the clear Serene he "opens" things out to that in their surroundings which causes joy. Through the joyful Serene he illumines the spirit of men,

251

so that their nature may be open to what is genuine in their fields, towns and houses. Through the high Serene he first lets the gloomy depth gape open to its illumination. What would depth be without lighting?

Even the "sorrowing ones" are again made joyful by the "Joyous One," though this be done "with slow hand." He does not take away the grief but changes it, whilst letting the sorrowing ones guess that the grief itself arises only out of "old joys." The Joyous One is the "father" of all that causes joy. He, who dwells in the Serene, now first allows himself to be named after this dwelling-place. The high is called "the heaven," Αἰθήρ. The wafting "air" and the clarifying "light" and the "earth" which blossoms with them are the "three in one," in which the Serene becomes serene and sends forth the Joyous and sends its greeting to men in the Joyous.

But how does the Serene reach men from its height? The Joyous One and the joyous heralds of the serenification, the father heaven and the angel of the house—earth—and the angel of the year—light—are capable of nothing by themselves. The three together, although for everything joyous they are the dearest that dwell within the range of the Serene, must in its "essence," namely in the serenification, almost exhaust themselves, if there is not at times one who first (and therefore alone) comes singing to meet the Joyous One and already forms part of him. That is why there occurs in the elegy "The Wanderer" (whose very name shows its connection with the later elegy "Homecoming") the following passage (IV, 105f):

> "And so I am alone. But thou, above the clouds,
> Father of the Fatherland! Mighty Heaven! And thou,
> Earth and Light! Ye three in one, who rule and love,
> Eternal Gods! The bonds shall never break that bind me to you.
> Gone forth from you, with you too have I wandered,
> And more experienced now, I bring you Joyous Ones back."

Earth and light, the angels of the house and year, are called here in "the voyage," "gods." Even in the first fair-copy of the elegy "Homecoming" Hölderlin still wrote "gods of the year" and "gods of the house." Similarly in the first fair-copy of the last stanza of "Homecoming" (I, 94), instead of "without the joyful ones" we read "without the gods." Is it that in the later conception of the poem the gods have been reduced to mere angels? Or have angels made their appearance as well as gods? No—it is that now by the name "angels" the essence of what were previously called "gods" is more purely expressed. For the gods are the serenifiers, who in the serenification announce the greeting which the Serene sends. The Serene is the origin of the greeting, i.e. of the angelic, wherein the innermost essence of the gods consists. By using this

253

word "gods" sparingly and hesitating to apply the name, the poet has made more apparent the peculiar quality of the gods, as being the heralds through whom the Serene sends greeting.

The returning wanderer has acquired more experience in the essence of the gods, i.e. of the joyous ones.

"That which thou seekest is near, and already coming to meet thee."

The poet has a much clearer view of the Serene. The Joyous which meets him in the sight of home, he now sees as what becomes serene only out of the Most Joyous and, coming from there alone, stays near. But if now "Whatever poets meditate or sing" is of more value "to him" than to any—to the high father heaven, must not the poet who is seeking the Most Joyous take up his residence there where the joyous ones dwell—in that place therefore where, according to the first stanza of the "Rhine Hymn" (IV, 172), there are the

". . . Steps of the alpine chain
   Which is for me the divinely built,
   The citadel of the heavenly ones
   As in the ancient belief, but where
   Much still determined secretly
   Reaches mankind; . . ."?

But now the "homecoming" plainly leads the poet away from the "Alpine chain" over the water of the lake to the shore of the land of his birth. The sojourn "beneath the Alps," the proximity to the Most Joyous, is entirely given up for the return home. Certainly it is even more strange that still above the waters which bear the poet away from the Alpine range, and beneath the wings of the vessel that carries him off, there appears the Joyous:

> "Far on the level of the lake was one joyous undulation
> Beneath the sails."

Joyousness bursts into flower at the farewell to the "citadel of the heavenly ones." The Bodensee is also called "the Swabian Sea," and if we think of it in a geographical or commercial context, or in connection with home, then we mean the lake which lies between the Alps and the upper reaches of the Danube and through which the youthful Rhine also flows. Thus we still think of this water unpoetically. And how much longer are we going to? How long are we going to imagine that there was first of all a part of nature existing for itself and a landscape existing for itself, and that then with the help of "poetic experiences" this landscape became coloured with myth? How long are we going to prevent ourselves from experiencing the actual as actual? How long will Germans ignore the message which Hölderlin gave in the first stanza of the "Patmos Hymn"?

> "Near and
> Hard to grasp is the god.
> But where danger is,

The deliverer too grows strong.
In the darkness dwell
The eagles and fearless
The sons of the Alps go out over the abyss
On lightly built bridges.
Therefore, since massed around are
The peaks of time
And the dear ones dwell near to one another,
Tired on mountains farthest apart,
Grant innocent water,
O give us wings, to go over
Loyal-mindedly and return."

The poet must "go over" to the "Alpine range"; but "loyal-mindedly" implies that out of loyalty to his homeland he will return there, where according to the phrase from "Homecoming" what is sought-after "is near." So, therefore, proximity to the Most Joyous (and that means also proximity to the source of all that is joyous) is not there "beneath the Alps." So there must be some mystery in this proximity to the source. Then the Swabian homeland, far removed from the Alps, must be that very place of proximity to the source. Yes, that is how it is. The first stanzas of the hymn "The Voyage" declare it to be so. Hölderlin published this hymn in 1802, together with the elegy "Homecoming," in a number of the Almanac "Flora." This hymn, which is full of riddles, begins by invoking the homeland. The poet deliberately gives it the old name "Suevien." By this means he invokes the oldest, innermost essence—still hidden, but long

since already prepared in advance—of home
(IV, 167).

The hymn "The Voyage" begins:

"Blissful Suevien, my mother,
Thou too, like the more splendid, the sister
    Lombarda yonder,
Traversed by a hundred streams!
And with trees enough, white-blossoming and
    rosy,
And full with darker, wild, deepgreen-grow-
    ing foliage,
And with the Swiss alpine range overshad-
    owing,
Surrounding you; for near the hearth of the
    house
Thou dwellest, and hearest how within
From silver offering-bowls
The spring rushes, poured out
By pure hands, when
Crystalline ice is touched
By warm rays and
The snowy peak, overthrown by the swift-
    inciting light,
Floods the earth over
With purest water. Therefore is
Loyalty innate in thee. Whatever dwells near
    the source
Will leave the place regretfully.
And thy children, the cities,
On the lake that vanishes in the distance,
On Neckar's pastures, on the Rhine,
They all feel there could be
Nowhere better to dwell."

Suevien, the mother, dwells near the hearth of the house. The hearth keeps watch over the ever-reserved glow of the fire, which when it bursts into flame, opens out the airs and light into the Serene. Around the fire of the hearth is the workshop, where the secretly-determined is forged. "Hearth of the house," i.e. of the maternal earth, is the source of the serenification, whose light first pours out in streams over the earth. Suevien dwells near the source. This fact, that it dwells near, is twice mentioned. The homeland itself dwells near. It is the point of proximity to the hearth and source. Suevien, the maternal voice, points towards the essence of the fatherland. It is in this proximity to the source that neighbourhood to the Most Joyous is founded. What is innermost and best in the homeland consists solely in being just this proximity to the source—and nothing else except that. Therefore, too, in this homeland loyalty to the source is innate. That is why anyone who has to forsake this point of proximity does so regretfully. But now, if the innermost essence of the homeland consists in being the point of proximity to the Most Joyous, then what is homecoming?

Homecoming is the return into the proximity of the source.

But such a return is only possible for one who has previously, and perhaps for a long time now, borne on his shoulders as the wanderer the burden of the voyage, and has gone over into the source, so that he could there experience what the nature of the Sought-For might be, and then be able to come back more experienced, as the Seeker.

> "That which thou seekest is near, and already coming to meet thee."

The now dominating proximity makes the Near be near and yet at the same time makes it the sought-after, and therefore not near. Otherwise we would take proximity to be the smallest possible measurement of the distance between two places. Now on the contrary the essence of proximity seems to consist in bringing near the Near, while keeping it at a distance. Proximity to the source is a mystery.

But now if homecoming means becoming at home in proximity to the source, then must not the return home consist chiefly, and perhaps for a long time, in getting to know this mystery, or even first of all in learning how to get to know it. But we never get to know a mystery by unveiling or analysing it; we only get to know it by carefully guarding the mystery *as* mystery. But how can it be carefully guarded—this mystery of proximity—without even being known? For the sake of this knowledge there must always be another who comes home for the first time and tells of the mystery.

> "But the best, the discovery, that lies beneath the arc
> Of holy peace, is reserved from youth and from age."

"The treasure," the innermost essence of the homeland, "all that is German," is reserved. Proximity to the source is a proximity which reserves something. It withholds the Most Joyous. It keeps it and stores it away for the Comers, but this proximity does not take the Most Joyous right away, it only causes it to appear just *in this character* of the Stored-Away. In the essence of proximity a clandestine process of reservation takes place. The fact that proximity to the Most Joyous reserves the Near, is the mystery of proximity. The poet knows that, in calling the discovery "the reserved," he is saying something which the ordinary understanding will struggle against. To say that something is near and that at the same time it remains at a distance—this is tantamount either to violating the fundamental law of ordinary thought, the principle of contradiction, or on the other hand to playing with empty words, or merely to making a presumptuous suggestion. That is why the poet, almost as soon as he has spoken the line about the mystery of the reserving proximity, has to descend to the phrase:

"Foolish is my speech."

But nevertheless he is speaking. The poet must speak, for

"It is joy."

Is it any unspecified joy over something, or is it joy which is only joy through comprehending in itself the essence of all joys? What is joy? The original essence of joy is the process of becoming at home in proximity to the source. For in this proximity there draws near in welcome the serenification, wherein the Serene makes its appearance. The poet comes home, in the act of coming into proximity with the source. The poet comes into this proximity, in the act of telling of the mystery of proximity to the Near. He tells of this, in the act of writing of the Most Joyous. The writing of poetry is not primarily a cause of joy to the poet, rather the writing of poetry *is* joy, is serenification, because it is in writing that the principal return home consists. The elegy "Homecoming" is not a poem about homecoming; rather the elegy itself, taken as the very poetry of which it is comprised, is the actual homecoming—a homecoming which is continually being enacted so long as its message sounds out like a bell in the speech of German people. To write poetry means to exist in that joy, which preserves in words the mystery of proximity to the Most Joyous. Joy is *the* joy of the poet, as he puts it when he says (line 100) "our joy." The joy in writing is the knowledge of the fact that in everything joyous which is already coming to meet one, the Most Joyous sends its greeting, while reserving itself. In order therefore that the reserving proximity to the Most Joyous may remain guarded, the poetic word must take care that what sends greeting out of the Joyous (but sends greeting as the Self-Reserving), must not be too precipitate or become lost. So it is that, since care must be taken to guard the self-reserving

261

proximity to the Most Joyous, care enters into the Joyous.

Therefore the joy of the poet is in fact the care of the singer, whose singing guards the Most Joyous as the reserved, and brings the sought-for near in a reserving proximity.

But how is the poet to tell of the Most Joyous, if care has entered into the Joyous? At the time of the elegy "Homecoming" and the hymn "The Voyage," Hölderlin noted in an "Epigram" how the song of the Most Joyous, i.e. of the reserved, and therefore too the "Song of the German," was to be sung; the epigram bears the title "Sophocles," and runs:

> "Many have sought in vain to tell joyously of the Most Joyous. Now at last it declares itself to me, now in this grief."

Now we understand why, at the time when he came home to the homeland which constituted the point of reserving proximity to the source, the poet had to translate "The Tragedies of Sophocles." Grief, separated from mere melancholy by a gap, is joy which is serenified for the Most Joyous, so long as it still reserves itself and hesitates. For from where else could proceed the far-reaching inner light of grief, if it did not covertly originate in joy for the Most Joyous?

Certainly Hölderlin's poetic dialogue with Sophocles in the "Translation" and "Notes" does indeed form a part of the poetic homecoming, but it does not comprise the whole of it. For this reason the dedication, with which Hölderlin launched his translation of the "Tragedies of Sophocles," ends with the declaration (V, 91):

"I wish too, if there is time, to sing of the parents of our princes, and of their thrones and of the angels of our holy fatherland."

The timid word "too" does duty here for "really." For both now and subsequently the song is of value "chiefly to the angels and to him." The High One who inhabits the Serene of the holy, draws near sooner than any within the reserving proximity, in which the sparing joy of the poet has become at home. But

"To grasp him, our joy is scarcely large enough."

"To grasp" means to name the High One himself. To name poetically means: to cause the High One himself to appear in words,[2] not merely to tell of his dwelling-place, the Serene, the holy, not merely to name him with reference to his dwelling-place. But for the naming of him himself, the very sorrowing joy itself will not suffice, even though it sojourns in fitting proximity to the High One.

Sometimes, certainly, "the holy" can be named and the word spoken out of its serenification. But these "holy" words are not "names" that really name:

". . . Holy names are lacking."

Who this actually is that dwells in the holy—to tell this and in telling it cause him to appear himself—for this the naming word is lacking. That is why the poetic "singing," because it lacks the real, the naming word, still remains a song without words—"lyre-music." Certainly the "song" of the lyre-player does throughout follow the High One. The singer's "soul" does indeed gaze into the Serene, but the singer does not see the High One himself. The singer is blind. In the poem "The Blind Singer," to which a phrase from Sophocles is prefaced, Hölderlin says (IV, 58):

"After him, my lyre! With him lives
My song, and, as the spring follows the stream,
Whithersoever he thinks, there must I away and
Follow the sure one on the wandering path."

"Lyre-music"—that is the tentative name for the hesitant singing of the troubled singer:

"But lyre music lends to each hour its sounds,
And perhaps rejoices the heavenly ones who draw near.
This makes ready. . . ."

To prepare joyously the fitting proximity to the Near for the greeting heralds, who bring greeting from the still-reserved discovery—that is what determines the vocation of the homecoming poet. The holy does indeed appear. But the god remains far off. The time of the reserved discovery is the age when the god is lacking.

264

This "failure" of the god is the reason for the lack of "holy names." Nevertheless, because the discovery in being reserved is at the same time near, the failing god sends greeting in the Near of the heavenly. That is why "god's failure" is yet no lack. Therefore too the people of the country may not attempt to make to themselves a god by cunning and thus put aside by force the supposed lack. But neither may they accommodate themselves merely by calling on an accustomed god. True, by this means the presence of the failure would be overlooked. But if the proximity were not determined by the failure and hence reserving, then the discovery could not be near in the way in which it is near. So for the poet's care there is only one possibility: without fear of the appearance of godlessness he must remain near the failure of the god, and wait long enough in the prepared proximity of the failure, until out of the proximity of the failing god the initial word is granted, which names the High One.

In the same number of the almanac in which the elegy "Homecoming" and the hymn "The Voyage" appeared, Hölderlin published a poem inscribed "The Poet's Vocation." This poem culminates in the stanza (IV, 147):

"But fearless man remains, as he must,
Alone before God, simplicity protects him,
And no weapon needs he, and no
Cunning, till the time when God's failure
helps."

The vocation of the poet is homecoming, by which the homeland is first made ready as the land of proximity to the source. To guard the mystery of the reserving proximity to the Most Joyous, and in the process of guarding it to unfold it—that is the care of homecoming. Therefore the poem ends with the lines:

"Cares like these, whether he wills or no, a singer
Must bear in his soul and often, but the others not."

Who are "the others" to whom that blunt "not" is spoken? The poem which ends thus, bears at its head the dedication "To Kindred Ones." But why should the "Homecoming" be spoken first to the people of the country, who have always been in the homeland? The homecoming poet is met by the hastening greeting of the people. They seem to be kindred, but they are not so yet—kindred, that is, with him, the poet. But supposing it was the others mentioned at the end who were to become first the kindred of the poet, then why does the poet exclude them from the care of the singer?

The blunt "not" does indeed exempt "the others" from the care of poetic speech, but it in no way exempts them from the care of hearing that which "poets meditate or sing" here in "Homecoming." The "not" is the mysterious call "to" the others in the fatherland, to become hearers, in order that for the first time they

266

should learn to know the essence of the homeland. "The others" must for the first time learn to consider the mystery of the reserving proximity. Thinking of this kind first produces the deliberating ones, who do not precipitate the reserved and (in the phrase of the poem) guarded discovery. Out of these deliberating ones will come the slow ones of the long-enduring spirit, which itself learns again to persevere with the still-continuing failure of the god. The deliberating ones and the slow ones are for the first time the careful ones. Because they think of that which is written of in the poem, they are directed with the singer's care towards the mystery of the reserving proximity. Through this single turning towards the same object the careful hearers are related with the care of the speaker, "the others" are the "kindred" of the poet.

Supposing then that those residing on the soil of the native land are not yet those who have come home to the peculiar essence of home; and supposing also that it is characteristic of the *poetic* essence of homecoming to be (above and apart from the merely casual possession of domestic things and the inner life) open to the source of the Joyous—supposing *both* of these things, then are not those sons of the homeland who though far distant from the soil of home, still gaze at the home shining towards them, and devote their life and sacrifice it lavishly for the still-reserved discovery—are not these sons of the homeland the nearest kindred of the poet? Their

267

sacrifice holds concealed the poetic call to the dearest in the homeland, even though the reserved discovery should remain reserved.

It does remain thus, if those "who are beset with care in the fatherland" are transformed into the careful ones. Then there is a kinship with the poet. Then there is a homecoming. But this homecoming is the future of the historical being of the German people.

They are the people of writing *and* of thinking. For now there must be thinkers in advance, so that the word of the writer may be heard. It is the thought of the careful ones alone—directed to the written mystery of the reserving proximity —that is the "remembrance of the poet." In this remembrance there is a first beginning, which will in time become a far-reaching kinship with the homecoming poet.

But—if through remembrance "the others" become kindred—then how are they not turned *towards* the poet? Does the blunt "not" with which "Homecoming" ends still apply to them? It does apply. But something else applies too. "The others," if they have become kindred, are also "the others" in yet another sense at the same time.

In hearkening to the spoken word and thinking about it so that it may be properly interpreted and retained, they are helping the poet. This help corresponds to the essence of the reserving proximity, in which the Most Joyous draws near. For just as the greeting heralds must help, in order that the Serene may reach men in the serenification, so too there must be among men a First, who poetically rejoices in the face of the greeting heralds, in order that he, alone and in advance, may first conceal the greeting in the word.

But because the word, once it has been spoken, slips out of the protection of the care-worn poet, he cannot easily hold fast in all its truth to the spoken knowledge of the reserved discovery and of the reserving proximity. Therefore the poet turns to the others, so that their remembrance may help towards an understanding of the poetic word, with the result that in the process of understanding each may have a homecoming in the manner appropriate for him.

On account of the protection, in which for the poet and his kindred the spoken word must remain, the singer of "Homecoming" mentions at the same time in the poem "The Poet's Vocation" the other relationship between the poet and "the others." There Hölderlin speaks the following lines about the poet and his knowledge of the mystery of the reserving proximity (IV, 147):

". . . But alone he cannot easily maintain it,
And the poet gladly joins with others,
So that they may understand how to help."

HÖLDERLIN AND THE
ESSENCE OF POETRY

THE FIVE POINTERS

1. Writing poetry: "That most innocent of all occupations." (III, 377.)

2. "Therefore has language, most dangerous of possessions, been given to man . . . so that he may affirm what he is. . . ." (IV, 246.)

3. "Much has man learnt.
   Many of the heavenly ones has he named,
   Since we have been a conversation
   And have been able to hear from one another." (IV, 343.)

4. "But that which remains, is established by the poets." (IV, 63.)

5. "Full of merit, and yet poetically, dwells
   Man on this earth." (VI, 25.)

Why has Hölderlin's work been chosen for the purpose of showing the essence of poetry? Why not Homer or Sophocles, why not Virgil or Dante, why not Shakespeare or Goethe? The essence of poetry is realised in the works of these poets too, and more richly even, than in the creative work of Hölderlin, which breaks off so early and abruptly.

This may be so. And yet Hölderlin has been chosen, and he alone. But generally speaking is it possible for the universal essence of poetry to be read off from the work of one single poet?

Whatever is universal, that is to say, what is valid for many, can only be reached through a process of comparison. For this, one requires a sample containing the greatest possible diversity of poems and kinds of poetry. From this point of view Hölderlin's poetry is only one among many others. By itself it can in no way suffice as a criterion for determining the essence of poetry. Hence we fail in our purpose at the very outset. Certainly—so long as we take "essence of poetry" to mean what is gathered together into a universal concept, which is then valid in the same way for every poem. But this universal which thus applies equally to every particular, is always the indifferent, that essence which can never become essential.

Yet it is precisely this essential element of the essence that we are searching for—that which compels us to decide whether we are going to take poetry seriously and if so how, whether and to what extent we can bring with us the presuppositions necessary if we are to come under the sway of poetry.

Hölderlin has not been chosen because his work, one among many, realises the universal essence of poetry, but solely because Hölderlin's poetry was borne on by the poetic vocation to write expressly of the essence of poetry. For us Hölderlin is in a pre-eminent sense *the poet of the poet.* That is why he compels a decision.

But—to write about the poet, is this not a symptom of a perverted narcissism and at the same time a confession of inadequate richness

271

of vision? To write about the poet, is that not a senseless exaggeration, something decadent and a blind alley?

The answer will be given in what follows. To be sure, the path by which we reach the answer is one of expediency. We cannot here, as would have to be done, expound separately each of Hölderlin's poems one after the other. Instead let us take only five pointers which the poet gave on the subject of poetry. The necessary order in these sayings and their inner connectedness ought to bring before our eyes the essential essence of poetry.

1.

In a letter to his mother in January 1799, Hölderlin calls the writing of poetry "that most innocent of all occupations" (III, 377). To what extent is it the "most innocent"? Writing poetry appears in the modest guise of *play*. Unfettered, it invents its world of images and remains immersed in the realm of the imagined. This play thus avoids the seriousness of decisions, which always in one way or another create guilt. Hence writing poetry is completely harmless. And at the same time it is ineffectual; since it remains mere saying and speaking. It has nothing about it of action, which grasps hold directly of the real and alters it. Poetry is like a dream, and not reality; a playing with words, and not the seriousness of action. Poetry is harmless and ineffectual. For what can be less dangerous than mere speech? But in taking poetry to be the "most innocent of all occupations," we have not yet comprehended its essence. At any rate this gives us an indication of where we must look for it. Poetry creates its works in the realm and out of the "material" of language. What does Hölderlin say about language? Let us hear a second saying of the poet.

2.

In a fragmentary sketch, dating from the same period (1800) as the letter just quoted, the poet says:

"But man dwells in huts and wraps himself in the bashful garment, since he is more fervent and more attentive too in watching over the spirit, as the priestess the divine flame; this is his understanding. And therefore he has been given arbitrariness, and to him, godlike, has been given higher power to command and to accomplish, and therefore has language, most dangerous of possessions, been given to man, so that creating, destroying, and perishing and returning to the ever-living, to the mistress and mother, he may affirm what he is—that he has inherited, learned from thee, thy most divine possession, all-preserving love." (IV, 246.)

Language, the field of the "most innocent of all occupations," is the "most dangerous of possessions." How can these two be reconciled? Let us put this question aside for the moment and consider the three preliminary questions: 1. Whose possession is language? 2. To what extent is it the most dangerous of possessions? 3. In what sense is it really a possession?

First of all we notice where this saying about language occurs: in the sketch for a poem which is to describe who man is, in contrast to the other beings of nature; mention is made of the rose, the swans, the stag in the forest (IV, 300 and 385). So, distinguishing plants from animals, the fragment begins: "But man dwells in huts."

And who then is man? He who must affirm what he is. To affirm means to declare; but at the same time it means: to give in the declaration a guarantee of what is declared. Man is *he* who he *is*, precisely in the affirmation of his own existence. This affirmation does not mean here an additional and supplementary expression of human existence, but it does in the process make plain the existence of man. But what must man affirm? That he belongs to the earth. This relation of belonging to consists in the fact that man is heir and learner in all things. But all these things are in conflict. That which keeps things apart in opposition and thus at the same time binds them together, is called by Hölderlin "intimacy." The affirmation of belonging to this intimacy occurs through the creation of a world and *i*ts ascent, and likewise through the destruction of a world and its decline. The affirmation of human existence and hence its essential consummation occurs through freedom of decision. This freedom lays hold of the necessary and places itself in the bonds of a supreme obligation. This bearing witness of belonging to all that is existent, becomes actual as history. In order that history may be possible, language has been given to man. It is one of man's possessions.

But to what extent is language the "most dangerous of possessions?" It is the danger of all dangers, because it creates initially the possibility of a danger. Danger is the threat to existence from what is existent. But now it is only by virtue of language at all that man is exposed to something manifest, which, *as* what is existent, afflicts and enflames man in his existence, and as what is non-existent deceives and disappoints. It is language which first creates the manifest conditions for menace and confusion to existence, and thus the possibility of the loss of existence, that is to say—danger. But language is not only the danger of dangers, but necessarily conceals in itself a continual danger for itself. Language has the task of making manifest in its work the existent, and of preserving it as such. In it, what is purest and what is most concealed, and likewise what is complex and ordinary, can be expressed in words. Even the essential word, if it is to be understood and so become a possession in common, must make itself ordinary. Accordingly it is remarked in another fragment of Hölderlin's: "Thou spokest to the Godhead, but this you have all forgotten, that the first-fruits are never for mortals, they belong to the gods. The fruit must become more ordinary, more everyday, and then it will be mortals' own." (IV, 238.) The pure and the ordinary are both equally something said. Hence the word as word never gives any direct guarantee as to whether it is an essential word or a counterfeit. On the contrary—an essential word often looks in its simplicity like an unessential one. And on the other hand that which is dressed up to look like the essential, is only something recited by heart or repeated. Therefore language must constantly present itself in an appearance which it itself attests, and hence endanger what is most characteristic of it, the genuine saying.

In what sense however is this most dangerous thing one of man's possessions? Language is his own property. It is at his disposal for the purpose of communicating his experiences, resolutions and moods. Language serves to give information. As a fit instrument for this, it is a "possession." [3] But the essence of language does not consist entirely in being a means of giving information. This definition does not touch its essential essence, but merely indicates an effect of its essence. Language is not a mere tool, one of the many which man possesses; on the contrary, it is only language that affords the very possibility of standing in the openness of the existent. Only where there is language, is there world, i.e. the perpetually altering circuit of decision and production, of action and responsibility, but also of commotion and arbitrariness, of decay and confusion. Only where world predominates, is there history. Language is a possession[4] in a more fundamental sense. It is good for the fact that (i.e. it affords a guarantee that) man can *exist* historically. Language is not a tool at his disposal, rather it is that event which disposes of the supreme possibility

276

of human existence. We must first of all be certain of this essence of language, in order to comprehend truly the sphere of action of poetry and with it poetry itself. How does language become actual? In order to find the answer to this question, let us consider a third saying of Hölderlin's.

3.

We come across this saying in a long and involved sketch for the unfinished poem which begins "Versöhnender, der du nimmergeglaubt . . ." (IV, 162ff. and 339ff.):

"Much has man learnt.
 Many of the heavenly ones has he named,
 Since we have been a conversation
 And have been able to hear from one another." (IV, 343.)

Let us first pick out from these lines the part which has a direct bearing on what we have said so far: "Since we have been a conversation . . ." We—mankind—are a conversation. The being of men is founded in language. But this only becomes actual in *conversation*. Nevertheless the latter is not merely a manner in which language is put into effect, rather it is only as conversation that language is essential. What we usually mean by language, namely, a stock of words and syntactical rules, is only a threshold of language. But now what is meant by "a conversation"? Plainly, the act of speaking with others about something. Then speaking also brings about the process of coming together. But Hölderlin says: "Since we

277

have been a conversation and have been able to hear from one another." Being able to hear is not a mere consequence of speaking with one another, on the contrary it is rather pre-supposed in the latter process. But even the ability to hear is itself also adapted to the possibility of the word and makes use of it. The ability to speak and the ability to hear are equally fundamental. We are a conversation—and that means: we can hear from one another. We are a conversation, that always means at the same time: we are a *single* conversation. But the unity of a conversation consists in the fact that in the essential word there is always manifest that one and the same thing on which we agree, and on the basis of which we are united and so are essentially ourselves. Conversation and its unity support our existence.

But Hölderlin does not say simply: we are a conversation—but: "Since we have been a conversation . . ." Where the human faculty of speech is present and is exercised, that is not by itself sufficient for the essential actualisation of language—conversation. Since when have we been a conversation? Where there is to be a *single* conversation, the essential word must be constantly related to the one and the same. Without this relation an argument too is absolutely impossible. But the one and the same can only be manifest in the light of something perpetual and permanent. Yet permanence and perpetuity only appear when what persists and is present begins to shine. But that happens in the moment when time opens out and extends. After man has placed himself in the presence of something perpetual, then only can he expose himself to the changeable, to that which comes and goes; for only the persistent is changeable. Only after "ravenous time" has been riven into present, past and future, does the possibility arise of agreeing on something permanent. We have been a single conversation since the time when it "is time." Ever since time arose, we have *existed* historically. Both—existence as a *single* conversation and historical existence—are alike ancient, they belong together and are the same thing.

Since we have been a conversation—man has learnt much and named many of the heavenly ones. Since language really became actual as conversation, the gods have acquired names and a world has appeared. But again it should be noticed: the presence of the gods and the appearance of the world are not merely a consequence of the actualisation of language, they are contemporaneous with it. And this to the extent that it is precisely in the naming of the gods, and in the transmutation of the world into word, that the real conversation, which we ourselves are, consists.

But the gods can acquire a name only by addressing and, as it were, claiming us. The word which names the gods is always a response to such a claim. This response always springs from the responsibility of a destiny. It is in the process by which the gods bring our existence to language, that we enter the sphere of the decision as to whether we are to yield ourselves to the gods or withhold ourselves from them.

Only now can we appreciate in its entirety what is meant by: "Since we have been a conversation . . ." Since the gods have led us into conversation, since time has been time, ever since then the basis of our existence has been a conversation. The proposition that language is the supreme event of human existence has through it acquired its meaning and foundation.

But the question at once arises: how does this conversation, which we are, begin? Who accomplishes this naming of the gods? Who lays hold of something permanent in ravenous time and fixes it in the word? Hölderlin tells us with the sure simplicity of the poet. Let us hear a fourth saying.

4.

This saying forms the conclusion of the poem "Remembrance" and runs:

"But that which remains, is established by the poets." (IV. 63.)

This saying throws light on our question about the essence of poetry. Poetry is the act of establishing by the word and in the word. What is established in this manner? The permanent. But can the permanent be established then? Is it not that which has always been present? No! Even the permanent must be fixed so that it will not be carried away, the simple must be wrested from confusion, proportion must be set before what lacks proportion. That which supports and dominates the existent in its entirety must become manifest. Being must be opened out, so that the existent may appear. But this very permanent is the transitory. "Thus, swiftly passing is everything heavenly; but not in vain." (IV, 163f.) But that this should remain, is "Entrusted to the poets as a care and a service" (IV, 145). The poet names the gods and names all things in that which they are. This naming does not consist merely in something already known being supplied with a name; it is rather that when the poet speaks the essential word, the existent is by this naming nominated as what it is. So it becomes known *as* existent. Poetry is the establishing of being by means of the word. Hence that which remains is never taken from the transitory. The simple can never be picked out immediately from the intricate. Proportion does not lie in what lacks proportion. We never find the foundation in what is bottomless. Being is never an existent. But, because being and essence of things can never be calculated and derived from what is present, they must be freely created, laid down and given. Such a free act of giving is establishment.

But when the gods are named originally and the essence of things receives a name, so that things for the first time shine out, human existence is brought into a firm relation and given a basis. The speech of the poet is establishment not only in the sense of the free act of giving, but at the same time in the sense of the firm basing of human existence on its foundation.

If we conceive this essence of poetry as the establishing of being by means of the word, then we can have some inkling of the truth of that saying which Hölderlin spoke long after he had been received into the protection of the night of lunacy.

5.

We find this fifth pointer in the long and at the same time monstrous poem which begins:

"In the lovely azure there flowers with its
  Metallic roof the church-tower." (VI, 24ff.)

Here Hölderlin says (line 32f.):

"Full of merit, and yet poetically, dwells
  Man on this earth."

What man works at and pursues is through his own endeavours earned and deserved. "Yet" —says Hölderlin in sharp antithesis, all this does not touch the essence of his sojourn on this earth, all this does not reach the foundation of human existence. The latter is fundamentally "poetic." But we now understand poetry as the inaugural naming of the gods and of the essence of things. To "dwell poetically" means: to stand in the presence of the gods and to be involved in the proximity of the essence of things. Existence is "poetical" in its fundamental aspect—which means at the same time: in so far as it is established (founded), it is not a recompense, but a gift.

Poetry is not merely an ornament accompanying existence, not merely a temporary enthusiasm or nothing but an interest and amusement. Poetry is the foundation which supports history, and therefore it is not a mere appearance of culture, and absolutely not the mere "expression" of a "culture-soul."

That our existence is fundamentally poetic, this cannot in the last resort mean that it is really only a harmless game. But does not Hölderlin himself, in the first pointer which we quoted, call poetry "That most innocent of all occupations?" How can this be reconciled with the essence of poetry as we are now revealing it? This brings us back to the question which we laid aside in the first instance. In now proceeding to answer this question, we will try at the same time to summarise and bring before the inner eye the essence of poetry and of the poet.

First of all it appeared that the field of action of poetry is language. Hence the essence of poetry must be understood through the essence of language. Afterwards it became clear that poetry is the inaugural naming of being and of the essence of all things—not just any speech, but that particular kind which for the first time brings into the open all that which we then discuss and deal with in everyday language. Hence poetry never takes language as a raw material ready to hand, rather it is poetry which first makes language possible. Poetry is the primitive language of a historical people. Therefore, in just the reverse manner, the essence of language must be understood through the essence of poetry.

The foundation of human existence is conversation, in which language does truly become actual. But primitive language is poetry, in which being is established. Yet language is the "most dangerous of possessions." Thus poetry is the most dangerous work—and at the same time the "most innocent of all occupations."

In fact—it is only if we combine these two definitions and conceive them as one, that we fully comprehend the essence of poetry.

But is poetry then truly the most dangerous work? In a letter to a friend, immediately before leaving on his last journey to France, Hölderlin writes: "O Friend! The world lies before me brighter than it was, and more serious. I feel pleasure at how it moves onward, I feel pleasure when in summer 'the ancient holy father with calm hand shakes lightnings of benediction out of the rosy clouds." For amongst all that I can perceive of God, this sign has become for me the chosen one. I used to be able to exult over a new truth, a better insight into that which is above us and around us, now I am frightened lest in the end it should happen with me as with Tantalus of old, who received more from the gods than he was able to digest." (V, 321.)

The poet is exposed to the divine lightnings. This is spoken of in the poem which we must recognise as the purest poetry about the essence of poetry, and which begins:

"When on festive days a countryman goes
To gaze on his field, in the morning . . ."

(IV, 151ff.)

There, the last stanza says:

"Yet it behoves us, under the storms of God,
Ye poets! with uncovered head to stand,
With our own hand to grasp the very light-
ning-flash
Paternal, and to pass, wrapped in song,
The divine gift to the people."

And a year later, when he had returned to his
mother's house, struck down with madness, Hölderlin wrote to the same friend, recalling his stay
in France:

"The mighty element, the fire of heaven and
the stillness of men, their life amid nature, and
their limitation and contentment, have constantly seized me, and, as it is told of the heroes,
I can truly say that I have been struck by
Apollo." (V, 327.) The excessive brightness has
driven the poet into the dark. Is any further evidence necessary as to the extreme danger of his
"occupation"? The very destiny itself of the poet
tells everything. The passage in Hölderlin's "Empedocles" rings like a premonition:

"He, through whom the spirit speaks, must
leave betimes." (III, 154.)

And nevertheless: poetry is the "most innocent
of all occupations," Hölderlin writes to this effect
in his letter, not only in order to spare his

mother, but because he knows that this innocent fringe belongs to the essence of poetry, just as the valley does to the mountain; for how could this most dangerous work be carried on and preserved, if the poet were not "cast out" ("Empedocles" III, 191) from everyday life and protected *against* it by the apparent harmlessness of his occupation?

Poetry looks like a game and yet it is not. A game does indeed bring men together, but in such a way that each forgets himself in the process. In poetry on the other hand, man is re-united on the foundation of his existence. There he comes to rest; not indeed to the seeming rest of inactivity and emptiness of thought, but to that infinite state of rest in which all powers and relations are active (cf. the letter to his brother, dated 1st January, 1799. III, 368f.).

Poetry rouses the appearance of the unreal and of dream in the face of the palpable and clamorous reality, in which we believe ourselves at home. And yet in just the reverse manner, what the poet says and undertakes to be, is the real. So Panthea, with the clairvoyance of a friend, declares of "Empedocles" (III, 78):

> "That he himself should be, is
> What is life, and the rest of us are dreams of
> it."

So in the very appearance of its outer fringe the essence of poetry seems to waver and yet stands firm. In fact it is itself essentially establishment— that is to say: an act of firm foundation.

286

Yet every inaugural act remains a free gift, and Hölderlin hears it said: "Let poets be free as swallows" (IV, 168). But this freedom is not undisciplined arbitrariness and capricious desire, but supreme necessity.

Poetry, as the act of establishing being, is subject to a *two-fold* control. In considering these integral laws we first grasp the essence entire.

The writing of poetry is the fundamental naming of the gods. But the poetic word only acquires its power of naming, when the gods themselves bring us to language. How do the gods speak?

". . . . And signs to us from antiquity are the language of the gods." (IV, 135.)

The speech of the poet is the intercepting of these signs, in order to pass them on to his own people. This intercepting is an act of receiving and yet at the same time a fresh act of giving; for "in the first signs" the poet catches sight already of the completed message and in his word boldly presents what he has glimpsed, so as to tell in advance of the not-yet-fulfilled. So:

". . . the bold spirit, like an eagle
Before the tempests, flies prophesying
In the path of his advancing gods." (IV, 135.)

The establishment of being is bound to the signs of the gods. And at the same time the poetic word is only the interpretation of the "voice of the people." This is how Hölderlin names the sayings in which a people remembers that it be-

longs to the totality of all that exists. But often
this voice grows dumb and weary. In general
even it is not capable of saying of itself what is
true, but has need of those who explain it. The
poem which bears the title "Voice of the People,"
has been handed down to us in two versions. It is
above all the concluding stanzas which are different, but the difference is such that they supple-
ment one another. In the first version the ending
runs:

"Because it is pious, I honour for love of the
heavenly ones
The people's voice, the tranquil,
Yet for the sake of gods and men
May it not always be tranquil too willingly!"
(IV, 141.)

And the second version is:

". . . and truly
Sayings are good, for they are a reminder
Of the Highest, yet something is also needed
To explain the holy sayings." (IV, 144.)

In this way the essence of poetry is joined on
to the laws of the signs of the gods and of the
voice of the people, laws which tend towards and
away from each other. The poet himself stands
between the former—the gods, and the latter—
the people. He is one who has been cast out—
out into that *Between*, between gods and men.
But only and for the first time in this Between
is it decided, who man is and where he is settling

his existence. "Poetically, dwells man on this earth."

Unceasingly and ever more securely, out of the fullness of the images pressing about him and always more simply, did Hölderlin devote his poetic word to this realm of Between. And this compels us to say that he is the poet of the poet.

Can we continue now to suppose that Hölderlin is entangled in an empty and exaggerated narcissism due to inadequate richness of vision? Or must we recognise that this poet, from an excess of impetus, reaches out with poetic thought into the foundation and the midst of being. It is to *Hölderlin himself* that we must apply what he said of Oedipus in the late poem "In the lovely azure there flowers . . .":

> "King Oedipus has one
> Eye too many perhaps." (VI, 26.)

Hölderlin writes poetry about the essence of poetry—but not in the sense of a timelessly valid concept. This essence of poetry belongs to a determined time. But not in such a way that it merely conforms to this time, as to one which is already in existence. It is that Hölderlin, in the act of establishing the essence of poetry, first determines a new time. It is the time of the gods that have fled *and* of the god that is coming. It is the time of need, because it lies under a double lack and a double Not: the No-more of the gods that have fled and the Not-yet of the god that is coming.

The essence of poetry, which Hölderlin establishes, is in the highest degree historical, because it anticipates a historical time; but as a historical essence it is the sole essential essence.

The time is needy and therefore its poet is extremely rich—so rich that he would often like to relax in thoughts of those that have been and in eager waiting for that which is coming and would like only to sleep in this apparent emptiness. But he holds his ground in the Nothing of this night. Whilst the poet remains thus by himself in the supreme isolation of his mission, he fashions truth, vicariously and therefore truly, for his people. The seventh stanza of the elegy "Bread and Wine" (IV, 123f.) tells of this. What it has only been possible to analyse here intellectually, is expressed there poetically.

"But Friend! we come too late. The gods are
     alive, it is true,
  But up there above one's head in another
     world.
  Eternally they work there and seem to pay
     little heed
  To whether we live, so attentive are the
     Heavenly Ones.
  For a weak vessel cannot always receive them,
  Only now and then does man endure divine
     abundance.
  Life is a dream of them. But madness
  Helps, like slumber and strengthens need and
     night,
  Until heroes enough have grown in the iron
     cradle,

Hearts like, as before, to the Heavenly in
    power.
Thundering they come. Meanwhile it often
    seems
Better to sleep than to be thus without com-
    panions,
To wait thus, and in the meantime what to
    do and say
I know not, and what use are poets in a time
    of need?
But, thou sayest, they are like the wine-god's
    holy priests,
Who go from land to land in the holy night."

Our subject is the essence of truth. The question as to the nature of truth is not concerned with whether truth is the truth of practical experience or of economic calculation, whether it is the truth of a technical consideration or of political shrewdness, or, more particularly, the truth of scientific research or of art, or even the truth of contemplative thought or of religious belief. The essential question disregards all this and fixes its attention on the one thing that is the mark of "truth" of every kind.

Yet, questioning as we do the nature of truth, are we not in danger of losing ourselves in the void of the commonplace, which suffocates all thought? Does not the presumptuousness of such a question expose the baselessness of all philosophy? All radical thinking, all thinking that is turned to reality, must aim first and foremost at establishing, without any digressions, the real truth which can give us a standard and a yardstick against the prevailing confusion of opinion and calculation. In the face of this real need, what is the good of an "abstract" enquiry into the nature of truth, an enquiry which is bound to turn away from all reality? Is not the question as to the essential nature of truth the most inessential, the least obligatory of all the questions that could possibly be asked?

Nobody can evade the obvious cogency of these considerations. Nobody can simply ignore their urgent seriousness. But what is it that speaks in these considerations? "Sound" common sense. It harps on the claims of what is palpably useful and inveighs against all knowledge of the nature of "what-is" [5]—that essential knowledge which has long been called "Philosophy."

Common sense has its own necessity; it exacts its due with the weapon appropriate and peculiar to it, namely an appeal to the "self-evident" nature of its claims and considerations. Philosophy, however, can never refute common sense since common sense is deaf to the language of philosophy. Nor may it even wish to do so, since common sense is blind to the things which philosophy sets before her essence-seeking eyes.

Moreover we ourselves keep to the prudence of common sense inasmuch as we fancy ourselves safe in the multifarious "truths" of experience and action, research, art, and faith. We ourselves support the "common sense" repudiation of all claims made by anything at all questionable.

If, therefore, we must ask after truth, then an answer is demanded to the question: "Where do we stand today?" We want to know what our position is. We call for the goal which shall be set for man, both *in* his history and *for* his history. We want the real "truth." Well, *truth* then!

But in calling for real "truth" we must already know what in fact is meant by truth. Or do we only know by "feeling" and in a "general" sort of way? Yet is not this vague "knowing" and this indifference to the vagueness of it even more wretched than plain ignorance of the nature of truth?

293

1. THE CONVENTIONAL CONCEPT OF TRUTH

What do we ordinarily understand by "truth"? This exalted but at the same time overworked and almost exhausted word "truth" means: that which makes something true into a truth. What is "something true"? We say, for example: "It is a true pleasure to collaborate in the accomplishment of this task." We mean, it is a pure, real joy. The True is the Real. In the same way we speak of "true coin" as distinct from false. False coin is not really what it seems. It is only a "seeming" and therefore unreal. The unreal stands for the opposite of the real. But counterfeit coin too is something real. Hence we say more precisely: "Real coin is genuine coin." Yet both are "real," the counterfeit coin in circulation no less than the genuine. Therefore the truth of the genuine coin cannot be verified by its reality. The question returns: What do "genuine" and "true" mean here? Genuine coin is that real thing whose reality agrees with (*in der Uebereinstimmung steht mit*) what we always and in advance "really" mean by "coin." Conversely, where we suspect false coin we say: "There is something not quite right here" (*Hier stimmt etwas nicht*). On the other hand we say of something that is "as it should be": "It's right" (*es stimmt*). The *thing* (*Sache*) is right.

We call "true" not only a real pleasure, genuine coin and all actualities of that sort, we also and principally call "true" or "false" our statements concerning such actualities as are themselves true or false in their kind, which may be thus or thus in their reality. A statement is true when what it means and says agrees with the thing of which it speaks. Here too we say: "It's right." Though now it is not the *thing* that is right but the *proposition* (*Satz*).

The True, then, be it a true thing or a true proposition, is that which is right, which corresponds (*das Stimmende*). Being true and truth here mean correspondence, and that in a double sense: firstly the correspondence of a thing with the idea of it as conceived in advance (*dem über sie Vorgemeinten*), and secondly the correspondence of that which is intended by the statement with the thing itself.[6]

The dual aspect of this correspondence is brought out very clearly by the traditional definition of truth: *veritas est adaequatio rei et intellectus*. Which can be taken to mean: truth is the approximation of thing (object) to perception. But it can also mean: truth is the approximation of perception to thing (object). Admittedly the above definition is usually employed only in the formula: *veritas est adaequatio intellectus ad rem*. Yet truth so understood, i.e. *propositional* truth, is only possible on the basis of *objective* truth, the *adaequatio rei ad intellectum*. Both conceptions of the nature of *veritas* always imply "putting oneself right by" (*sich richten nach*) something and thus conceive truth as *rightness* (*Richtigkeit*).

All the same, the one is not just the inversion

of the other. Rather is it the case that *intellectus* and *res* are thought of differently each time. In order to appreciate this we must trace the accepted formula for the conventional concept of truth back to its immediate (i.e. medieval) origins. *Veritas* as *adaequatio rei ad intellectum* does not imply the later, transcendental conception of Kant—possible only on the basis of man's subjectivity—that "objects conform to *(sich richten nach)* our perception," but rather the Christian theological belief that things are only what they are, if they are, to the extent that they, as created things *(ens creatum)* correspond to an *idea* preconceived in the *intellectus divinus,* that is to say, in the mind of God, and thus conform to the idea (are right) and are in this sense "true." The *intellectus humanus* is likewise an *ens creatum.* It must, as a faculty conferred by God on man, satisfy His idea. But the intellect only conforms to the idea in that it effects in its propositions that approximation of thought to thing, which, in its turn, must also conform to the idea. The possibility of human knowledge being true (granted that all that "is" is "created") has its basis in the fact that thing and proposition are to an equal extent in conformity with the idea and thus find themselves conforming to one another in the unity of the divine creative plan. *Veritas* as *adaequatio rei (creandæ) ad intellectum (divinum)* guarantees *veritas* as *adaequatio intellectus (humani) ad rem (creatum).* *Veritas* always means in its essence: *convenientia,* the accord of "what-is" itself, as creature, with the Creator, an accordance with the destiny of the creative order.

But this order, divorced from the idea of creation, can also be conceived in a general and indefinite way as world-order. The creative order as conceived by theology is supplanted by the possibility of planning everything with the aid of earthly reasoning (*Weltvernunft*), which is a law unto itself and can claim that its workings are immediately intelligible (what we call "logical"). Therefore, it is thought not to require any further proof that the essence of propositional truth consists in the rightness of the proposition. Even where, with conspicuous lack of success, we try to explain just how rightness may be achieved, we are already postulating rightness as the essence of truth. Similarly, objective truth always implies conformity of the object in question with the essential or "rational" idea of it. The impression is given—wrongly—that this definition of the essence of truth is independent of the explanation of the essential nature of all that "is," of its very *being* (*Sein alles Seienden*)—which explanation always involves a corresponding explanation of the essential nature of man as the vehicle and perfecter of the *intellectus*. Thus the formula for the essence of truth (*veritas est adaequatio intellectus et rei*) acquires a universal validity evident at once to everyone. Dominated by the self-evident nature of this concept of truth, the essentials of which remain for the most part

297

unperceived, we take it as equally self-evident that truth has an opposite and that there is such a thing as untruth. Propositional untruth (incorrectness) is the non-conformity of statement with thing. Objective untruth (non-genuineness: *Unechtheit*) is the non-conformity of what-is with its essence. In both cases untruth can be understood as a failure to agree. This failure is an exclusion from the nature of truth. For this reason untruth as the opposite of truth can be left out of account when it is a matter of coming to grips with the pure essence of truth.

But then, is there really any need for a special revelation of the nature of truth? Is not the pure essence of truth demonstrated adequately enough in the commonly accepted idea of it, which is vitiated by no theory and protected by its self-evident nature? If, on top of this, we take the reduction of propositional truth to objective truth for what it appears at first sight, namely a theological explanation, and if, further, we keep the philosophical definition completely free from all admixture of theology and limit the concept of truth to propositional truth, then we are at once brought face to face with an old, if not the oldest, tradition of thought, according to which truth is the *likeness* or *agreement* (*Uebereinstimmung*: ὁμοίωσις) of a statement (λόγος) to or with a given thing (πρᾶγμα). What is it that still remains in question, provided that we know what is meant by the "likeness or agreement of a statement to or with the thing"? Do we know that?

2. THE INNER POSSIBILITY OF AGREEMENT[7]

We speak of "agreement" in different senses. We say, for example, seeing two half-crowns lying on the table, that they agree with one another, are like one another. Both agree in identity of appearance. They have this in common and are therefore in this respect alike. Further, we speak of agreement when we say of one of these half-crowns: this coin is round. Here the statement "agrees" with the subject or thing. The relationship now obtains not between thing and thing, but between statement and thing. But in what do statement and thing agree, seeing that the referents are obviously different in appearance? The coin is of metal. The statement is in no sense material. The coin is round. The statement has absolutely nothing spatial about it. With the coin you can buy something. The statement about it can never be legal tender. But despite the disparity between the two, the above statement agrees with and is true of the coin. And, according to the accepted idea of truth, this agreement is supposed to be an approximation (*Angleichung*). How can something completely unlike —the statement—approximate to the coin? It would have to *become* the coin and present itself entirely in that form. No statement can do that. The moment it succeeded in doing so the statement, as statement, could no longer agree with the thing. In any approximation the statement has to remain, indeed it has first to become, what it is. In what does its nature, so entirely different from any other thing, consist? How can the statement, precisely by insisting on its own nature, approximate to something else, to the thing?

"Approximation" in this instance cannot mean a material likeness between two things unlike in kind. The nature of the approximation is rather determined by the kind of relationship obtaining between statement and thing. So long as this "relationship" remains indeterminate and its nature unfathomed, all argument as to the possibility or impossibility, the kind and degree of approximation, leads nowhere.

The statement about the coin relates "itself" to this thing by representing it[8] and saying of the thing represented "how it is," "what it is like," in whatever respect is important at that moment. The representative statement has its say about the thing represented, stating it to be *such as* it is. This "such-as" (*so-wie*)[9] applies to the representation and what it represents. "Representation" means here, if we disregard all "psychological" and "theory of consciousness" preconceptions, *letting something take up a position opposite to us, as an object.* The thing so opposed must, such being its position, come across the open towards us[10] and at the same time stand fast in itself as the thing and manifest itself as a constant. This manifestation of the thing in making a move towards us is accomplished in the open, within the realm of the Overt (*das Offene*),[11] the overt character (*Offenheit*) of

300

which is not initially created by the representation but is only entered into and taken over each time as an area of relationships (*Bezugsbereich*). The relation between representative statement and thing serves to implement that condition (*Verhältnis*) which originally started to vibrate, and now continues to vibrate, as *behaviour* (*Verhalten*). But all behaviour is characterised by the fact that, obtaining as it does in the open, it must always relate to something manifest *as such* (*ein Offenbares als ein solches*). What is thus, and solely in this narrow sense, made manifest was experienced in the early stages of Western thought as "that which is present" and has long been termed "that which is" (*das Seiende*).

All behaviour is "overt" (lit. "stands open": *offenständig*) to what-is, and all "overt" relationship is behaviour. Man's "overtness" varies with the nature of what-is and the mode of behaviour. All working and carrying out of tasks, all transaction and calculation, sustains itself in the open, an overt region within which what-is can expressly take up its stand *as* and *how* it is *what* it is, and thus become capable of expression. This can only occur when what-is represents itself (*selbst vorstellig wird*) with the representative statement, so that the statement submits to a directive enjoining it to express what-is "such-as" or just as it is. By following this directive the statement "rights itself" (*sich richtet nach*) by what-is. Directing itself in this way the statement is right (true). And what is thus stated is rightness (truth).

The statement derives its rightness from the overtness of behaviour, for it is only through this that anything manifest can become the criterion for the approximation implicit in the representative statement. Overt behaviour must apply this criterion to itself. Which means: it must be for a start something of a criterion for all representation. This is implicit in the overtness of behaviour. But if rightness (truth) of statement is only made possible by the overt character of behaviour, then it follows that the thing that makes rightness possible in the first place must have a more original claim to be regarded as the essence of truth.

Thus the traditional practice of attributing truth exclusively to the statement as its sole and essential place of origin, falls to the ground. Truth does not possess its original seat in the proposition. At the same time the question arises: on what basis does it become inwardly possible for overt behaviour to postulate a criterion—a possibility which alone invests propositional rightness with sufficient status to achieve, in any measure, the essence of truth?

3. THE BASIS OF THE INNER POSSIBILITY OF RIGHTNESS

Whence does the representative statement receive its command to "right itself" by the object and thus to be in accord with rightness? Why does this accord (*Stimmen*) at the same time determine (*bestimmen*) the nature of truth? How, in fact, can there be such a thing at all as approximation to a pre-established criterion, or a directive enjoining such an accord? Only because this postulate (*Vorgeben*) has already freed itself (*sich freigegeben hat*) and become open to a manifestation operating in this openness—a manifestation which is binding on all representation whatsoever. This "freeing" for the sake of submitting to a binding criterion is only possible as freedom to reveal something already overt (*zum Offenbaren eines Offenen*). Being free in this way points to the hitherto uncomprehended nature of freedom. The overt character of behaviour in the sense that it makes rightness a possibility, is grounded in freedom. *The essence of truth is freedom.*

But does not this proposition regarding the nature of rightness merely substitute one self-evident fact for another? In order to be able to turn an action, and thus the action of the representative statement and indeed that of agreeing or not agreeing, into a "truth," the agent must of course be free. Even so, our proposition in no way implies that voluntary action has any part in the completion of the statement, or the communication and adoption of it. The proposition says: Freedom is the *essence* of truth itself. "Essence" is understood here as the basis of the inner possibility of whatever is accepted in the first place and generally admitted as "known." In our ordinary conception of freedom we do not think of truth, let alone its essence. The proposition

303

that the essence of truth (rightness of statement) is freedom must therefore appear strange.

But to turn truth into freedom—is that not to abandon truth to the caprice of man? Can truth be more basically undermined than by being delivered up to the whim of this wavering reed? The thing that has forced itself time and again on our sound judgment during the course of this exposition so far, now becomes all the more evident: truth is brought down to the subjective level of the human subject. Even if this subject can attain to some kind of objectivity, it still remains human in its subjectivity and subject to human control.

Admittedly, guile and dissimulation, lies and deception, fraud and pretence, in short, all manner of untruth, are ascribed to man. But untruth is the opposite of truth, for which reason it is, as the very negation of truth, its "dis-essence" [12] rightly kept at a remove from the field of enquiry into the pure essence of truth. This human origin of untruth merely confirms by contrast the essential nature of truth "as such" which holds sway "over" man and which metaphysics regard as something imperishable and eternal, something that can never be founded on the transitoriness and fragility of humankind. How then can the essence of truth possibly have a stable basis in human freedom?

Resistance to the proposition that the essence of truth is freedom is rooted in prejudices, the most obstinate of which contends that freedom is a property of man and that the nature of freedom neither needs nor allows of further questioning. As for man, we all know what *he* is.

4. THE ESSENTIAL NATURE OF FREEDOM

The indication, however, of the essential connection between truth *as rightness,* and freedom, shatters these preconceived notions, provided of course that we are prepared to change our way of thinking. Consideration of the natural affinity between truth and freedom induces us to pursue the question as to the nature of man in one of its aspects—an aspect vouched for by our experience of a hidden ground in man's nature and being, so that we are transported in advance into the original living realm of truth. But at this point it also becomes evident that freedom is the basis of the inner possibility of rightness only because it receives its own essence from that thing of earlier origin: the uniquely essential truth.

Freedom was initially defined as freedom for the revelation of something already overt. How are we to think of the essence of freedom so conceived? The Manifest (*das Offenbare*), to which a representative statement approximates in its rightness, is that which obviously "is" all the time and has some manifest form of behaviour. The freedom to reveal something overt lets whatever "is" at the moment *be* what it is. Freedom reveals itself as the "letting-be" of what-is.

We usually talk of "letting be" when, for instance, we stand off from some undertaking we have planned. "We let it be" means: not touching it again, not having anything more to do with it. "Letting be" here has the negative sense of disregarding something, renouncing something, of indifference and even neglect.

The phrase we are now using, namely the "letting-be" of what-is, does not, however, refer to indifference and neglect, but to the very opposite of them. To let something be (*Seinlassen*) is in fact to have something to do with it (*sich einlassen auf*). This is not to be taken merely in the sense of pursuing, conserving, cultivating and planning some actuality casually met with or sought out. To let what-is *be* what it is means participating in something overt and its overtness, in which everything that "is" takes up its position and which entails such overtness. Western thought at its outset conceived this overtness as τὰ ἀληθέα, the Unconcealed. If we translate ἀλήθεια by "unconcealment" or "revealment" [13] instead of truth, the translation is not only more "literal" but it also requires us to revise our ordinary idea of truth in the sense of propositional correctitude and trace it back to that still uncomprehended quality: the revealedness (*Entborgenheit*) and revelation (*Entbergung*) of what-is. Participation in the revealed nature of what-is does not stop there, it develops into a retirement before it so that what-is may reveal itself as *what* and *how* it is, and the approximation which represents it in the statement may take it for a criterion. In this manner "letting-be" exposes itself (*setzt sich aus*) to what-is-as-such and brings all behaviour into the open (*versetzt ins Offene*). "Letting-be," i.e. freedom, is in its own self "ex-posing" (*aus-setzend*) and "ex-sistent" (*ek-sistent*).[14]

The nature of freedom, seen from the point of view of the nature of truth, now shows itself as an "exposition" into the revealed nature of what-is.

Freedom is not what common sense is content to let pass under that name: the random ability to do as we please, to go this way or that in our choice. Freedom is not licence in what we do or do not do. Nor, on the other hand, is freedom a mere readiness to do something requisite and necessary and thus in a sense "actual" (*Seiendes*). Over and above all this ("negative" and "positive" freedom) freedom is a participation in the revealment of what-is-as-such (*das Seiende als ein solches*). The revelation of this is itself guaranteed in that ex-sistent participation whereby the overtness of the overt (*die Offenheit des Offenen*), i.e. the "There" (*Da*) of it, *is* what it is.

In this Da-sein[15] there is preserved for mankind that long unfathomed and essential basis on which man is able to ex-sist. "Existence" in this case does not signify *existentia* in the sense of the "occurrence" (*Vorkommen*) and "being" (*Dasein*), i.e. "presence" (*Vorhandensein*) of an "existent" (*eines Seienden*). Nor does "existence" mean, "existentially" speaking, man's moral preoccupation with himself—a preoccupation arising out of his psycho-physical constitution. Existence, grounded in truth as freedom, is nothing less than exposition into the revealed nature of

what-is-as-such. Still unfathomed and not even
conscious of the need for any deeper fathoming
of its essence, the ex-sistence of historical man begins at that moment when the first thinker to ask
himself about the revealed nature of what-is,
poses the question: What is what-is? With this
question unconcealment and revealment are experienced for the first time. What-is-in-totality
(*das Seiende im Ganzen*) reveals itself as φύσις,
"Nature," which does not as yet mean a particular field of what-is, but what-is-as-such-in-totality
(*das Seiende als solches im Ganzen*) and, moreover, in the sense of an unfolding presence
(*aufgehenden Anwesens*). Only where what-is is
expressly raised to the power of its own revelation and preserved there, only where this preservation is conceived as the quest for what-is-as-
such, only there does history begin. The initial
revelation of what-is-in-totality, the quest for
what-is-as-such, and the beginning of the history
of the West, are one and the same thing and
are contemporaneous in a "time" which, itself
immeasurable, alone opens the Manifest to every
kind of measurement.

But if ex-sistent *Da-sein*, understood as the
letting-be of what-is, sets man free for his "freedom" which confronts him, then and only then,
with a choice between actual possibilities and
which imposes actual necessities upon him, then
freedom is not governed by human inclination.
Man does not "possess" freedom as a property, it
is the contrary that is true: freedom, or ex-sistent,
revelatory *Da-sein* possesses man and moreover in

so original a manner that it alone confers upon him that relationship with what-is-in-totality which is the basis and distinctive characteristic of his history. Only ex-sistent man is historical. "Nature" has no history.

Freedom, so understood as the letting-be of what-is, fulfils and perfects the nature of truth in the sense that truth is the unconcealment and revealment of what-is. "Truth" is not the mark of some correct proposition made by a human "subject" in respect of an "object" and which then—in precisely what sphere we do not know—counts as "true"; truth is rather the revelation of what-is, a revelation through which something "overt" comes into force. All human behaviour is an exposition into that overtness. Hence man *is* in virtue of his ex-sistence.

Because all modes of human behaviour (*Verhalten*) are, each in its own way, overt and always relate to that which they must (*wozu es sich verhält*), it follows that the restraint (*Verhaltenheit*) of "letting things be," i.e. freedom, must necessarily have given man an inner directive to approximate his ideas (representations: *Vorstellen*)[16] to what-is at any moment. Man ex-sists, and this now means: historical man has his history and all its possibilities guaranteed him in the revelation of what-is-in-totality. The manner in which the original nature of truth operates (*west*) gives rise to the rare and simple decisions of history.

But because truth is in essence freedom, historical man, though he lets things be, cannot really let what-is be just *what* it is and *as* it is. What-is

309

is then covered up and distorted. Illusion comes into its own. The essential negation of truth, its "dis-essence" (*Unwesen*), makes its appearance. But because ex-sistent freedom, being the essence of truth, is not a property of man (it being rather the case that man only ex-sists as the property of this freedom and so becomes capable of history), it follows that the dis-essence of truth cannot, in its turn, simply arise *a posteriori* from the mere incapacity and negligence of man. On the contrary, untruth must derive from the essence of truth. Only because truth and untruth are not *in essence* indifferent to one another, can a true proposition contrast so sharply with its correspondingly untrue proposition. Our quest for the nature of truth only extends into the original realm of interrogation when, having gained a preliminary insight into the complete essence of truth, we now include a consideration of untruth in the revelation of "essence." The enquiry into the dis-essence of truth is not a subsequent filling of the gap; it is the decisive step towards any adequate posing of the question as to the nature of truth. Yet, how are we to conceive truth's dis-essence as part of its essence? If the essence of truth is not fully displayed in the rightness of a statement, then neither can untruth be equated with the wrongness of an opinion.

5. THE ESSENCE OF TRUTH

The essence of truth has revealed itself as freedom. This is the ex-sistent, revelatory "letting-be" of what-is. Every overt mode of behaviour vibrates (*schwingt*) with this "letting-be" and relates itself to this or that actuality. In the sense that freedom means participation in the revealment of what-is-in-totality, freedom has attuned (*abgestimmt*) all behaviour to this from the start. But this attunement (*Gestimmtheit*) or "mood" (*Stimmung*) can never be understood as "experience" and "feeling" because, were it so understood, it would at once be deprived of its being (*Wesen*) and would only be interpreted in terms of, say, "life" and "soul"—which only *appear* to exist in their own right (*Wesensrecht*) so long as they contain any distortion and misinterpretation of that attunement. A mood of this kind, i.e. the ex-sistent exposition into what-is-in-totality, can only be "experienced" or "felt," as we say, because the "experient," without having any idea of the nature of the mood, is participating in an attunement revelatory of what-is-in-totality. The whole behaviour of historical man, whether stressed or not, whether understood or not, is tuned and by this attunement raised up to the plane of what-is-in-totality. The manifest character of what-is-in-totality is not identical with the sum of known actualities. On the contrary, it is just where few actualities are known or where they are known hardly at all by science or only very roughly, that the manifest character of what-is-in-totality can operate far more essentially than where the Known and always Knowable has become impossible to survey and can no longer resist the activity of knowing, because the technical control of things seems limitless in its scope. It is precisely this proliferation and standardisation of knowledge, this desire to know everything, that causes the manifest character of what-is to sink into the apparent void of indifference or, worse still, oblivion.

The determining principle of letting-be pervades and anticipates all overt behaviour which it has set vibrating in tune with it. Man's behaviour is attuned to the manifest character of what-is-in-totality. But this "in-totality" appears, in the field of vision of our daily calculations and activities, as something incalculable and incomprehensible. It cannot be understood in terms of what manifestly "is," whether this be part of nature or of history. Although itself ceaselessly determining all things, this "in-totality" nevertheless remains something indeterminate and indeterminable, and is thus generally confused with what is readiest at hand and most easily thought of. At the same time this determining factor is not just *nothing:* it is a concealment of what-is *in* totality. Precisely because "letting be" always, in each case, lets each thing be in its proper relationship and thus reveals it, it immediately conceals what-is in totality (*verbirgt es das Seiende im Ganzen*). "Letting things be" is at once a concealment (*Verbergen*).[17] In the existent freedom of *Da-sein* there is accomplished a dissimulation of what-is in totality and therein lies the concealment (*Verborgenheit*).[18]

6. UNTRUTH AS DISSIMULATION

Concealment denies revelation to ἀλήθεια but does not yet admit it as στέρησις (privation, loss); rather, it makes its own specific property the property of ἀλήθεια. From the point of view of truth conceived as revelation, then, concealment is non-revelation (*Un-entborgenheit*) and thus the untruth which is specific of and peculiar to the nature of truth. The concealment of what-is in totality is not *successive* to our always fragmentary knowledge of what-is. This concealment, or authentic (*eigentlich*) untruth, is anterior to all revelation of this or that actuality. It is even anterior to the letting-be of what-is, which, by revealing, conceals and thus establishes the dissimulation. What is it that keeps letting-be correlated in this way to dissimulation? Nothing less than the dissimulation of the dissimulated (*die Verbergung des Verborgenen*) in totality, the dissimulation of what-is-as-such i.e. the mystery. Not an isolated mystery concerning this thing or that, but the single fact that absolute mystery, mystery as such (the dissimulation of the dissimulated), pervades the whole of man's *Da-sein*.

Letting things be in totality—a process which reveals and conceals at the same time—brings it about that dissimulation appears as the initial thing dissimulated.[19] *Da-sein,* insofar as it ex-sists, reaffirms the first and most extreme non-revelation of all: authentic untruth. The authentic "dis-essence" of truth—that is the mystery. Dis-

essence is not to be taken here as something reduced to, and contrasted with,[20] "essence" in the
sense of what is common or general (κοινόν, γένος),
the possibility of dis-essence and the basis of this
possibility. Dis-essence is meant here in the sense
of pre-essence, something that precedes essence
(*das vorwesende Wesen*). But first and foremost it
means a de-naturing (*Verunstaltung*) of that already reduced essence. The point, however, is
that in all these significations dis-essence still remains essential to essence and never becomes
inessential in the sense of something indifferent
to it. Yet to speak in this way of dis-essence and
untruth flies too much in the face of common
opinion (δόξα) and looks like the dragging in of
far-fetched paradoxes. Because it is difficult to
avoid the appearance of this we shall refrain
from speaking in this way, which is "paradoxical" only for the accepted modes of thinking.
For those who know, the "dis-" of the initial dis-
essence of truth, as also the "un-" of untruth,
point into the still unexplored region of the
truth of Being (*Sein*), and not merely of what-is
(*das Seiende*).

Understood as the letting-be of what-is, freedom is essentially a *relationship of open resolve*
and not one locked up within itself.[21] All behaviour is grounded in this relationship and
receives from it a directive to turn to what-is, a
command to reveal it. Yet this affinity with revelation conceals itself inasmuch as it gives precedence to a continual forgetting of the mystery,
so that the relationship vanishes in this forget-

314

fulness. Although man is all the time related to what-is, he almost always acquiesces in this or that particular manifestation of it. He is still in the region of what he can touch and control, even when the ultimates are in question. And when he sets out to enlarge the manifestation of what-is in his various fields of activity, to change it, to possess himself of it afresh and secure it, he is still taking his directives from the sphere of practical plans and requirements.

But this fixation in the realm of the practicable is itself an unwillingness to let the dissimulation of the dissimulated have full dominion. Even in the practicable world there are enigmas, unclarified issues, things undecided or left in question. But these questions, although so sure of themselves, are only thoroughfares, halting-places on our journey through the practicable, and are thus not important. Wherever the dissimulation of what-is in totality is admitted only by the way, as a boundary which occasionally impinges, dissimulation as the ground-phenomenon of *Da-sein* is lost in oblivion.

But the forgotten mystery of *Da-sein* is not obviated by being forgotten; on the contrary, forgetting gives the apparent disappearance of the forgotten a presence of its own. Inasmuch as the mystery denies itself in and for the sake of forgetfulness, it leaves historical man to rely on his own resources in the realm of the practicable. Abandoned thus, humanity builds up its "world" out of whatever intentions and needs happen to be the most immediate, filling it out with projects and plans. From these in their turn man, having forgotten what-is-in-totality, adopts his measures. He insists (*beharrt*) on them and continually provides himself with new ones, without giving a thought to the reasons for taking measures or the nature of measurement.[22] Despite his advance towards new measures and goals he mistakes their essential genuineness. He is the more mistaken the more exclusively he takes himself as the measure of all things.

With that measureless and presumptuous (*vermessen*) forgetfulness of his he clings to the certainties of selfhood, to whatever happens to be immediately accessible. This insistence (*Beharren*) is—unknown to him—supported by the circumstance that his *Da-sein* not only *ex-sists* but *in-sists*[23] at the same time, i.e. obstinately holds fast to (*besteht auf*) that which actuality (*das Seiende*), as though open of and in itself, offers him.

As ex-sistent, Da-sein is in-sistent. But the mystery dwells also in in-sistent existence,[24] though here the mystery is the forgotten essence of truth, now become "inessential."[25]

7. UNTRUTH AS ERROR[26]

In-sisting, man is turned to the most readily accessible part of what-is. But he in-sists only as already ex-sisting, taking what-is for his measure. Yet in the measures he takes he is turned away from the mystery. That insistent turning towards the practicable and accessible and this ex-sistent turning away from the mystery, go together. They are one and the same thing. Nevertheless this back and forth movement follows the peculiar rhythm of *Da-sein*. Man's drifting from the mystery to the practicable and from one practicability to the next, always missing the mystery, is *erring (das Irren)*.

Man errs. He does not merely fall into error, he lives in error always because, by ex-sisting, he in-sists and is thus already in error. The error in which he lives is not just something that runs along beside him like a ditch, something he occasionally falls into. No, error is part of the inner structure of *Da-sein,* in which historical man is involved. Error is the theatre for that variable mode of being (*Wende*) where in-sistent ex-sistence, turning and turning about, perpetually forgets and mistakes itself. The dissimulation of what-is concealed in totality comes into force through the revelation of what-is at any moment, and this revelation, because it is a forgetting of the dissimulation, leads to error.

Error is the essential counter-essence (*das wesentliche Gegenwesen*) of the original essence of truth. It opens out as the manifest theatre for all counter-play to essential truth. Error is the open ground, the basis of Wrong (*Irrtum*). Wrong is not just the isolated mistake, it is the empire, the whole history of all the complicated and intricate ways of erring.

All modes of behaviour have, according to their overtness and correlation to what-is-in-totality, each their way of erring. Wrong ranges from the commonest mistake, oversight, miscalculation to going astray and getting utterly lost when it comes to adopting important attitudes and making essential decisions. What we ordinarily understand by "wrong" and moreover, according to the teachings of philosophy— namely the wrongness (*Unrichtigheit*) of a judgment and the falseness of a perception, is only one, and that the most superficial, way of erring. The error in which historical man must always walk, which makes his road erratic (*irrig*) is essentially one with the manifest character of what-is. Error dominates man through and through by leading him astray. But, by this selfsame aberration (*Beirrung*), error collaborates in the possibility which man has (and can always extract from his ex-sistence) of *not allowing* himself to be led astray, of himself experiencing error and thus not overlooking the mystery of *Da-sein*.

Because man's in-sistent ex-sistence leads to error, and because error always oppresses in one way or another and out of this oppression becomes capable of commanding the mystery, albeit forgotten, it follows that man in his *Da-sein* is *especially* subject to the rule of mystery and his own affliction. Between them, *he lives in an extremity of compulsion*.[27] The total essence of truth, which contains in its own self its "disessence," keeps *Da-sein* ever turning this way and that but always into misery. *Da-sein* is, in fact, a turning to misery, a turning into need. From man's *Da-sein* and from this alone comes the revelation of necessity and, as a result, the possibility of turning this necessity into something *needed,* something unavoidable.

The revelation of what-is-as-such is at the same time the concealment of what-is in totality. In this simultaneity of revealing and concealing error has sway. The dissimulation of the dissimulated, and error, belong to the original essence of truth. Freedom, consisting in the in-sistent ex-sistence of *Da-sein,* is the essence of truth (in the sense of propositional rightness) only because freedom itself springs from the original essence of truth, from the reign of mystery in error. The letting-be of what-is is accomplished in the sphere of overt relationship. But the letting-be of what-is-as-such in totality is only accomplished in conformity with the essence of it when the latter (i.e. what-is-as-such in totality) is assumed (*übernommen*) in its original essence. Then the "open resolve" for the mystery is well on the way to error as such. Then the question concerning the essential nature of truth is being asked more profoundly and originally. Then the reason why the essence of truth is bound up with the truth of essence stands revealed. Gazing out of error into the mystery is a questioning in the sense of the only question that exists: What is that which is as such in totality? This question meditates the essentially confusing and, because of its multifarious aspects, still unmastered question regarding the *Being* of what-is (*das Sein des Seienden*). The thought of Being, which is the original source of all such questioning, has, ever since Plato's day, been conceived as "Philosophy," later acquiring the title of "Metaphysics."

8. THE PROBLEM OF TRUTH AND PHILOSOPHY

In this thought of Being, man's freedom for ex-sistence (a freedom which is the basis of all history) is put into words. This is not to be understood as the "expression" of an "opinion"; rather this word (Being) is the well-preserved structure of the truth of what-is-in-totality. How many have ears for this word matters little. Those who hear it determine man's place in history. But at that moment in the world when philosophy came to birth there also began, and not before, the *express* domination of common sense (Sophism).

Sophism appeals to the non-problematical character of what is manifest and interprets all intellectual interrogation as an attack upon sound common sense and its unhappy susceptibilities.

But what philosophy is in the estimation of sound common sense (which is perfectly justified in its own domain) does not affect its essence, which is determined solely by its relations with the original truth of what-is-as-such in totality. But because the complete essence of truth also includes its "dis-essence" and because it functions primarily as dissimulation, philosophy, regarded as the quest for this truth, has a two-fold nature. Its meditations have the calm dignity of gentleness, not denying the dissimulation of what-is in totality. At the same time they have the "open resolve" of hardness, which, while not shattering the dissimulation, forces its essence whole and intact into the open, into our understanding, and so to reveal its own truth.

In the gentle hardness and hard gentleness with which it lets what-is-as-such *be* in totality, philosophy becomes a questioning which not merely holds fast to what-is, but can admit no outside authority. Kant had some idea of the inmost extremity of such thinking when he said of philosophy: "We now see philosophy in a doubtful position indeed, a position which is supposed to be a firm one regardless of the fact that neither in heaven nor on earth is it attached to or supported by anything whatsoever. In this position philosophy has to demonstrate its sincerity as the keeper of its own laws, not as the herald of laws which ingrained sense or some kind of guardian Nature whispers in its ear."

With this interpretation of the nature of philosophy Kant, whose work is a prelude to the latest phase of Western metaphysics, looks out into a sphere which, because his metaphysics were rooted in subjectivity, he could only understand in subjective terms and was bound to understand as keeping its own laws. All the same, the glimpse he had of the function of philosophy is still sufficiently broad to reject all enslavement of philosophical thought, the most helpless of which is to be found in the subterfuge of letting philosophy assert itself merely as an "expression" of "culture" (Spengler), as the ornament of a creative humanity.

321

Whether philosophy is after all fulfilling its initially decisive role as "keeper of its own laws," or whether it is not primarily maintained by, and itself destined to maintain, the truth of that whereof the laws are eternal laws, this is an issue to be decided out of that initial source (*aus der Anfänglichkeit:* lit. "initiality") where the original essence of truth becomes essential to philosophical enquiry.

The present essay leads the question concerning the nature of truth beyond the accustomed confines of our fundamental ideas and helps us to consider whether this question of the essence of truth is not at the same time necessarily the question of the truth of essence. Philosophy, however, conceives "essence" as Being. By tracing the inner possibility of a statement's "rightness" back to the ex-sistent freedom of "letting-be" as the very basis of that statement, and by suggesting that the essential core of this basis is to be found in dissimulation and error, we may have indicated that the nature of truth is not just the empty, "general" character of some "abstract" commonplace, but something that is unique in history (itself unique): the self-dissimulation of the unveiling of the "meaning" of what we call "Being," which we have long been accustomed to think of only as "what-is-in-totality."

NOTE

The foregoing enquiry into the essence of truth was first communicated in a public lecture delivered in 1930 in Bremen, Marburg and Freiburg and again in 1932 in Dresden. Such extracts from the lecture as had bearing on a consideration of the truth of *essence* were then repeatedly revised, though the arrangement, structure and general trend of it were preserved.

The crucial question (viz. my "Sein und Zeit," 1927) regarding the "meaning," that is to say ("Sein und Zeit," p. 151) the realm of projection (*Entwurfsbereich*), that is to say the manifest character (*Offenheit*), that is to say the truth, of Being and not merely of "what-is," has been deliberately left undeveloped. The line of thought follows to all appearances the road of metaphysics, but at the same time, as regards its decisive steps—those leading from truth as rightness to ex-sistent freedom and from this to untruth as dissimulation and error—it effects a change in the direction of the enquiry, a change which properly belongs to the *conquest (Ueberwindung)* of metaphysics.

The knowledge arrived at in the lecture comes to flower in the essential experience that only in and from *Da-sein,* as a thing to which we have entry, can any approximation to the truth of Being evolve for historical man. Not only is every sort of "anthropology" and every sort of subjectivity (of man regarded as a subject) abandoned, as was already the case in "Sein und Zeit," and the truth of Being pursued as the "ground" of a fundamentally new attitude to history, but an effort is made in the course of this lecture to think in terms of this other "ground," i.e. *Da-*

sein. The sequence of questions is itself a mode of thinking which, instead of supplying concepts merely, feels and tests itself as a new mode of relationship to Being.

WHAT IS METAPHYSICS?

"What is metaphysics?" The question leads one to expect a discussion about metaphysics. Such is not our intention. Instead, we shall discuss a definite metaphysical question, thus, as it will appear, landing ourselves straight into metaphysics. Only in this way can we make it really possible for metaphysics to speak for itself.

Our project begins with the presentation of a metaphysical question, then goes on to its development and ends with its answer.

THE PRESENTATION OF A METAPHYSICAL QUESTION

Seen from the point of view of sound common sense, Philosophy, according to Hegel, is the "world stood on its head." Hence the peculiar nature of our task calls for some preliminary definition. This arises out of the dual nature of metaphysical questioning.

Firstly, every metaphysical question always covers the whole range of metaphysical problems. In every case it is itself the whole. Secondly, every metaphysical question can only be put in such a way that the questioner as such is by his very questioning involved in the question.

From this we derive the following pointer: metaphysical questioning has to be put as a whole and has always to be based on the essential situation of existence, which puts the question. We question here and now, on our own account. Our existence—a community of scientists, teachers and students—is ruled by science. What essential things are happening to us in the foundations of our existence, now that science has become our passion?

The fields of the sciences lie far apart. Their methodologies are fundamentally different. This disrupted multiplicity of disciplines is today only held together by the technical organisation of the Universities and their faculties, and maintained as a unit of meaning by the practical aims of those faculties. As against this, however, the root of the sciences in their essential ground has atrophied.

And yet—insofar as we follow their most specific intentions—in all the sciences we are related to what-is. Precisely from the point of view of the sciences no field takes precedence over another, neither Nature over History nor vice versa. No one methodology is superior to another. Mathematical knowledge is no stricter than philological or historical knowledge. It has merely the characteristic of "exactness," which is not to be identified with strictness. To demand exactitude of history would be to offend against the idea of the kind of strictness that pertains to the humanistic sciences. The world-relationship which runs through all the sciences as such constrains them to seek what-is *in itself,* with a view to rendering it, according to its quiddity (*Wasgehalt*) and its modality (*Seinsart*), an object of investigation and basic definition. What the sciences accomplish, ideally speaking, is an approximation to the essential nature of all things.

This distinct world-relationship to what-is in itself is sustained and guided by a freely chosen attitude on the part of our human existence. It is true that the pre-scientific and extra-scientific activities of man also relate to what-is. But the distinction of science lies in the fact that, in an altogether specific manner, it and it alone explicitly allows the object itself the first and last word. In this objectivity of questioning, definition and proof there is a certain limited submission to what-is, so that this may reveal itself. This submissive attitude taken up by scientific theory becomes the basis of a possibility: the possibility of science acquiring a leadership of its own, albeit limited, in the whole field of human existence. The world-relationship of science and the attitude of man responsible for it can, of course, only be fully understood when we see and understand what is going on in the world-relationship so maintained. Man—one entity (*Seiendes*) among others—"pursues" science. In this "pursuit" what is happening is nothing less than the irruption of a particular entity called "Man" into the whole of what-is, in such a way that in and through this irruption what-is manifests itself *as* and *how* it is. The manner in which the revelatory irruption occurs is the chief thing that helps what-is to become what it is.

This triple process of world-relationship, attitude, and irruption—a radical unity—introduces something of the inspiring simplicity and intensity of *Da-sein* into scientific existence. If we now explicitly take possession of scientific *Da-*

sein as clarified by us, we must necessarily say:

That to which the world-relationship refers is what-is—and nothing else.

That by which every attitude is moulded is what-is—and nothing more.

That with which scientific exposition effects its "irruption" is what-is—and beyond that, nothing.

But is it not remarkable that precisely at that point where scientific man makes sure of his surest possession he should speak of something else? What is to be investigated is what-is—and nothing else; only what-is—and nothing more; simply and solely what-is—and beyond that, nothing.

But what about this "nothing"? Is it only an accident that we speak like that quite naturally? Is it only a manner of speaking—and nothing more?

But why worry about this Nothing? "Nothing" is absolutely rejected by science and abandoned as null and void (*das Nichtige*). But if we abandon Nothing in this way are we not, by that act, really admitting it? Can we, though, speak of an admission when we admit Nothing? But perhaps this sort of cross-talk is already degenerating into an empty wrangling about words.

Science, on the other hand, has to assert its soberness and seriousness afresh and declare that it is concerned solely with what-is. Nothing—how can it be for science anything other than a horror and a phantasm? If science is right then one thing stands firm: science wishes to know nothing of Nothing. Such is after all the strictly scientific approach to Nothing. We know it by wishing to know nothing of Nothing.

Science wishes to know nothing of Nothing. Even so the fact remains that at the very point where science tries to put its own essence in words it invokes the aid of Nothing. It has recourse to the very thing it rejects. What sort of schizophrenia is this?

A consideration of our momentary existence as one ruled by science has landed us in the thick of an argument. In the course of this argument a question has already presented itself. The question only requires putting specifically: What about Nothing?

THE DEVELOPMENT OF THE QUESTION

The development of our enquiry into Nothing is bound to lead us to a position where either the answer will prove possible or the impossibility of an answer will become evident. "Nothing" is admitted. Science, by adopting an attitude of superior indifference, abandons it as that which "is not."

All the same we shall endeavour to enquire into Nothing. What is Nothing? Even the initial approach to this question shows us something out of the ordinary. So questioning, we postulate Nothing as something that somehow or other "is" —as an entity (*Seiendes*). But it is nothing of the sort. The question as to the what and wherefore of Nothing turns the thing questioned into its opposite. The question deprives itself of its own object.

Accordingly, every answer to this question is impossible from the start. For it necessarily moves in the form that Nothing "is" this, that or the other. Question and answer are equally non-sensical in themselves where Nothing is concerned.

Hence even the rejection by science is super-fluous. The commonly cited basic rule of all thinking—the proposition that contradiction must be avoided—and common "logic" rule out the question. For thinking, which is essentially always thinking about something, would, in thinking of Nothing, be forced to act against its own nature.

Because we continually meet with failure as soon as we try to turn Nothing into a subject, our enquiry into Nothing is already at an end— always assuming, of course, that in this enquiry "logic" is the highest court of appeal, that reason is the means and thinking the way to an original comprehension of Nothing and its possible reve-lation.

But, it may be asked, can the law of "logic" be assailed? Is not reason indeed the master in this enquiry into Nothing? It is in fact only with reason's help that we can define Nothing in the first place and postulate it as a problem—though a problem that consumes only itself. For Nothing is the negation (*Verneinung*) of the totality of what-is: that which is absolutely not. But at this point we bring Nothing into the higher category of the Negative (*Nichthaftes*) and therefore of what is negated. But according to the overriding and unassailable teachings of "logic" negation is a specific act of reason. How, then, in our enquiry into Nothing and into the very possibility of holding such an enquiry can we dismiss reason? Yet is it so sure just what we are postulating? Does the Not (*das Nicht*), the state of being negated (*die Verneintheit*) and hence negation itself (*Verneinung*), in fact represent that higher category under which Nothing takes its place as a special kind of thing negated? Does Nothing "exist" only because the Not, i.e. negation exists? Or is it the other way about? Does negation and the Not exist only because Nothing exists? This has not been decided—indeed, it has not even been explicitly asked. We assert: "Nothing" is more original than the Not and negation.

If this thesis is correct then the very possibility of negation as an act of reason, and consequently reason itself, are somehow dependent on Nothing. How, then, can reason attempt to decide this issue? May not the apparent nonsensicality of the question and answer where Nothing is concerned only rest, perhaps, on the blind obstinacy of the roving intellect?

If, however, we refuse to be led astray by the formal impossibility of an enquiry into Nothing and still continue to enquire in the face of it, we must at least satisfy what remains the fundamental pre-requisite for the full pursuit of any enquiry. If Nothing as such is still to be enquired into, it follows that it must be "given" in advance. We must be able to encounter it.

Where shall we seek Nothing? Where shall we find Nothing? In order to find something must we not know beforehand that it is there? Indeed we must! First and foremost we can only look if we have presupposed the presence of a thing to be looked for. But here the thing we are looking for is Nothing. Is there after all a seeking without pre-supposition, a seeking complemented by a pure finding?

However that may be, we do know "Nothing" if only as a term we bandy about every day. This ordinary hackneyed Nothing, so completely taken for granted and rolling off our tongue so casually—we can even give an off-hand "definition" of it:

Nothing is the complete negation of the totality of what-is.

Does not this characteristic of Nothing point, after all, in the direction from which alone it may meet us?

The totality of what-is must be given beforehand so as to succumb as such to the negation from which Nothing is then bound to emerge.

But, even apart from the questionableness of this relationship between negation and Nothing, how are we, as finite beings, to render the whole of what-is in its totality accessible *in itself*—let alone to ourselves? We can, at a pinch, think of the whole of what-is as an "idea" and then negate what we have thus imagined in our thoughts and "think" it negated. In this way we arrive at the formal concept of an imaginary Nothing, but never Nothing itself. But Nothing is nothing, and between the imaginary and the "authentic" (*eigentlich*) Nothing no difference can obtain, if Nothing represents complete lack of differentiation. But the "authentic" Nothing—is this not once again that latent and nonsensical idea of a Nothing that "is"? Once again and for the last time rational objections have tried to hold up our search, whose legitimacy can only be attested by a searching experience of Nothing.

As certainly as we shall never comprehend absolutely the totality of what-is, it is equally certain that we find ourselves placed in the midst of what-is and that this is somehow revealed in totality. Ultimately there is an essential difference between comprehending the totality of what-is and finding ourselves in the midst of what-is-in-totality. The former is absolutely impossible. The latter is going on in existence all the time.

Naturally enough it looks as if, in our everyday activities, we were always holding on to this or that actuality (*Seiendes*), as if we were lost in this or that region of what-is. However fragmentary the daily round may appear it still maintains what-is, in however shadowy a fashion, within the unity of a "whole." Even when, or rather, precisely when we are not absorbed in things or in our own selves, this "wholeness" comes over us—for example, in real boredom. Real boredom is still far off when this book or that play, this activity or that stretch of idleness merely bores us. Real boredom comes when "one is bored." This profound boredom, drifting hither and thither in the abysses of existence like a mute fog, draws all things, all men and oneself along with them, together in a queer kind of indifference. This boredom reveals what-is in totality.

There is another possibility of such revelation, and this is in the joy we feel in the presence of the being—not merely the person—of someone we love.

Because of these moods in which, as we say, we "are" this or that (i.e. bored, happy, etc.) we find ourselves (*befinden uns*) in the midst of what-is-in-totality, wholly pervaded by it. The affective state in which we find ourselves not only discloses, according to the mood we are in, what-is in totality, but this disclosure is at the same time far from being a mere chance occurrence and is the ground-phenomenon of our *Da-sein*.

Our "feelings," as we call them, are not just the fleeting concomitant of our mental or volitional behaviour, nor are they simply the cause and occasion of such behaviour, nor yet a state that is merely "there" and in which we come to some kind of understanding with ourselves.

Yet, at the very moment when our moods thus bring us face to face with what-is-in-totality they hide the Nothing we are seeking. We are now less than ever of the opinion that mere negation of what-is-in-totality as revealed by these moods of ours can in fact lead us to Nothing. This could only happen in the first place in a mood so peculiarly revelatory in its import as to reveal Nothing itself.

Does there ever occur in human existence a mood of this kind, through which we are brought face to face with Nothing itself?

This may and actually does occur, albeit rather seldom and for moments only, in the key-mood of dread (*Angst*). By "dread" we do not mean "anxiety" (*Aengstlichkeit*), which is common enough and is akin to nervousness (*Furchtsamkeit*)—a mood that comes over us only too easily. Dread differs absolutely from fear (*Furcht*). We are always *afraid* of this or that definite thing, which threatens us in this or that definite way. "Fear of" is generally "fear about" something. Since fear has this characteristic limitation—"of" and "about"—the man who is afraid, the nervous man, is always bound by the thing he is afraid of or by the state in which he finds himself. In his efforts to save himself from this "something" he becomes uncertain in relation to other things; in fact, he "loses his bearings" generally.

In dread no such confusion can occur. It would be truer to say that dread is pervaded by a peculiar kind of peace. And although dread is always "dread of," it is not dread of this or that. "Dread of" is always a dreadful feeling "about" —but not about this or that. The indefiniteness of *what* we dread is not just lack of definition: it represents the essential impossibility of defining the "what." The indefiniteness is brought out in an illustration familiar to everybody.

In dread, as we say, "one feels something un-canny." [28] What is this "something" (*es*) and this "one"? We are unable to say what gives "one" that uncanny feeling. "One" just feels it gen-erally (*im Ganzen*). All things, and we with them, sink into a sort of indifference. But not in the sense that everything simply disappears; rather, in the very act of drawing away from us every-thing turns towards us. This withdrawal of what-is-in-totality, which then crowds round us in dread, this is what oppresses us. There is nothing to hold on to. The only thing that remains and overwhelms us whilst what-is slips away, is this "nothing."

Dread reveals Nothing.

In dread we are "in suspense" (*wir schweben*). Or, to put it more precisely, dread holds us in suspense because it makes what-is-in-totality slip away from us. Hence we too, as existents in the midst of what-is, slip away from ourselves along with it. For this reason it is not "you" or "I" that has the uncanny feeling, but "one." In the trepi-dation of this suspense where there is nothing to hold on to, pure *Da-sein* is all that remains.

Dread strikes us dumb. Because what-is-in-to-tality slips away and thus forces Nothing to the fore, all affirmation (lit. "Is"-saying: *"Ist"-Sagen*) fails in the face of it. The fact that when we are caught in the uncanniness of dread we often try to break the empty silence by words spoken at random, only proves the presence of Nothing. We ourselves confirm that dread reveals Nothing —when we have got over our dread. In the lucid vision which supervenes while yet the experience is fresh in our memory we must needs say that what we were afraid of was "actually" (*eigentlich*: also "authentic") Nothing. And indeed Nothing itself, Nothing as such, was there.

With this key-mood of dread, therefore, we have reached that event in our *Da-sein* which reveals Nothing, and which must therefore be the starting-point of our enquiry.

What about Nothing?

THE ANSWER TO THE QUESTION

The answer which alone is important for our purpose has already been found if we take care to ensure that we really do keep to the problem of Nothing. This necessitates changing man into his *Da-sein*—a change always occasioned in us by dread—so that we may apprehend Nothing as and how it reveals itself in dread. At the same time we have finally to dismiss those characteristics of Nothing which have not emerged as a result of our enquiry.

"Nothing" is revealed in dread, but not as something that "is." Neither can it be taken as an object. Dread is not an apprehension of Nothing. All the same, Nothing is revealed in and through dread, yet not, again, in the sense that Nothing appears as if detached and apart from what-is-in-totality when we have that "uncanny" feeling. We would say rather: in dread Nothing functions as if *at one with* what-is-in-totality. What do we mean by "at one with"?

In dread what-is-in-totality becomes untenable (*hinfällig*). How? What-is is not annihilated (*vernichtet*) by dread, so as to leave Nothing over. How could it, seeing that dread finds itself completely powerless in face of what-is-in-totality! What rather happens is that Nothing shows itself as essentially belonging to what-is while this is slipping away in totality.

In dread there is no annihilation of the whole of what-is in itself; but equally we cannot negate what-is-in-totality in order to reach Nothing. Apart from the fact that the explicitness of a negative statement is foreign to the nature of dread as such, we would always come too late with any such negation intended to demonstrate Nothing. For Nothing is anterior to it. As we said, Nothing is "at one with" what-is as this slips away in totality.

In dread there is a retreat from something, though it is not so much a flight as a spell-bound (*gebannt*) peace. This "retreat from" has its source in Nothing. The latter does not attract: its nature is to repel. This "repelling from itself" is essentially an "expelling into": a conscious gradual relegation to the vanishing what-is-in-totality (*das entgleitenlassende Verweisen auf das versinkende Seiende im Ganzen*). And this total relegation to the vanishing what-is-in-totality—such being the form in which Nothing crowds round us in dread—is the essence of Nothing: nihilation.[29] Nihilation is neither an annihilation (*Vernichtung*) of what-is, nor does it spring from negation (*Verneinung*). Nihilation cannot be reckoned in terms of annihilation or negation at all. Nothing "nihilates" (*nichtet*) of itself.

Nihilation is not a fortuitous event; but, understood as the relegation to the vanishing what-is-in-totality, it reveals the latter in all its till now undisclosed strangeness as the pure "Other"—contrasted with Nothing.

Only in the clear night of dread's Nothingness is what-is as such revealed in all its original overtness (*Offenheit*): that it "is" and is not Nothing. This verbal appendix "and not Nothing" is, however, not an *a posteriori* explanation but an *a priori* which alone makes possible any revelation of what-is. The essence of Nothing as original nihilation lies in this: that it alone brings *Dasein* face to face with what-is as such.

Only on the basis of the original manifestness of Nothing can our human *Da-sein* advance towards and enter into what-is. But insofar as *Dasein* naturally relates to what-is, as that which it is not and which itself is, Da-sein *qua Da-sein* always proceeds from Nothing as manifest.[30]

Da-sein means *being projected into* Nothing (*Hineingehaltenheit in das Nichts*).

Projecting into Nothing, *Da-sein* is already beyond what-is-in-totality. This "being beyond" (*Hinaussein*) what-is we call Transcendence. Were *Da-sein* not, in its essential basis, transcendent, that is to say, were it not projected from the start into Nothing, it could never relate to what-is, hence could have no self-relationship.

Without the original manifest character of

Nothing there is no self-hood and no freedom.

Here we have the answer to our question about Nothing. Nothing is neither an object nor anything that "is" at all. Nothing occurs neither by itself nor "apart from" what-is, as a sort of adjunct. Nothing is that which makes the revelation of what-is as such possible for our human existence. Nothing not merely provides the conceptual opposite of what-is but is also an original part of essence (*Wesen*). It is in the Being (*Sein*) of what-is that the nihilation of Nothing (*das Nichten des Nichts*) occurs.

But now we must voice a suspicion which has been withheld far too long already. If it is only through "projecting into Nothing" that our *Dasein* relates to what-is, in other words, has any existence, and if Nothing is only made manifest originally in dread, should we not have to be in a continual suspense of dread in order to exist at all? Have we not, however, ourselves admitted that this original dread is a rare thing? But above all, we all exist and are related to actualities which we ourselves are not and which we ourselves are—without this dread. Is not this dread, therefore, an arbitrary invention and the Nothing attributed to it an exaggeration?

Yet what do we mean when we say that this original dread only occurs in rare moments? Nothing but this: that as far as we are concerned and, indeed, generally speaking, Nothing is always distorted out of its original state. By what? By the fact that in one way or another we completely lose ourselves in what-is. The more we turn to what-is in our dealings the less we allow it to slip away, and the more we turn aside from Nothing. But all the more certainly do we thrust ourselves into the open superficies of existence.

And yet this perpetual if ambiguous aversion from Nothing accords, within certain limits, with the essential meaning of Nothing. It—Nothing in the sense of nihilation—relegates us to what-is. Nothing "nihilates" unceasingly, without our really knowing what is happening—at least, not with our everyday knowledge.

What could provide more telling evidence of the perpetual, far-reaching and yet ever-dissimulated overtness of Nothing in our existence, than negation? This is supposed to belong to the very nature of human thought. But negation cannot by any stretch of imagination produce the Not out of itself as a means of distinguishing and contrasting given things, thrusting this Not between them, as it were. How indeed could negation produce the Not out of itself, seeing that it can only negate when something is there to be negated? But how can a thing that is or ought to be negated be seen as something negative (*nicht-haft*) unless all thinking as such is on the look-out for the Not? But the Not can only manifest itself when its source—the nihilation of Nothing and hence Nothing itself—is drawn out of concealment. The Not does not come into being through negation, but negation is based on the Not, which derives from the nihilation of Nothing.

341

Nor is negation only a mode of nihilating behaviour, i.e. behaviour based *a priori* on the nihilation of Nothing.

Herewith we have proved the above thesis in all essentials: Nothing is the source of negation, not the other way about. If this breaks the sovereignty of reason in the field of enquiry into Nothing and Being, then the fate of the rule of "logic" in philosophy is also decided. The very idea of "logic" disintegrates in the vortex of a more original questioning.

However often and however variously negation—whether explicit or not—permeates all thinking, it cannot *of itself* be a completely valid witness to the manifestation of Nothing as an essential part of *Da-sein*. For negation cannot be cited either as the sole or even the chief mode of nihilation, with which, because of the nihilation of Nothing, *Da-sein* is saturated. More abysmal than the mere propriety of rational negation is the harshness of opposition and the violence of loathing. More responsible the pain of refusal and the mercilessness of an interdict. More oppressive the bitterness of renunciation.

These possible modes of nihilating behaviour, through which our *Da-sein* endures, even if it does not master, the fact of our being thrown upon the world [31] are not modes of negation merely. That does not prevent them from expressing themselves in and through negation. Indeed, it is only then that the empty expanse of negation is really revealed. The permeation of

Da-sein by nihilating modes of behaviour points to the perpetual, ever-dissimulated manifestness of Nothing, which only dread reveals in all its originality. Here, of course, we have the reason why original dread is generally repressed in *Da-sein*. Dread is there, but sleeping. All *Da-sein* quivers with its breathing: the pulsation is slightest in beings that are timorous, and is imperceptible in the "Yea, yea!" and "Nay, nay!" of busy people; it is readiest in the reserved, and surest of all in the courageous. But this last pulsation only occurs for the sake of that for which it expends itself, so as to safeguard the supreme greatness of *Da-sein*.

The dread felt by the courageous cannot be contrasted with the joy or even the comfortable enjoyment of a peaceable life. It stands—on the hither side of all such contrasts—in secret union with the serenity and gentleness of creative longing.

Original dread can be awakened in *Da-sein* at any time. It need not be awakened by any unusual occurrence. Its action corresponds in depth to the shallowness of its possible cause. It is always on the brink, yet only seldom does it take the leap and drag us with it into the state of suspense.

Because our *Da-sein* projects into Nothing on this basis of hidden dread, man becomes the "stand-in" (*Platzhalter*) for Nothing. So finite are we that we cannot, of our own resolution and will, bring ourselves originally face to face with

Nothing. So bottomlessly does finalisation (*Verendlichung*) dig into existence that our freedom's peculiar and profoundest finality fails.

This projection into Nothing on the basis of hidden dread is the overcoming of what-is-in-totality: Transcendence.

Our enquiry into Nothing will, we said, lead us straight to metaphysics. The name "metaphysics" derives from the Greek τὰ μετὰ τὰ φυσικά. This quaint title was later interpreted as characterising the sort of enquiry which goes μετά—trans, beyond—what-is as such.

Metaphysics is an enquiry over and above what-is, with a view to winning it back again as such and in totality for our understanding.

In our quest for Nothing there is similar "going beyond" what-is, conceived as what-is-in-totality. It therefore turns out to be a "metaphysical" question. We said in the beginning that such questioning had a double characteristic: every metaphysical question at once embraces the whole of metaphysics, and in every question the being (*Da-sein*) that questions is himself caught up in the question.

To what extent does the question about Nothing span and pervade the whole of metaphysics?

Since ancient times metaphysics has expressed itself on the subject of Nothing in the highly ambiguous proposition: *ex nihilo nihil fit*—nothing comes from nothing. Even though the proposition as argued never made Nothing itself the real problem, it nevertheless brought out very explicitly, from the prevailing notions about

Nothing, the over-riding fundamental concept of what-is.

Classical metaphysics conceives Nothing as signifying Not-being (*Nichtseiendes*), that is to say, unformed matter which is powerless to form itself into "being" [32] and cannot therefore present an appearance (εἶδος). What has "being" is the self-creating product (*Gebilde*) which presents itself as such in an image (*Bild*), i.e. something seen (*Anblick*). The origin, law and limits of this ontological concept are discussed as little as Nothing itself.

Christian dogma, on the other hand, denies the truth of the proposition *ex nihilo nihil fit* and gives a twist to the meaning of Nothing, so that it now comes to mean the absolute absence of all "being" [33] outside God: *ex nihilo fit—ens creatum:* the created being is made out of nothing. "Nothing" is now the conceptual opposite of what truly and authentically (*eigentlich*) "is"; it becomes the *summum ens*, God as *ens increatum*. Here, too, the interpretation of Nothing points to the fundamental concept of what-is. Metaphysical discussion of what-is, however, moves on the same plane as the enquiry into Nothing. In both cases the questions concerning Being (*Sein*) and Nothing as such remain unasked. Hence we need not be worried by the difficulty that if God creates "out of nothing" he above all must be able to relate himself to Nothing. But if God is God he cannot know Nothing, assuming that the "Absolute" excludes from itself all nullity (*Nichtigkeit*).

This crude historical reminder shows Nothing as the conceptual opposite of what truly and authentically "is," i.e. as the negation of it. But once Nothing is somehow made a problem this contrast not only undergoes clearer definition but also arouses the true and authentic metaphysical question regarding the Being of what-is. Nothing ceases to be the vague opposite of what-is: it now reveals itself as integral to the Being of what-is.

"Pure Being and pure Nothing are thus one and the same." This proposition of Hegel's ("The Science of Logic," I, WW III, p. 74) is correct. Being and Nothing hang together, but not because the two things—from the point of view of the Hegelian concept of thought—are one in their indefiniteness and immediateness, but because Being itself is finite in essence and is only revealed in the Transcendence of *Da-sein* as projected into Nothing.

If indeed the question of Being as such is the all-embracing question of metaphysics, then the question of Nothing proves to be such as to span the whole metaphysical field. But at the same time the question of Nothing pervades the whole of metaphysics only because it forces us to face the problem of the origin of negation, that is to say, forces a decision about the legitimacy of the rule of "logic" in metaphysics.

The old proposition *ex nihilo nihil fit* will then acquire a different meaning, and one appropriate to the problem of Being itself, so as to run: *ex nihilo omne ens qua ens fit:* every being, so far as it is a being, is made out of nothing. Only in the Nothingness of *Da-sein* can what-is-in-totality—and this in accordance with its peculiar possibilities, i.e. in a finite manner —come to itself. To what extent, then, has the enquiry into Nothing, if indeed it be a metaphysical one, included our own questing *Da-sein*?

Our *Da-sein* as experienced here and now is, we said, ruled by science. If our *Da-sein*, so ruled, is put into this question concerning Nothing, then it follows that it must itself have been put in question by this question.

The simplicity and intensity of scientific *Da-sein* consist in this: that it relates in a special manner to what-is and to this alone. Science would like to abandon Nothing with a superior gesture. But now, in this question of Nothing, it becomes evident that scientific *Da-sein* is only possible when projected into Nothing at the outset. Science can only come to terms with itself when it does not abandon Nothing. The alleged soberness and superiority of science becomes ridiculous if it fails to take Nothing seriously. Only because Nothing is obvious can science turn what-is into an object of investigation. Only when science proceeds from metaphysics can it conquer its essential task ever afresh, which consists not in the accumulation and classification of knowledge but in the perpetual discovery of the whole realm of truth, whether of Nature or of History.

Only because Nothing is revealed in the very basis of our *Da-sein* is it possible for the utter strangeness of what-is to dawn on us. Only when the strangeness of what-is forces itself upon us does it awaken and invite our wonder. Only because of wonder, that is to say, the revelation of Nothing, does the "Why?" spring to our lips. Only because this "Why?" is possible as such can we seek for reasons and proofs in a definite way. Only because we can ask and prove are we fated to become enquirers in this life.

The enquiry into Nothing puts us, the enquirers, ourselves in question. It is a metaphysical one.

Man's *Da-sein* can only relate to what-is by projecting into Nothing. Going beyond what-is is of the essence of *Da-sein*. But this "going beyond" is metaphysics itself. That is why metaphysics belongs to the nature of man. It is neither a department of scholastic philosophy nor a field of chance ideas. Metaphysics is the ground-phenomenon of *Da-sein*. It is *Da-sein* itself. Because the truth of metaphysics is so unfathomable there is always the lurking danger of profoundest error. Hence no scientific discipline can hope to equal the seriousness of metaphysics. Philosophy can never be measured with the yard-stick of the idea of science.

Once the question we have developed as to the nature of Nothing is really asked by and among our own selves, then we are not bringing in metaphysics from the outside. Nor are we simply "transporting" ourselves into it. It is completely out of our power to transport ourselves into metaphysics because, in so far as we exist, we **are** already there. Φύσει γὰρ, ὦ φίλει, ἔνεστί τις φιλοσοφία τῇ τοῦ ἀνδρὸς διανοίᾳ (Plato: Phaedrus 279a). While man exists there will be philosophising of some sort. Philosophy, as we call it, is the setting in motion of metaphysics; and in metaphysics philosophy comes to itself and sets about its explicit tasks. Philosophy is only set in motion by leaping with all its being, as only it can, into the ground-possibilities of being as a whole. For this leap the following things are of crucial importance: firstly, leaving room for what-is-in-totality; secondly, letting oneself go into Nothing, that is to say, freeing oneself from the idols we all have and to which we are wont to go cringing; lastly, letting this "suspense" range where it will, so that it may continually swing back again to the ground-question of metaphysics, which is wrested from Nothing itself:

Why is there any Being at all—why not far rather Nothing?

POSTSCRIPT

Metaphysics is the word before which, however abstract and near to thinking it be, most of us flee as from one smitten with the plague. Hegel (1770-1831), Works XVII, p. 400.

The question "What is Metaphysics?" remains a question. For those who persevere with this question the following postscript is more of a foreword. The question "What is Metaphysics?" asks a question that goes beyond metaphysics. It arises from a way of thinking which has already

349

entered into the overcoming of metaphysics. It is of the essence of such transitions that they are, within certain limits, compelled to speak the language of that which they help to overcome. The particular circumstances in which our enquiry into the nature of metaphysics is held should not lead us to the erroneous opinion that this question is bound to make the sciences its starting-point. Modern science, with its completely different ways of conceiving and establishing what-is, has penetrated to that basic feature of truth according to which everything that "is" is characterised by the will to will, as the prototype of which—"the will to power"—all appearance began. "Will," conceived as the basic feature of the "is-ness" (*Seiendheit*) of what-is, is the equation of what-is with the Real, in such a way that the reality of the Real becomes invested with the sovereign power to effect a general objectivisation. Modern science neither serves the purpose originally entrusted to it, nor does it seek truth in itself. As a method of objectivising what-is by calculation it is a condition, imposed by the will to will, through which the will to will secures its own sovereignty. But because all objectivisation of what-is ends in the provision and safeguarding of what-is and thus provides itself with the possibility of further advance, the objectivisation gets stuck in what-is and regards this as nothing less than Being (*Sein*). Every relationship to what-is thus bears witness to a knowledge of Being, but at the same time to its own inability by and of itself to authenticate the truth of this knowledge. This truth is merely the truth about what-is. Metaphysics is the history of this truth. It tells us what what-is is by conceptualising the "is-ness" of what-is. In the is-ness of what-is metaphysics thinks the thought of Being, but without being able to reflect on the truth of Being with its particular mode of thought. Metaphysics moves everywhere in the realm of the truth of Being, which truth remains the unknown and unfathomable ground. But supposing that not merely what-is comes from Being but that, in a manner still more original, Being itself reposes in its truth and that the truth of Being is a function of the Being of truth, then we must necessarily ask what metaphysics is in its own ground. Such a question must think metaphysically and, at the same time, think in terms of the ground of metaphysics, i.e. no longer metaphysically. All such questions must remain equivocal in an essential sense.

Any attempt to follow the train of thought of the preceding lecture is bound, therefore, to meet with obstacles. That is good. It will make our questioning more genuine. All questions that do justice to the subject are themselves bridges to their own answering. Essential answers are always but the last step in our questioning. The last step, however, cannot be taken without the long series of first and next steps. The essential answer gathers its motive power from the inwardness (*Inständigkeit*) of the asking and is only the beginning of a responsibility where the asking arises with renewed originality. Hence even the most genuine question is never stilled by the answer found.

The obstacles to following the thought of the lecture are of two kinds. The first arise from the enigmas which lurk in this region of thought. The others come from the inability and often the reluctance to think. In the region of cerebral enquiry even fleeting intimations can sometimes help, although real help only comes from those that have been carefully thought out. Gross errors may also bear fruit, flung out, perhaps, in the heat of blind controversy. Only, reflection must take everything back again in the calm mood of patient meditation.

The chief misgivings and misconceptions to which the lecture gives rise may be grouped under three heads. It is said that:

1. The lecture makes "Nothing" the sole subject of metaphysics. But since Nothing is simply the nugatory (*das Nichtige*), this kind of thinking leads to the idea that everything is nothing, so that it is not worth while either to live or to die. A "Philosophy of Nothing" is the last word in "Nihilism."

2. The lecture raises an isolated and, what is more, a morbid mood, namely dread, to the status of the one key-mood. But since dread is the psychic state of nervous people and cowards, this kind of thinking devalues the stout-hearted attitude of the courageous. A "Philosophy of Dread" paralyses the will to act.

3. The lecture declares itself against "logic." But since reason contains the criteria for all cal-

culation and classification, this kind of thinking delivers all judgments regarding the truth up to a chance mood. A "Philosophy of Pure Feeling" imperils "exact" thinking and the certainty of action.

The right attitude to these propositions will emerge from a renewed consideration of the lecture. It may show whether Nothing, which governs the whole nature of dread, can be exhausted by an empty negation of what-is, or whether that which never and nowhere "is" discloses itself as that which differs from everything that "is," i.e. what we call "Being." No matter where and however deeply science investigates what-is it will never find Being. All it encounters, always, is what-is, because its explanatory purpose makes it insist at the outset on what-is. But Being is not an existing quality of what-is, nor, unlike what-is, can Being be conceived and established objectively. This, the purely "Other" than everything that "is," is that-which-is-not (*das Nicht-Seiende*). Yet this "Nothing" functions as Being. It would be premature to stop thinking at this point and adopt the facile explanation that Nothing is merely the nugatory, equating it with the nonexistent (*das Wesenlose*). Instead of giving way to such precipitate and empty ingenuity and abandoning Nothing in all its mysterious multiplicity of meanings, we should rather equip ourselves and make ready for one thing only: to experience in Nothing the vastness of that which gives every being the warrant to be. That is Being itself. Without Being, whose unfathomable and unmanifest essence is vouchsafed us by Nothing in essential dread, everything that "is" would remain in Beinglessness (*Sein-losigkeit*). But this too, in its turn, is not a nugatory Nothing, assuming that it is of the truth of Being that Being may be without what-is, but never what-is without Being.

An experience of Being as sometimes "other" than everything that "is" comes to us in dread, provided that we do not, from dread of dread, i.e. in sheer timidity, shut our ears to the soundless voice which attunes us to the horrors of the abyss. Naturally if, in this matter of essential dread, we depart at will from the train of thought of the lecture; if we detach dread conceived as the mood occasioned by that voice from its relationship to Nothing, then dread is left over as an isolated "feeling" which we can analyse and contrast with other feelings in the well-known assortment of psychological stock-types. Using the simple distinction between "upper" and "lower" as a clue we can then group the various "moods" into classes: those which are exalting and those which are lowering. But this zealous quest for "types" and "counter-types" of "feelings," for the varieties and sub-varieties of these "types," will never get us anywhere. It will always be impossible for the anthropological study of man to follow the mental track of the lecture, since the latter, though paying attention to the voice of Being, thinks beyond it into the attunement occasioned by this voice—an attunement which takes possession of the essential man so that he may come to experience Being in Nothing.

Readiness for dread is to say "Yes!" to the inwardness of things, to fulfil the highest demand which alone touches man to the quick. Man alone of all beings, when addressed by the voice of Being, experiences the marvel of all marvels: that what-is *is*. Therefore the being that is called in its very essence to the truth of Being is always attuned in an essential sense. The clear courage for essential dread guarantees that most mysterious of all possibilities: the experience of Being. For hard by essential dread, in the terror of the abyss, there dwells awe (*Scheu*). Awe clears and enfolds that region of human being within which man endures, as at home, in the enduring.

Dread of dread, on the other hand, may stray so far as to mistake the simple relationships obtaining in the essence of dread. What would all courage avail did it not find continual hold in the experience of essential dread? To the degree that we degrade this essential dread and the relationship cleared within it for Man to Being, we demean the essence of courage. Courage can endure Nothing: it knows, in the abyss of terror, the all but untrodden region of Being, that "clearing" whence everything that "is" returns into *what* it is and is able to be. Our lecture neither puts forward a "Philosophy of Dread" nor seeks to give the false impression of being an "heroic" philosophy. Its sole thought is that thing which has dawned on Western thinking from the beginning as the one thing that has to be thought—Being. But Being is not a product of thinking. It is more likely that essential thinking is an occurrence of Being.

For this reason the scarcely formulated question now forces itself on us as to whether this kind of thinking conforms to the law of its truth when it only follows the thinking whose forms and rules constitute "logic." Why do we put this word in inverted commas? In order to indicate that "logic" is only *one* exposition of the nature of thinking, and one which, as its name shows, is based on the experience of Being as attained in Greek thought. The animus against "logic"—the logical degeneration of which can be seen in "logistics," derives from the knowledge of that thinking which has its source not in the observation of the objectivity of what-is, but in the experience of the truth of Being. "Exact" thinking is never the strictest thinking, if the essence of strictness lies in the strenuousness with which knowledge keeps in touch with the essential features of what-is. "Exact" thinking merely binds itself to the calculation of what-is and ministers to this alone.

All calculation makes the calculable "come out" in the sum so as to use the sum for the next count. Nothing counts for calculation save what can be calculated. Any particular thing is only what it "adds up to," and any count ensures the further progress of the counting. This process is continually using up numbers and is itself a continual self-consumption. The "coming out" of the calculation with the help of what-is counts as the explanation of the latter's Being. Calculation uses everything that "is" as units of computation, in advance, and, in the computation, uses up its stock of units. This consumption of what-is reveals the consuming nature of calculation. Only because number can be multiplied indefinitely —and this regardless of whether it goes in the direction of the great or the small—is it possible for the consuming nature of calculation to hide behind its "products" and give calculative thought the appearance of "productivity"— whereas it is of the prime essence of calculation, and not merely in its results, to assert what-is only in the form of something that can be arranged and used up. Calculative thought places itself under compulsion to master everything in the logical terms of its procedure. It has no notion that in calculation everything calculable is already a whole before it starts working out its sums and products, a whole whose unity naturally belongs to the incalculable which, with its mystery, ever eludes the clutches of calculation. That which, however, is always and everywhere closed at the outset to the demands of calculation and, despite that, is always closer to man in its enigmatic unknowableness than anything that "is," than anything he may arrange and plan, this can sometimes put the essential man in touch with a thinking whose truth no "logic" can grasp. The thinking whose thoughts not only do not calculate but are absolutely determined by what is "other" than what-is, might be called essential thinking. Instead of counting *on* what-is

357

with what-is, it expends itself in Being for the truth of Being. This thinking answers to the demands of Being in that man surrenders his historical being to the simple, sole necessity whose constraints do not so much necessitate as create the need (*Not*) which is consummated in the freedom of sacrifice. The need is: to preserve the truth of Being no matter what may happen to man and everything that "is." Freed from all constraint, because born of the abyss of freedom, this sacrifice is the expense of our human being for the preservation of the truth of Being in respect of what-is. In sacrifice there is expressed that hidden *thanking* which alone does homage to the grace wherewith Being has endowed the nature of man, in order that he may take over in his relationship to Being the guardianship of Being. Original thanking is the echo of Being's favour wherein it clears a space for itself and causes the unique occurrence: that what-is is. This echo is man's answer to the Word of the soundless voice of Being. The speechless answer of his thanking through sacrifice is the source of the human word, which is the prime cause of language as the enunciation of the Word in words. Were there not an occasional thanking in the heart of historical man he could never attain the thinking—assuming that there must be thinking (*Denken*) in all doubt (*Bedenken*) and memory (*Andenken*) —which originally thinks the thought of Being. But how else could humanity attain to original thanking unless Being's favour preserved for man, through his open relationship to this favour, the splendid poverty in which the freedom of sacrifice hides its own treasure? Sacrifice is a valediction to everything that "is" on the road to the preservation of the favour of Being. Sacrifice can be made ready and can be served by doing and working in the midst of what-is, but never consummated there. Its consummation comes from the inwardness out of which historical man by his actions—essential thinking is also an act—dedicates the *Da-sein* he has won for himself to the preservation of the dignity of Being. This inwardness is the calm that allows nothing to assail man's hidden readiness for the valedictory nature of all sacrifice. Sacrifice is rooted in the nature of the event through which Being claims man for the truth of Being. Therefore it is that sacrifice brooks no calculation, for calculation always miscalculates sacrifice in terms of the expedient and the inexpedient, no matter whether the aims are set high or low. Such calculation distorts the nature of sacrifice. The search for a purpose dulls the clarity of the awe, the spirit of sacrifice ready prepared for dread, which takes upon itself kinship with the imperishable.

The thought of Being seeks no hold in what-is. Essential thinking looks to the slow signs of the incalculable and sees in this the unforeseeable coming of the ineluctable. Such thinking is mindful of the truth of Being and thus helps the Being of truth to make a place for itself in man's history. This help effects no results because it has no need of effect. Essential thinking helps as the simple inwardness of existence, insofar as this inwardness, although unable to exercise such thinking or only having theoretical knowledge of it, kindles its own kind.

Obedient to the voice of Being, thought seeks the Word through which the truth of Being may be expressed. Only when the language of historical man is born of the Word does it ring true. But if it does ring true, then the testimony of the soundless voice of hidden springs lures it ever on. The thought of Being guards the Word and fulfils its function in such guardianship, namely care for the use of language. Out of long-guarded speechlessness and the careful clarification of the field thus cleared, comes the utterance of the thinker. Of like origin is the naming of the poet. But since like is only like insofar as difference allows, and since poetry and thinking are most purely alike in their care of the word, the two things are at the same time at opposite poles in their essence. The thinker utters Being. The poet names what is holy.

We may know something about the relations between philosophy and poetry, but we know nothing of the dialogue between poet and thinker, who "dwell near to one another on mountains farthest apart." [34]

One of the essential theatres of speechlessness is dread in the sense of the terror into which the abyss of Nothing plunges us. Nothing, conceived as the pure "Other" than what-is, is the veil of Being. In Being all that comes to pass in what-is is perfected from everlasting.

The last poem of the last poet of the dawn-period of Greece—Sophocles' "Oedipus in Colonos"—closes with words that hark back far beyond our ken to the hidden history of these people and marks their entry into the unknown truth of Being:

ἀλλ᾿ ἀποπαύετε μηδ᾿ ἐπὶ πλείω
θρῆνον ἐγείρετε.
πάντων γὰρ ἔχει τάδε κῦρος.

But cease now, and nevermore
Lift up the lament:
For all this is determined.

NOTES

[1] From here onwards Heidegger uses "the Serene" in the feminine gender, instead of the neuter as hitherto.

[2] The power of the Father (the High One) has departed from the gods and from men and alone remains existent in the Word. The patriarchal power absent from reality comes for the last time to existence *as language*. Heidegger says "I am what I say." Man after he has taken the final step of thinking within death and of expressing in language his consciousness of death will *exist as death*. Schizophrenic man, having outlived his own Eros, and thus no longer disturbed by the spiritual problems and conflicts of sublimation, will exist solely as a physical instrument to be wrought upon by the totality of death and expressing in the fact of his own existence the external annihilation of libido already accomplished by him. Heidegger draws attention to the movement of man towards death-in-the-world, the sole future existence open to man. It is the existential demand of the dying unconscious to die in a dying world in which the psyche can live out its introverted death with itself. That is homecoming. In the return to life of death as a known and understood power, in the recognition of the future not as future but as the necessity of the living and the dead to continually re-present themselves to participate in the obsessional compulsion of misery and dread without end in the world, can humanity having lost Existence-in-life find Existence-in-death. Death will mean dying into the world and not beyond it. Only those who are, as it were, dead-in-the-world will have an easy death; those who still possess libido will have, in their dying, to take over into consciousness

363

the whole agonising and angry libido of death.
The only task left to philosophy before the
end is to understand death and to bring the
totality of anxiety into full individual consciousness thus achieving Existence as Being-
in-the-world-of nothingness.

3 The German word *"Gut,"* which has been translated throughout as "possession," also has the
meaning of "a good thing"; it is thus related
to the English word "goods" as in "goods and
chattels."

4 See note 3.

5 Both here and wherever it occurs in the sequel,
the term *Seiendes* or *das Seiende* is rendered
by "what-is" or, on occasion, by "actuality."
The literal meaning is "that which is," and in
ordinary parlance we speak of it as "existence"
or "being" in general (τὸ ὄν), or again, specifically, as *"a* being," "an existent," "an
entity" (*ens*). In the Heideggerian system,
however, the German equivalents of "existence" and "being" are used in a special sense,
as will be made clear when we come to them.

6 As will be seen later in this section, the type of
correspondence, traced back to its last relevant
historical origin, is rooted in the concept *intellectus divinus*, the second type of correspondence, in that of the *intellectus humanus*
either as created by God or as a law unto itself.

7 *Uebereinstimmung* can be translated in any number of ways in English, but the two words
which would seem to catch most adequately
its operative meaning in this chapter are *likeness* and *agreement*. One would like to translate individual nuances by synonyms or
near-synonyms such as *accord, accordance,
conformity, concurrence, assimilation,* etc.,
but these have been avoided wherever possible
for the sake of a uniform terminology.

8 *Vorstellen* ("to represent") is literally "to place

before." Heidegger here and elsewhere writes it *vor-stellen,* thus bringing out the original dynamic meaning of the word. It would only be confusing to hyphenate *re-present,* since the reiterative character of the prefix "re-" would tend to outweigh the "presentation," which is the primary signification involved here. On the other hand it is clear that "the statement" does rather more than merely "present" the thing—it also "represents" it. The latter term has therefore been chosen.

9 *So-wie* also means "like." Here the thread is taken up again with the sense of "likeness" in *Übereinstimmung.*

10 *Ein offenes Entgegen durchmessen:* literally, "traverse an open Against (and/or Towards)." *Entgegen* has both meanings. It would appear that Heidegger intends to convey the double "movement" of a thing: its motion towards us, by which it "presents" itself, and its recoil, by which it rests *in* itself.

11 The words which immediately suggest themselves for the series of terms that now follows (*das Offene, die Offenheit, das Offenbare, Offenständigkeit,* etc.) are "obvious" and "evident." These have been avoided because neither has any etymological connection with the concept "open" ("evident" from L. *videre* and "obvious" from L. *via*).

12 *Unwesen:* which means the "negation" (*Un-*) of "essence" or "nature," a condition of complete chaos, negativity, blankness, etc. One might have translated it by "anti-essence" were it not for the fact that the term *Gegenwesen* ("counter-essence") occurs later on. It is hoped that the periphrasis employed above has captured the operative meaning.

13 *Unverborgenheit* can be translated either way, since "revealment" or indeed "revelation" has,

etymologically, the sense of throwing *back* the
veil, hence of *un*-veiling, dis-covering.

14 That is to say that freedom in the sense of
"letting-be" unveils things for us and exposes
them to our regard in that region of clarity or
"overtness" mentioned earlier. It does this in
virtue of its "ex-sistence," the innate capacity
of all earthly or human "existence" (*Da-sein*)
to "stand out from" (L. *exsistere:* to stand
forth, come forth, arise, hence *be*) or transcend
itself, transport itself out of itself and the
whole of *Da-sein* into the "Overt." "Ex-sistence" is later (end of Section 6) contrasted
with "In-sistence," q.v.

15 It is proposed to leave this key-term in German
as a *terminus technicus heideggerianus.* Alex-
andre Koyré, Heidegger's French translator,
observes that M. Corbin ("Qu-est-ce que la
Métaphysique," Martin Heidegger, Paris), renders *Da-sein* by "réalité humaine," which, although "juste sans doute," has the defect of
"anthropologising the Heideggerian doctrine."
"Le *Da-sein*," M. Koyré goes on, "est une
'structure' ou, pour employer un terme plus
habituel, une 'essence' qui s'actualise dans
l'homme, mais qui pourrait (et peut-être le
fait-elle) s'actualiser dans d'autres 'étants,' ou
même ne pas s'actualiser du tout . . . En
effet, en langage courant, autant que dans la
langue philosophique préheideggerienne, le
substantif *Dasein* veut dire: existence (*existentia*) et ne veut dire rien d'autre. Aussi parle-
t-on du 'Dasein Gottes' exactement dans le
même sens dans lequel on parle de l'existence
de Dieu." *Dasein*, the noun, is thus in ordinary
parlance "existence" and like the verb (*da
sein*) simply means "to be there" (in the world).
In view, however, of Heidegger's special use of
the term "ex-sistence," it has been decided, lest
confusion arise, not to employ the word "ex-

istence" at all for *Da-sein,* and not to translate it by "being," which term is reserved exclusively for *Sein.* M. Corbin's "human reality" could hardly be improved on as an interpretation, though an alternative might be suggested in "human being," in the sense of the state of "being human" with all that this state, for Heidegger, involves.

16 See note 8.

17 There is hardly any difference between *Verbergen* and *Verbergung.* Both can be translated either by "concealment" or "dissimulation." In the main "dissimulation" has been kept for *Verbergung* and "concealment" for *Verbergen.*

18 Literally "concealedness," "hiddenness."

19 Meaning that we do not know of the dissimulation, are unaware that anything is dissimulated at all: we are always deceived.

20 *abgefallen zum Wesen* contains both meanings.

21 *das Entschlossene, d.h. das sich nicht verschliessende Verhältnis. Entschlossenheit* is the ordinary word for "resolution," compounded of the negative prefix *ent-* ("de," "un-") and *(Ge)schlossenheit* ("closedness"). Its antonym is *Verschlossenheit* (the state of being locked up, hence "reserve," "taciturnity"). Our words "decision" and "resolve" represent a similar process, namely that of "cutting away" or "loosening." The end-result is the same. As M. Koyré comments: "Resolution keeps us open for the mystery."

22 *ohne noch den Grund der Maass-nahme selbst und das Wesen der Maassgabe zu bedenken.* Literally: "without considering the ground (basis) of measure-taking itself and the nature of measure-giving." *Maassgabe* is "proportion," "standard"—that which gives measure.

23 *in-sistiert.* Heidegger is here using the word in the obsolete sense of "standing in or on" (*insistere*).

367

24 *Existenz* in the ordinary sense.

25 "unwesentlich," which could also be taken to mean (from *Unwesen*) "dis-essential," i.e. the essence of truth has become "de-essentialised" or "de-natured" by having been forgotten.

26 *Die Irre.* M. Koyré holds that this is incorrectly rendered by "error," and prefers, after much cogitation, the term les ténèbres (the dark). He is right insofar as German has the popular expression *er geht in die Irre,* which means "he goes astray," "he wanders in the dark," "he gets confused or lost" rather than, specifically, "he falls into error." Nevertheless the above states do *imply* falling into error. M. Koyré goes on to say that by *die Irre* Heidegger means that state, or region, of total confusion, of vague obscurity where we lose all our bearings and where we "err." In that state or region we follow an *Irrgang*—an erratic course. Further, it is undeniable that the correct word for "error" is *Irrtum,* which has been translated by "Wrong." Despite these considerations, however, "error" for *die Irre* and "to err" for *irren* have been decided on, since there would appear to be no alternative, which would not involve excessive circumlocution.

27 *in der Not der Nötigung. Not* means misery, need: hence "extremity."

28 *ist es einem unheimlich.* Literally, "it is uncanny to one."

29 *Nichtung.* The word "nihilation" has been coined in the hope of conveying Heidegger's meaning. His thought, which is also expressed in the verb *nichten* at the end of this paragraph and elsewhere, is very difficult to reproduce in the negative terms of its German formulation. *Nichtung* is a causative process, and *nichten* a causative and intransitive verb. Ordinarily we would express the process in positive terms and would speak, for instance, of the "be-

368

coming" of Nothing or the "de-becoming" of something, as would be clear in a term like *Nichtswerdung* or the *Entwerdung* of Meister Eckhart. A concept as important to philosophy as was the acceptance by psychology of an independent dynamic death-instinct (*Todes- trieb*).

30 Cf. "Tao Te Ching" XL: for though all creatures under heaven are the products of Being, Being itself is the product of Not-being. Trans.

31 *Geworfenheit*. Literally "thrownness." M. Corbin, in his French version of this essay, renders the term by *déréliction*. The underlying thought would appear to be that in *Da-sein* we are "thrown there" and left derelict, like a thing cast up by the waves on the seashore.

32 Here *Seiendes* has been translated by "being," with the proviso that it be understood as "being" in simple contrast to "not-being." Heidegger's *Sein* is always rendered as "Being" with a capital B.

33 See note 32.

34 Hölderlin, "Patmos."

Gateway Titles

AQUINAS, ST. THOMAS, *Providence and Predestination*

AQUINAS, ST. THOMAS, *The Teacher—The Mind*

AQUINAS, ST. THOMAS, *Treatise on Law*

ARISTOTLE, *Ethics I, Politics I*

ARISTOTLE, *Poetics*

AUGUSTINE, ST., *The Enchiridion on Faith, Hope and Love*

AUGUSTINE, ST., *The Political Writings*

AUGUSTINE, ST., *Of True Religion*

BELL, BERNARD I., *Crowd Culture*

BERNS, WALTER F., *Freedom, Virtue and the First Amendment*

BOGAN, LOUISE, *Achievement in American Poetry*

BURKE, EDMUND, *Reflections on the Revolution in France*

BURKE, EDMUND, *Speech on Conciliation with the Colonies*

BURNHAM, JAMES, *The Machiavellians: Defenders of Freedom*

BUTLER, RICHARD, *The Life and World of George Santayana*

CLAUDEL, PAUL, *Break of Noon*

CLAUDEL, PAUL, *The Tidings Brought to Mary*

CLAUSEWITZ, KARL von, *War, Politics and Power*

COLLINS, JAMES, *The Existentialists*

COLLINS, JAMES, *God in Modern Philosophy*

COLLINS, JAMES, *The Mind of Kierkegaard*

CUSTINE, ASTOLPHE I., *Journey for Our Time*

DOWNER, ALAN, *Fifty Years of American Drama*

DUVERGER, MAURICE, *The Idea of Politics*

EPICTETUS, *Enchiridion* (with MARCUS AURELIUS, *Meditations*)

FORD, FORD MADOX, *Portraits from Life*

FREUD, SIGMUND, *The Origin and Development of Psychoanalysis*

GENTZ, FRIEDRICH, & POSSONY, *Three Revolutions*

HANNA, THOMAS, *The Thought and Art of Albert Camus*

HARVEY, WILLIAM, *On the Motion of the Heart and Blood*

HEIDEGGER, MARTIN, *Existence and Being*

HITTI, PHILIP K., *The Arabs—A Short History*

HOBBES, THOMAS, *Leviathan I*

HOFFMAN, FREDERICK J., *Modern Novel in America*

HUME, DAVID, *Enquiry Concerning Human Understanding; Abstract of A Treatise on Human Nature*

JASPERS, KARL, *Nietzsche and Christianity*

JOHNSON, HOWARD A. AND NIELS THULSTRUP, *A Kierkegaard Critique*

JOHNSON, SAMUEL, *Lives of the English Poets*

JUENGER, F. G., *The Failure of Technology*

KIRK, RUSSELL, *The Conservative Mind*

KLAASEN, ADRIAN, *The Invisible Hand*

LEONHARD, WOLFGANG, *Child of the Revolution*

LEWIS, WYNDHAM, *Self Condemned*

LOCKE, JOHN, *Essay Concerning Human Understanding* (Abridged)

LOCKE, JOHN, *Of Civil Government*

LOCKE, JOHN, *On the Reasonableness of Christianity*

MACHIAVELLI, NICCOLO, *The Prince*

MAISTRE, JOSEPH de, *On God and Society*

MARCEL, GABRIEL, *Man Against Mass Society*

MARCEL, GABRIEL, *Metaphysical Journal*

MARCEL, GABRIEL, *The Mystery of Being*, Vols. I & II

MARCUS AURELIUS, *Meditations* (with EPICTETUS, *Enchiridion*)

MARX, KARL, *Das Kapital* (Abridged)

MARX, KARL, *Communist Manifesto*

MAYER, PETER, ed., *The Pacifist Conscience*

MILL, JOHN STUART, *Considerations on Representative Government*

MILL, JOHN STUART, *On Liberty*
MORLEY, FELIX, *Freedom and Federalism*
NIETZSCHE, FRIEDRICH, *Beyond Good and Evil*
NIETZSCHE, FRIEDRICH, *Philosophy in the Tragic Age of the Greeks*
NIETZSCHE, FRIEDRICH, *Schopenhauer as Educator*
NIETZSCHE, FRIEDRICH, *Thus Spoke Zarathustra*
O'CONNOR, WILLIAM VAN, *An Age of Criticism*
PICARD, MAX, *Man and Language*
PICARD, MAX, *The World of Silence*
PICO della MIRANDOLA, GIOVANNI, *Oration on the Dignity of Man*
PLATO, *Euthyphro, Crito, Apology, Symposium*
RICOEUR, PAUL, *Fallible Man*
ROUSSEAU, JEAN JACQUES, *The Social Contract*
RUEFF, JACQUES, *The Age of Inflation*
SARTRE, JEAN PAUL, *Existential Psychoanalysis*
SENESI, MAURO, *Longshadow and Nine Stories*
SMITH, ADAM, *The Wealth of Nations* (Selections)
SOROKIN, PITIRIM A., *Fads and Foibles in Modern Sociology*
SOROKIN, PITIRIM A., *The Ways and Power of Love* (first 15 chapters)
SOSEKI, NATSUME, *Kokoro*
SPENGLER, OSWALD, *Aphorisms*
SPENGLER, OSWALD, *Selected Essays*
STEVENSON, ROBT. LOUIS, *Selected Essays*
SUMNER, WM. GRAHAM, *The Conquest of the United States by Spain and Other Essays*
THURSTON, HERBERT, *Ghosts and Poltergeists*
TILGHER, ADRIANO, *Homo Faber: Work Through the Ages*
UNAMUNO, MIGUEL de, *Able Sanchez & Other Stories*
VIVAS, ELISEO, *Creation and Discovery*
VIVAS, ELISEO, *The Moral Life and the Ethical Life*
WEAVER, RICHARD M., *The Ethics of Rhetoric*
WRIGHT, DAVID MCCORD, *Capitalism*

A   25 00 80 1140 0